Dialogical Apolo

Dialogical Apologetics

A Person-Centered Approach to Christian Defense

DAVID K. CLARK

Baker Books

A Division of Baker Book House Co
Grand Rapids, Michigan 49516

Published by Baker Books
a division of Baker Book House Company
P.O. Box 6287, Grand Rapids, MI 49516-6287

Second printing, April 1999

Printed in the United States of America

Library of Congress Cataloging-in-Publication Data

Clark, David K.
    Dialogical apologetics : a person-centered approach to Christian defense / David K. Clark.
      p.   cm.
    Includes bibliographical references and index.
    ISBN 0-8010-2573-7
    1. Apologetics—20th century.   I. Title.
BT1102.C55   1993
239—dc20   92-31661

For information about academic books, resources for Christian leaders, and all new releases available from Baker Book House, visit our web site:
http://www.bakerbooks.com

CONTENTS

Introduction: Apologetics and Real Life   vii

Part One   Foundations for Dialogical Apologetics

1   Faith and the World of Thought   3

2   Philosophy in Calvin's Heritage   27

3   The Challenge of Science   52

4   The Question of Questions   76

5   Apologetics as Dialogue   102

Part Two   Strategies for Dialogical Apologetics

6   The Word on Words   129

7   The Man's Got an Attitude   155

8   Conversation at the Cultural Crossroad   179

9   Tipping the Scale   205

Conclusion: Who You Are Counts Most   233

Index   237

INTRODUCTION

Apologetics and Real Life

"Cindy, you're a very rigid person," said John. "I used to think you were pretty flexible and open-minded. But lately you've been scrutinizing everything I say."

Bright, attractive, and single, Cindy was under the gun. She wanted to project her Christian faith in her office and make a difference in the lives of her co-workers. But a lot was happening under the surface; things were getting very confusing.

Cindy Weinberger heard of me from her cousin, who attended sessions I led on the New Age movement. She called me one day about a problem that stemmed from her work in a doctor's office. The physician had decided that theirs would be a "holistic practice," and so he brought in John.

As a "facilitator," John used work-released time to lead the nursing and clerical staffs in group exercises and personal meditations. These activities, in the context of John's pop psychology, would make their clinic "holistic." John had big plans to link Cindy's office with a network of "holistic health practices" to blanket their southern city. But John's teachings and instructions began sounding very New Agey. What should she do?

When I met with Cindy, we began by going over John's specific teachings. She wondered whether they were New Age. (They were.) We talked about how to rebut his grandiose and unwarranted claims. But gradually our conversation shifted to nonphilosophical aspects of Cindy's situation. The conceptual defects in John's pontificating took a back seat to the interpersonal dynamics in Cindy's office. Who were the opinion leaders? What did they think of John? How did others look at Cindy? Did they respect her? Like her? Were there others sympathetic to Cindy's Christian beliefs? Personal factors like these formed the all-important context in which Cindy sought to defend her faith.

How much help could Cindy have received from a usual course in apologetics? Apologetic reflection, study, and pedagogy have traditionally abstracted apologetics from the dynamics of personal encounter. The context provided by the conceptual, attitudinal, cultural, and psychological aspects of real people in discussion are generally ignored. Apologetics has traditionally centered on the philosophical to the exclusion of the personal. This is true both in cases like Cindy's, where she wanted to defend her Christian point of view before a group, and in one-on-one conversation. Apologetics has too long been disconnected from that multifaceted complex called Real Life.

The strength of Christianity's intellectual foundations is important. Christians do not exercise faith in Christ and participate in Christian community simply because doing so touches the emotions or meets felt needs. They trust Jesus, not just because they think Christianity is beneficial, but because they believe it is true. Of course, faith does produce benefits, and this is all to the good. But because they emphasize truth, Christians believe that the study of the ground for Christian truth is singularly important. This study depends on fields like philosophy, history, and the social sciences to provide intellectual mooring for the Christian world view.

To meet this need, apologists rightly consider the intellectual dimensions of Christianity in abstraction from the larger Christian life. But while they appropriately isolate the cognitive aspects of the Christian life, they should also carefully return them to the context where they are lived out. Naturalists may capture an endangered fish, then weigh it, check its health, and tag it to help preserve the species. But of course they must put the fish back into the water. Taking the intellectual aspects of Christian faith out of life for purposes of reflection and examination is all well and good. But apologists must not permanently disconnect thought from life.

One important way to relate apologetics to life is to take this fact into account: *every assessment of the case for Christianity is made by real people who have unique agendas firmly in place.* As a reasoned defense of the Christian world view, apologetics should appeal to objective evidence and reasons. But the evidential weight of such appeals is not perceived and evaluated in a single, purely abstract way by humanity in general. It is assessed in a variety of concrete ways by unique individuals. Dialogical apologetics is a new conception of apologetics. It is unique in recognizing the variety of ways in which real people will evaluate apologetic arguments. This fact begs for analysis. Thus dialogical apologetics is audience-sensitive or person-centered apologetics.

This book has two major parts. The first five chapters, on the theoretical side, introduce several exciting developments in the world of scholarship that are opening for apologists windows of intellectual opportunity that have been closed for three centuries.[1] Part 1 will lay an indispensable foundation for the practice of dialogical apologetics as I conceive it. The next four chapters, on the more practical side, borrow the results of several important fields to enrich the practice of apologetic dialogue. Part 2 will build toward a strategy for dialogical apologetics.

I believe these two parts fit together. Theorists will feel tempted to stop half way through. But good theory should blossom in effective practice. Mulching a garden is pointless if I never plant flowers or vegetables. Academic types must not skip Part 2. Conversely, practitioners will want to jump right to the second part, looking for a few tips to enhance persuasiveness. But understanding the first half of this book will provide a much needed base for apologetic practice. Good practice grows from the strong root system of good theory, even though roots are invisible. Plants gain strength from systematic mulching. People types must work through Part 1.

More specifically, here is what each chapter argues: Faith as personal trust is an act of the whole person. Since this includes the mind, faith is consistent with reason (chap. 1). Significant developments in philosophy are reaffirming the rational viability of Christian thinking (chap. 2). Important results from philosophy of science are breaking down the barriers between science and other kinds of thought. Science does not preclude theology (chap. 3). Apologists can use a flexible yet rational epistemology that claims neither too much nor too little (chap. 4). Other religions do not rule out a Christian defense, for genuine dialogue with other persons is possible and rewarding (chap. 5).

If these intellectual movements clear the path for apologetics, then how should dialogical apologetics proceed? Apologists must assess dialogues as to their conceptual structure. Logic, although it will

---

1. See Thomas Oden, *Two Worlds: Notes on the Death of Modernity in America and Russia* (Downers Grove: InterVarsity, 1992), and Diogenes Allen, *Christian Belief in a Postmodern World: The Full Wealth of Conviction* (Louisville: Westminster/John Knox, 1989), for discussions of the opportunities afforded by the new intellectual situation.

challenge many readers, is profitable (chap. 6). Attitudes play a key role in apologetics. An apologist's attitudes toward the dialogue partner as well as the partner's attitudes toward both Christianity and the apologist all powerfully affect dialogue (chap. 7). All conversations are saturated with racial, social, and cultural dimensions. These must not be ignored (chap. 8). Persuasion is not mere salesmanship, but a strategy for presenting legitimate reasons for faith when they are most likely to be heard (chap. 9).

In seeking a new strategy with flexibility to fit many different apologetic contexts, we must begin by building intellectual foundations. The most basic issue is the relation between the commitment of faith and its intellectual content. We turn therefore to this question: How do faith and reason relate?

PART ONE

Foundations for Dialogical Apologetics

1

Faith and the World of Thought

I wanted a vehicle with an airbag. This latest technological wizardry could reassure a person who often drives home from meetings late at night in the Minnesota snow. But I wanted to see how the airbag worked. So I asked the salesman, John, whether I could test it.

"No," said John, "the airbag works only once. Once it deploys in an accident, it quickly deflates. Then the mechanics install a new bag as they repair the vehicle."

"But how do I know it will work?" I wondered out loud. I had read in the owner's manual that a little computer chip checks the electronic circuits in the system. It flashes the red *Airbag* light on the dashboard when I turn on the ignition. But how could I know for sure whether to trust the mechanical parts?

"Well," John finally blurted. "It's like God. You just have to believe even though you have no evidence!"

Is John's epistemology right? Do Christian beliefs, which connect the believer to another world, relate in any way to usual sorts of evidence? This dilemma mirrors a broader problem in Christian life. Some sing the old gospel song, "This world is not my home, I'm just a-passin' through. My treasures are laid up, somewhere beyond the blue." They withdraw from the world and risk criticism for irrelevance. Others prefer the hymn, "This Is My Father's World." They plunge into the world, but are in danger of censure for compromise.

Just as Christians wonder how to relate the behavioral demands of Christianity to the ethical norms of society, so they struggle to connect the truth claims of the faith to the philosophical axioms of culture. How does Christian thought connect to human reasoning about other things? Can we ground beliefs about God in everyday sorts of evidence?

3

Historical Perspectives

Christians' responses to the world of ideas have varied greatly. Witness the traditional (and tortuous) problem of faith and reason. Historically, Christians used the words *faith* and *reason* for different sources for knowledge of God. Very roughly put, faith involves special theology built on supernatural revelation confirmed by the Holy Spirit. Reason, on the other hand, concerns natural theology, that is, theology built on natural revelation as observed and interpreted by the human mind. Very generally, faith emphasizes God's role in knowledge, while reason stresses human initiative.

Christian thinkers have related faith and reason in a variety of ways. The various perspectives range along two continua. The first continuum highlights the *degree of relative independence* between faith and reason. This accents the question, Are faith and reason isolated from each other or are they intimately related? The second continuum spotlights whether *priority* is given to faith or to reason. This focuses on the question, Which comes first—reason or faith? Historical examples will show that thinkers have defended every possible view—proof that, at least on the face of it, Christians have not found unanimity on the relation of faith and reason.

Reason without Faith

One perspective sharply divides faith from reason and then gives no role to faith. Only reason provides a secure foundation for religious knowledge. The title of Immanuel Kant's (1724–1804) little book, *Religion within the Limits of Reason Alone*, suggests this position.

Kant displayed characteristics typical of his era, the Enlightenment, a period roughly equal to the eighteenth century. He stressed human individualism, reason, and freedom while disparaging inherited authority, especially clerical authority. He refused to ground religious claims in revelation or miracle. While he conceded that these may be minimally helpful in getting a religion started, they are essentially superstitious. Kant therefore sought a more secure foundation for religion.

In a famous statement, Kant wrote, "Two things fill the mind with ever new and increasing admiration and awe . . . : the starry heavens above me and the moral law within me."[1] Isaac Newton's scientific advances explaining the "starry heavens above" impressed Kant. These successes pressed Kant to meet two important challenges. First, he sought to justify the methods scientists use. Like a carpenter who uses but does not forge a hammer, Newton *used* scientific methods, but his scientific heroics did not *demonstrate* that those methods are justified. A nonscientific argument justifies scientific methods. Kant tried to develop such an argument.

Second, Kant tried to reconcile scientific explanations of events ("the starry heavens above") with personal and moral interpretations ("the moral law within"). Newtonian science saw all events as products of necessity, and necessity *excludes* freedom. The human experience of moral obligation, however, *requires* real human freedom.

Kant resolved this tension by limiting the range to which science has access. He posited two kinds of reason, theoretical and practical. Theoretical reason deals with the *world as it appears*; practical reason deals with the *world as it is*. Since it is part of theoretical reason, science deals with the *world as it appears* to the mind, not with the *world as it really is*. Practical reason, on the other hand, posits that the *world as it is* in itself differs from the *world as it appears* to us. One can *assume* that the human person, the soul as it is in itself, is free. But he cannot *know* that scientifically. Given this distinction, Kant constructed his case for religion in the area of practical reason, that is, on reason rooted in the human experience of moral obligation.

Kant's religion, built on practical reason, is a religion of moral duty. It has no need of speculative theology or institutional procedures. Miracles, prayer, and ritual are all superfluous superstitions. *Religion within the Limits of Reason Alone* outlines a religion that all good persons may follow. It is primarily a matter of morally right living supported by purity of heart. Though Kant limited theoretical reason (including science) to make room for religion, his religious perspective still depends heavily on practical reason. Faith, in the sense of special revelation, plays no role in Kant's religious philosophy. Faith and reason have no connection.

1. Immanuel Kant, *Critique of Practical Reason*, conclusion; *in Critique of Practical Reason and Other Writings in Moral Philosophy*, trans. Lewis White Beck (Chicago: University of Chicago Press, 1949), 258.

Faith without Reason

Like Kant's view, a second option sees faith and reason as relatively isolated from each other. But unlike Kant's, this perspective gives priority to faith. Perhaps the most famous line representing this position comes from the church father Tertullian (c. 160–230), who wrote, "The Son of God died; it is by all means to be believed, because it is absurd."[2] Tertullian's line has not always been properly understood, for he does not advocate total irrationality. As Richard Swinburne noted, "There are logical limits to the possibilities for human irrationality, and even Tertullian cannot step outside them."[3]

Like Tertullian, the great theologian Karl Barth (1886–1968) represented this view, holding that reason is secondary to faith. As a young man, Barth abandoned the nineteenth-century liberal theology he learned during his formal education, and this decision permanently marked his views on faith and reason. (In fact, Kant's view of religion had helped to shape the liberalism from which Barth retreated.) Barth argued that God is "knowable to us in His grace, and because in His grace, only in His grace." God is "visible only to faith and can be attested only by faith."[4]

The liberal theology Barth rejected emphasizes the primacy of human reason and religious experience over divine revelation. It sees God at work immanently in the world, but it resists the idea of a literally divine Son of God coming into the world. It sees humans as basically good and consequently asserts that Christ's teachings are more central to his mission than is redemption through his death on the cross. Liberals focus their attention on the social and ethical aspects of the Christian life. For them, Christianity is primarily a this-worldly matter: faith is following the moral teachings of Jesus.

Barth reacted violently against this liberal mentality. The best-known eruption of these passions is his debate with fellow theologian Emil Brunner. In 1934, he spelled out his argument with Brunner in the book *Nein!* (German for *No!*). This emphatic title is Barth's answer to the question, Can human thought begin in natural revelation

2. Tertullian, *On the Flesh of Christ*, 5; in *The Ante-Nicene Fathers, Translations of the Writings of the Fathers Down to* A.D. *325*, 10 vols., ed. Alexander Roberts and James Donaldson (reprint ed.; Grand Rapids: Eerdmans, 1950–51), 3:525.

3. Richard Swinburne, *Faith and Reason* (Oxford: Clarendon, 1981), 25.

4. Karl Barth, *Church Dogmatics*, vol. II/1, trans. T. H. L. Parker and others (Edinburgh: T. & T. Clark, 1957), 172, 190.

and arrive at God? Or, to put it simply, Is natural theology possible? (Natural theology is theology built on natural revelation; it is reason as distinct from faith.) Barth felt compelled to reject human reasoning in favor of grace. Knowledge of God is entirely and only God's free act on behalf of his creatures.

Despite the fame of *Nein!*, Barth had already clarified his view in what he called his most satisfying book, *Anselm: Faith in Search of Understanding* (1931). Later in life he wrote, "the *deepening* [of my theological position] consisted in this: in these years I have had to rid myself of the last remnants of a philosophical, i.e., anthropological (in America one says "humanistic" or "naturalistic") foundation and exposition of Christian doctrine."[5] A central element of Barth's theological agenda was the repudiation of human-centered theology in favor of God-focused theology.

Barth did reluctantly admit that the Bible speaks of a knowledge of God in nature in its "side statements." But, he insisted, according to the "main line" of biblical teaching, anyone who gains access to this knowledge must already know God through the Word (by which he meant Christ primarily).[6] Barth's reaction against the liberalism he learned in school, a theology taught by greats like Albrecht Ritschl and Adolf von Harnack, accounts for his reluctant attitude toward natural revelation.

According to Barth, Christian salvation must consist entirely of grace, and theology must have Christ at its center. Consequently, church proclamation and theology have no use for natural theology: "it can be treated only as nonexistent. In this sense, . . . it must be excused without mercy."[7] Though he certainly used his mind to understand theology, Barth decisively expelled reason, in the sense of philosophical knowledge about God, from his theology.

Faith Supported by Reason

Unlike the first two views, the third and fourth options affirm a more intimate connection between faith and reason. The third gives a certain priority to reason so that the human intellect can build genuine knowledge of God prior to and independent of God's gift of special revelation. Something like this view is often assumed by both

5. Karl Barth, *How I Changed My Mind* (Richmond: John Knox, 1966), 42–43.
6. Barth, *Church Dogmatics*, vol. II/1, 105–13.
7. Ibid., 170.

believers and others. First one proves Christianity with facts, and then she trusts in Jesus. In his classic discussion of faith and reason, the great Catholic thinker Thomas Aquinas (1225–1274) articulated a very sophisticated version of this general view.

Thomas taught that philosophy can demonstrate important theological truths to anyone who makes the effort to study its proofs. For instance, by rigorous thinking Thomas thought he could show that God exists and that he is one. Thomas used his famous Five Ways (which are five theistic arguments) to prove the existence of God. The Five Ways are classic examples of natural theology. Thomas defended the use of reason, by which he meant gaining knowledge through experiencing the world via the senses and then moving rationally from that experience to knowledge of God's existence.

The result of natural theology is a knowledge about God that is available to believers and unbelievers alike. In Thomas's view, someone who gains this knowledge *knows* a truth; he does not merely *believe* it. If he knows it, he cannot believe it; if he believes it, he cannot know it. Thus, once he works through the theistic proofs, a person *knows*, he does not merely *believe*, that God exists.[8] Knowing everything that can be known *philosophically* (e.g., *that* God exists) does not mean knowing *everything* about him (e.g., *what* God is). Though we learn some truths about God by reason, we gain other truths about God only by faith. For example, that God is triune, that Jesus Christ is the incarnate Son of God, that the body will rise again, that heaven and hell exist—these we come to believe only by faith. Since these are to be believed, they cannot, strictly speaking, be known. *Faith,* therefore, means accepting a belief on the basis of the authority of the church and the Bible.

Interestingly, the knowledge some people gain through philosophy can also be acquired by others through faith. Those who do not have the ability, time, or interest to follow the rigors of natural theology may legitimately accept the existence of God based on church authority. They may accept by faith what others understand by reason. In fact, not only is believing on authority acceptable, it actually provides greater certitude than philosophizing. Therefore, the *same truth* (e.g., that God exists) can be both believed (through faith) by

8. Thomas Aquinas, *Summa Theologica,* II/II.1.4; in *Great Books of the Western World,* 54 vols., ed. Robert Maynard Hutchins, trans. Fathers of the English Dominican Province, rev. Daniel J. Sullivan (Chicago: Encyclopedia Brittanica, 1952), 20:382–83.

some and known (through reason) by others. But the *same person* cannot both believe and know the same thing.

Those less able or interested in natural theology can acquire by faith all they need to believe. Those who embark on the path of natural theology, however, can only begin their journey with philosophy. When they go as far as philosophy goes, they must switch to faith, which then completes the journey to a full understanding of God. In this way, philosophically minded persons begin with reason and then flesh out their understanding with faith.

What benefits accrue from this intellectual faith? Thomas did not teach that this faith leads to salvation. He accepted a common medieval distinction between formed and unformed faith. Faith—that is, whatever one believes on authority—must be "formed by love." That is, one must supplement faith by a firm commitment to do the works that the love of God elicits. This includes, for example, a willingness to serve God. Faith itself, therefore, is a cognitive function. Only formed faith brings salvation.[9] As Thomas said, "faith is a habit of the mind, whereby eternal life is begun in us, making the intellect assent to what is non-apparent."[10]

In Thomas's view, then, faith (the unformed kind) and reason are compatible and complementary means to gain an understanding about God. For philosophers, reason precedes and leads to faith. For others, faith replaces reason. In either case, when reason can no longer produce knowledge, faith takes over.

Reason Dependent on Faith

Like Thomas, those who take this final perspective on faith and reason accept a close relationship between faith and reason. The difference, of course, is that those who hold this view reverse the sequence, moving first to faith. Reason follows faith, explaining or confirming what is already believed. Saint Augustine (354–430) held this view, expressing it in his well-known line, "faith is understanding's step; and understanding faith's [reward]."[11]

John Calvin (1509–1564) developed this Augustinian tradition. He taught that God scattered the light of his truth throughout

---

9. Ibid., II/II.4.1–5; 20:402–6.

10. Ibid., II/II.4.1; 20:403.

11. Augustine, *Sermons on New Testament Lessons*, 76.1; in *The Nicene and Post-Nicene Fathers*, 1st series, 14 vols., ed. Philip Schaff (reprint ed.; Grand Rapids: Eerdmans, 1956), 6:481.

creation. The truth about God as *creator* is everywhere, visible to all, both learned and ignorant alike. God's truth is displayed in nature and engraved deeply in the marrow of the human mind. But despite this abundance of light, human sin obscures the eyes of those who do not believe, preventing the brilliant light from illuminating their minds: "It is therefore in vain that so many burning lamps shine . . . to show forth the glory of [their] Author. Although they bathe us wholly in their radiance, yet they can of themselves in no way lead us into the right path."[12]

Because of this failure, humans desperately need another guide to truth. God responds by giving the Scripture. As the spectacles of the visually impaired help them see the world, so the Bible aids believers to see God: "Scripture, gathering up the otherwise confused knowledge of God in our minds, having dispersed our dullness, clearly shows us the true God."[13] The Bible alone gives completely certain knowledge.

This claim naturally raises a question: How can one know that the Scriptures are in fact true? Why use *these* spectacles and not some others? In Calvin's view, the Bible does not depend on the authority of the church (for the church depends on the Scripture). The Bible does not rest on human intellect or reasoning (for reason is subject to the Scripture). Instead, the Holy Spirit confirms the Bible with utter certainty. Those who read the Bible and receive the witness of the Spirit understand that the Bible authenticates itself.[14] In Calvin's view, knowledge of God as *creator* does not lead to faith. He defines faith in the context of knowledge of God as *redeemer*. Faith is not primarily intellectual, like Thomas's unformed faith. Indeed, the very idea of unformed faith (i.e., a merely intellectual apprehension of Christian knowledge) irritates Calvin considerably. It implies that "the perfect scoundrel may yet be a man of faith."[15] Absurd! For the reformer, faith is "a firm and certain knowledge of God's benevolence toward us, founded upon the truth of the freely given promise in Christ, both revealed to our minds and sealed upon our hearts through the Holy Spirit."[16]

---

12. John Calvin, *The Institutes of the Christian Religion*, 1.5.14; in *The Library of Christian Classics*, 26 vols., ed. John T. McNeill, trans. Ford Lewis Battles (Philadelphia: Westminster, 1960), 20:68.

13. Ibid., 1.6.1; 20:70.

14. Ibid., 1.7.5; 20:80.

15. Swinburne, *Faith and Reason*, 113.

16. Calvin, *Institutes*, 3.2.7; 20:551.

Despite the phrase, a "firm and certain knowledge," Calvin repudiated Thomas's more intellectually oriented definition of unformed faith. For Calvin, therefore, the knowledge that is faith is clearly a "higher knowledge," not a merely intellectual apprehension. He asserted that the knowledge of faith is more like assurance than it is mere comprehension. It includes the heart, for once the Holy Spirit illuminates truth in the mind, he then confirms it in the heart. "The Word of God," Calvin said, "is not received by faith if it flits about in the top of the brain."[17] A believer does not come to knowledge through his own intellectual resources. Knowledge of God comes through the operation of the Holy Spirit who brings faith to the believer through the Bible.

Assessing the Varieties of Usage

This too brief survey should underscore the variety of perspectives found in history on the problem of faith and reason. The possibilities may seem overwhelming at first, and finding a synthesis may seem nearly impossible. Yet the stance a person takes on this question will powerfully influence his approach to apologetics. This issue is so central to apologetic method that we cannot skirt it.

Semantic Problems

An evaluation of the views of these great men clearly reveals one fact: different thinkers use words differently. Generally, in traditional usage, *reason* means knowing God through natural revelation, and *faith* means knowing him through special revelation. But the thinkers we considered did not use exactly parallel meanings for the two words. This complicates the task of assessment. If we sort out these perspectives in light of each writer's basic agenda, however, we might find that they agreed on certain general points (although, of course, they did not agree completely). I cannot take time for complete historical assessments, but only for two suggestions. On the one hand, each saw some role for the process of human thinking. On the other hand, each recognized that this human thinking is not by itself sufficient for salvation.

17. Ibid., 3.2.14, 36; 20:560, 583.

Uses of Reason

One way to get at the meaning of *reason* is to examine two related words, *philosophy* and *logic*. These words have two general connotations. The first is negative or positive regarding Christian claims while the second is more nearly neutral. I begin with the word *philosophy*.

People use *philosophy* in several senses:

It can refer to the *academic discipline* that studies positions and viewpoints in areas like logic, metaphysics, epistemology, aesthetics, or ethics. The department of philosophy at any university will include many disparate ideas and methods, so this first general meaning is by no means simple.

The word can mean a *world view* or philosophy of life. (The fancy German word is *Weltanschauung*.) A world view is a *total interpretation*,[18] a comprehensive set of ideas by which someone explains the totality of life. In this sense, secular humanism is a world view.

Philosophy can denote a second-level exercise. As such it analyzes the goals, purposes, and methods of some first-level enterprise. A teacher might develop a philosophy of teaching to guide her work. Her *teaching* is at the first level, but her *philosophy of teaching* is at the second. Philosophy of science discusses the nature, goals, and methods of science.

The word can express a *method of clear thinking*, the process of analysis, careful evaluation, and critical thought. The analytic tradition in academic philosophy stresses this function.

To a large extent, the varied attitudes toward human reason are reflected in the differing uses of *philosophy*. In some senses, especially the first two, the word often connotes particular beliefs or sets of ideas (e.g., Marxist philosophy) that can either support or contradict Christian teachings. Christians who reject philosophy are usually thinking of one of these meanings for the word. However, in other senses—primarily the second two—philosophy signifies methods of thought that are more nearly neutral toward all perspectives, includ-

18. John Hick, *Faith and Knowledge* (Ithaca, N.Y.: Cornell University Press, 1957), 127ff.

ing Christian ones. Almost all Christians are open to philosophy in these senses.

The meanings of *logic* and *reason* reflect this same sort of distinction. Typically, *logic* denotes the study of proper standards of inference. It seeks appropriate guidelines for reasoning. These standards function to confirm or test novel truth claims by comparing them to other beliefs already accepted as true. Suppose someone asks, Is idea X logical? The answer requires comparing X to some reference point, either other claims or some larger framework of thought, perhaps even a world view. Thus, logic does not *generate* X out of thin air. It is not the beginning point or foundation of thought. Logic *tests* X against other ideas.

I once heard a Christian say, "I base my theology on faith in God's Word, not on human logic." This man was trying to say that he grounds his Christian beliefs primarily in the Bible, not in human observation. He would not trust reflection divorced from special revelation. But his comment was wrongly put.

The man assumed that *logic* must stand for "thought generated from human observations, intuitions, assumptions, and experiences without reference to special revelation." I agree that thinking of this kind undermines proper Christian thought. But the man's error is simple: the word *logic* does not normally denote "human thinking divorced from special revelation." Generally it is used more neutrally to mean the guidelines for processing and assessing ideas. In this proper sense, therefore, logic is necessary to all thought, Christian or otherwise. (By the way, a wise apologist will detect and understand others' use of this word. She will also use it correctly herself, but exercise restraint in correcting others' misuse.)

The word *reason*, however, is a little different. *Reason* can properly mean something like "human thoughts developed apart from special revelation." The Enlightenment, with its thirst for freedom from divine and religious authority, celebrated reason in this sense. Christian thinkers of all stripes rightly reject reason of this sort. Some see it as an expression of rebellion against God. Unlike the word *logic*, however, *reason* has good historical precedent for meaning "thinking that operates independently of God."

But like the word *logic*, *reason* can legitimately carry more neutral connotations. One of these is like the last two meanings of *philosophy*, in that it simply refers to the human function of mentally processing experiences and ideas, an activity that is necessary to all human thought. Another of these is Thomas's sense of reason: an honest person using God's gift of human intellect to understand God's natural revelation. In neither of these senses does reason constitute rebellion against God.

Francis Schaeffer brought clarity to this confusion when he coined the phrase *autonomous reason*.[19] He uses the phrase to denote human reasoning that insists on independence from God and claims priority and ultimacy for itself. This is the sense of the word *reason* exalted in the Enlightenment and rightly rejected by Christian thinkers. But reason need not be autonomous. Reason in its neutral senses is God's gift to humans, to be used to understand him rightly.

Sorting out the words *philosophy*, *logic*, and *reason* leads to this general conclusion: the words are used with two essentially different connotations. In some uses, the words point to a kind of thinking that seeks knowledge independently of God and places itself in opposition to him. In this sense, no Christian could build a world view on human reason. But in other uses, the words refer to human information processing. In this sense, human reason is necessary to any thinking or understanding at all, and this includes all Christian thought. Each of the thinkers surveyed above puts different degrees of emphasis on these points. But each recognizes, as he must, some legitimate role for the (relatively) neutral processes of human thinking.

Uses of Faith

Like *reason*, the word *faith* is ambiguous. It has two main senses, the one more intellectual and the other more personal. The complaint Calvin lodged against Thomas's distinction between unformed and formed faith highlights the two senses of *faith*. Thomas understood unformed faith to be a kind of knowledge that a person could gain by cognitively accepting as true the authoritative teachings of the church. Formed faith, however, is faith joined with a promise to do the works that a genuine love for God properly triggers.

This distinction mirrors the two emphases the word *faith* has taken on in history. The first is the more intellectual sense of the word. For instance, note the phrase, *the Christian faith*. This usually denotes the interlocking network of basic Christian truth claims. The second is the more personal sense. For example, George Mueller, a Christian

19. Francis A. Schaeffer, *How Should We Then Live? The Rise and Decline of Western Thought and Culture* (Old Tappan, N.J.: Revell, 1976), 81.

known for his powerful praying, was a *man of faith*. This way of speaking does not mean primarily that Mueller thought a certain way or acknowledged certain truths. It says he was a man who exercised a strong allegiance to or trust in God.

Like the word *faith*, the word *believe* is confusing because it has two different but related uses. To *believe that* is to come to hold or accept certain ideas as true. If I say, "I believe that God exists," I mean that I think it is true that there is a God. It means I assent in a primarily intellectual way to the statement *God exists*. Here the intellectual dimension of my person primarily is engaged.[20] This leaves largely unanswered the question of any personal involvement I may have with the object of that intellectual belief. Some who believe that God exists are minimally involved with God personally; others are deeply engaged.

To *believe in*, however, is a somewhat broader thing. If I say, "I believe in God," I mean that I have a personal trust in God, I have committed myself to him, and I am exercising a strong allegiance toward him. This stance of faith necessarily involves my whole person. My mind participates in this relation of faith, but ideally all other dimensions of my life will also connect vitally to this allegiance. When I *believe in* God, my entire person *in its wholeness* takes the lead. I would never say *my mind* believes in God. Rather *I* believe in God.

Distinguishing the intellectual senses of *faith* and *believe* from the personal meanings of these words is critical for practical reasons. A student of mine once reported trying to share with a woman his reasons for faith in God. Toward the end of the conversation, he suggested to her that she too should believe in God. She responded by affirming that she already believed that there is a God.

"But you must believe in God in your heart," said my frustrated pupil.

"But I do believe in my heart that God is really there," retorted the confused woman. These two hapless conversants missed each oth-

---

20. I must say *primarily* because knowledge and commitment always influence each other. All intellectual beliefs do involve at least minimal personal commitment. And deeply held beliefs are intimately integrated into other aspects of the person. Arthur F. Holmes, *Contours of a World View*, Studies in a Christian World View (Grand Rapids: Eerdmans, 1983), 137. Elsewhere Holmes puts it this way: "Thinking is rather a function of living than life is a function of impersonal thought." *All Truth Is God's Truth* (Grand Rapids: Eerdmans, 1977), 104.

er's thoughts completely. Neither could see the difference between understanding (believing that) and personally trusting (believing in).

Clarifying these words may help untangle the faith and reason question. Each of the thinkers surveyed above acknowledged that understanding or thinking about God is not sufficient for the practice of the Christian religion. Some writers, like Thomas, used *faith* in the intellectual sense. Others, like Calvin and Barth, rejected this vehemently. But each of the four understood that while living the Christian life is built on thinking of a certain kind, it requires more than thinking. Thus, despite important differences in vocabulary and emphasis, each recognized that human thinking is necessary, but not sufficient for salvation.

Toward a Solution

My claim so far is that Christian thinkers can find areas of general agreement on the faith and reason issue. Swinburne wrote, "despite appearances, advocates of the different views are not necessarily commending very different conduct or affirming very different doctrines from each other."[21] Christians of many hues know that thinking alone is not what God wants; philosophy will not by itself yield the fruit of the Spirit. They also know that clear-headed thinking is important; after all, God created the human mind and speaks intelligibly in the Bible. God's children must think in certain ways, but they must do other things as well.

Biblical Faith

If faith and reason do relate in some way, what sort of connection exists between them? To answer this question demands proper understanding of the word *faith*. History offers two main alternatives, the intellectual and the personal views of faith. Heirs of the Reformation typically take their cue from the Bible. So which general approach does the Bible commend?

I often hear Christian people take the intellectual view of faith. They say things like this: "I don't have any evidence that God exists, so I just take it by faith." These people apparently assume two ways of knowing:

---

21. Swinburne, *Faith and Reason*, 105.

Knowledge can be supported by evidence (which is best).

In the absence of good evidence, knowledge can be grounded in faith (which is not very good, but sometimes the best that we can expect). Faith is a *substitute* for evidence.

The second view seems to be what John the car salesman assumed and what Mark Twain had in mind when he wrote that the school boy knows "faith is believing something you know ain't so." Twain agreed with Christians who see faith as essentially cognitive assent to ideas that lack intellectual credentials. This view reflects the theory taught by Thomas Aquinas.

I argue that, from a biblical point of view, this distinction is defective. First, those who take this view turn faith into a kind of intellectual knowing or cognitive assent. This has an important consequence. Defining faith as a replacement for evidence places faith and evidence in an inverse relationship. (In other words, having more faith means needing less evidence. Conversely, having more evidence means needing less faith.) Given this mentality, *apologetics and theology are dangerous*: by trying to give rational moorings to faith, we actually *reduce* the need for faith. Now Thomas willingly admitted this: either one knows something philosophically or one believes it by faith, *but not both*.

This may seem acceptable on the surface, but it carries a untenable corollary. The one who sees God face to face in heaven will presumably have maximal evidence. But if faith and evidence are inversely related, then seeing God (Thomas called this the Beatific Vision) means that faith becomes obsolete in heaven. But the Bible says that *faith will abide* while *knowledge will fade* (1 Cor. 13:8, 13). Faith in God, faith in the sense of personal trust and loyalty, will continue and deepen in heaven. It is better, therefore, *not* to relate faith and evidence inversely. And this entails that faith is not a substitute for evidence.

Some people may quote 2 Corinthians 5:7 in defense of this intellectual view of faith. Here Paul wrote, "We live by faith, not by sight." But this means only that at times a Christian may rightly allow faith, in the sense of trust in God, to guide his thinking even though he has *no direct* evidence. For instance, if I trust my friend and he says he will do something for me, I may rightly believe he will do it, even when I lack direct evidence that he will fulfill his promise. Loyalty and allegiance, based partly on past experience, may rightly guide my thinking and acting. By contrast, the man who regularly suspects his friends is "blamed for a meanness of character, not admired for the excellence of his logic."[22]

But all this does not prove that faith is a substitute for evidence such that gaining evidence renders faith useless. Faith can function in cases of minimal evidence and in cases of maximal evidence. This is because exercising personal allegiance is not *directly* related in any way, either positively or inversely, to accumulating evidence. To take a parallel case, how much money a person earns is not *directly* related to his generosity—some rich persons are misers, others are philanthropists. Similarly, some people with lots of knowledge have little faith, but others have great faith. Some giants of faith have great knowledge, while others have little. How much faith a person has and how much knowledge she has just do not correlate directly.

Second and more importantly, the New Testament does not use *faith* primarily in this way. Now some Christians who take the intellectual view claim to have found a biblical definition of *faith* in Hebrews 11:1: "Faith is being sure of what we hope for and certain of what we do not see." But what makes them think this is a definition? Not every statement of the form "A is B" is a definition. Some are merely descriptions. Consider these examples:

(1) A car is an object with glass windows.

(1) is a description. A definition delineates the exact limits of some word or thing. It gives its exact nature. A definition is a complete description that differentiates the word from all others.

(2) A home is an object with glass windows.

(2) shows why (1) is merely a description. (1) is not sufficient to differentiate *car* from other objects. It is true as a description, but it is not a definition.

(3) A car is a four-wheeled, motorized vehicle intended primarily for carrying passengers on roadways.

Unlike (1) and (2), (3) is a definition. It is not a perfect definition, but it does delineate *car* in contrast to all other objects in the world, while (1) and (2) do not.

22. C. S. Lewis, "On Obstinacy in Belief," in *They Asked for a Paper* (London: G. Bles, 1962), 193.

In the context of Hebrews 10:32–39, Hebrews 11:1 is an exhortation to confidence and courage in the face of ambiguity. Those who have faith will continue to look forward to what has been promised but not yet been given, even when persecution causes emotional stress and cognitive uncertainty. Those who have faith do expect to see something for which they have not yet found direct evidence. But this does not mean that this is the *meaning* of the word *faith*. This confident expectation is *characteristic* of those who do have faith.

In the New Testament, *to believe* or *have faith* as a verb works off the personal meaning of the term. *Pisteúo* denotes trusting, relying, or believing. With *eis*, the form *pisteúein* means *believing in* in a strong sense. As a noun, *pístis* means faithfulness or trust. In sharp contrast to works or law, where salvation depends on human efforts, faith for Paul means a commitment to Christ that leads to salvation. For John, faith is accepting the message about Jesus, and this entails believing in Jesus himself, coming to, loving, and receiving him. Faith does involve assent to the truth of the Christian message, but it is not the impersonal acknowledgment of abstract truths. Rather, it is a personal attachment to the person who is the content of the message.[23]

New Testament faith is a complex combination of thinking and acting. The acting side of the equation is critical. The Bible makes it clear that many who think or speak with theological correctness do not exhibit the appropriate attitudes and actions. Such people face an uncertain future. The Old Testament prophets condemned the religious leaders of their day because they acted wrongly even though they knew about God intellectually (Jer. 23:11; Ezek. 22:26; Zeph. 1:4, 5). In the parable of the sheep and goats, the goats rightly identify the righteous judge as *Lord*, but their actions condemn them (Matt. 25:31–46). James speaks forcefully about those who do not follow up their intellectual understanding with appropriate action. Such faith is dead faith, not saving faith (James 2:14–26).

A critical element in biblical faith, then, is trusting or relying on God. Faith is a trustful reliance based on personal commitment to God revealed in Jesus Christ. It is much more like exercising loyalty to a friend than like understanding quantum physics. The best illustration of this commitment is the marriage vow. Exercising faith in God is like saying "I do" at the altar. These words are performatory; in the proper context, they bring a new reality into existence. A mar-

---

23. "Faith," in *Theological Dictionary of the New Testament*, ed. Gerhard Kittel and Gerhard Friedrich, trans. Geoffrey W. Bromiley, 10 vols. (Grand Rapids: Eerdmans, 1964–76), 6:203–28.

riage bond is created, and the personal experience of loyalty, trust, commitment, and love are formalized in a new relationship. Exercising faith in God is not merely thinking Christianly (though that is presupposed). It is saying "I do" to God and becoming a part of the bride of Christ.[24]

Reason in Christian Thinking

If the personal side dominates in biblical faith, how does the intellectual aspect fit in? In the New Testament, accepting the gospel message is a vital part of a relationship with God. Faith derives its value not from the intensity of the believer but from the genuineness of the one she believes in. True faith is faith in the right object; faith in an unfaithful person is worthless or worse. Faith in God as revealed in Jesus Christ is the epitome of wisdom, for God is unswervingly faithful. In general, therefore, trusting in the right object of faith is critical.

Given this, reason in the neutral sense is necessary to finding the right message. Humans use reason to comprehend language and meaning when they hear or read the Christian message. They use their reason in evaluating claims to prophetic revelation (Deut. 18:21–22; Gal. 1:6–9; 1 John 4:1–3). Judging in this way means using a test like consistency to decide the genuineness of a revelation claim by comparing it against what one already knows. Paul said the Jews had zeal but that their zeal proved insufficient for it was not based on knowledge (Rom. 10:2). In contrast, Luke commended the citizens of Berea who joyfully accepted Paul's message even as they evaluated it critically to see whether it conformed to the Old Testament they already knew (Acts 17:11).

This view of reason could raise several objections. First, some people believe that giving too high a place to human reason contradicts Christ's admonition to have childlike faith. It places the human mind in a position to make judgments about God's pronouncements. But that is entirely inappropriate, they claim. Humans are not to judge God's truth; they should cherish it, submit to it, and obey it.

I think this objection involves good intentions, but it is seriously confused. Jesus and Paul both encouraged childlikeness. But they

---

24. In Ephesians 5:21–33, Paul develops this analogy between marriage commitment and faith in Christ. In verses 31–32, he uses the sexual union, "the two become one flesh," as a profoundly mysterious picture of Christ's relationship to his bride.

challenged Christians to be like children *morally*, not *intellectually*. Disciples of Jesus should exhibit childlikeness in being sensitive to evil and sin, in being humble and contrite in spirit. At the same time, living and serving in a world of cunning men and women demands tough-mindedness. As he sent out the Twelve, Jesus told them, "'I am sending you out like sheep among wolves. Therefore be as shrewd as snakes and as innocent as doves'" (Matt. 10:16; cf. 1 Cor. 14:20).

Second, others argue that too much focus on rational assessment exalts human logic. It places human thought on a par with God's thought. But logic is simply a human invention, they argue. To think that something mere humans concocted (or Aristotle created) could somehow capture God is the height of folly.

This argument is also well-intentioned but seriously flawed. For one thing, seeking to grasp what God says of himself does not impose human logic on God. As I have argued, logic is relatively neutral as to world view. Logical principles help a person move appropriately from what he knows to what he does not know. They solidify patterns of thinking that humans have found reliable and that they use every time they think about anything. These patterns, I believe, reflect the Mind who created the human mind. Logical principles are human discoveries, therefore, not human inventions. Aristotle, who is given credit for organizing logical principles, no more invented logic than Newton invented gravity.

Fundamentally, I understand the attempts to think clearly about God as our small efforts to think God's great thoughts after him. God speaks in language that humans can understand just as a mother with a Ph.D. in physics speaks to her two-year-old in his vernacular. Humans can think because that is what God made their minds to do— although he did not give his creatures the ability to grasp him *completely*. This calls for a balance of two ideas: humans understand God truly, but they never capture him fully. The first idea requires courage, the second humility. As Paul Tillich noted, the best symbols for God both express his ultimacy and warn that the symbols themselves are not ultimate.[25] Tillich's warning is well taken: no one can domesticate God in any way, least of all with human concepts. The human capacity for understanding is limited; human finiteness means all persons are vulnerable to error and misinterpretation. Surely the knowledge of the wisest person is a flea bite compared to the totality of

25. Paul Tillich, *Dynamics of Faith* (New York: Harper and Row, Harper Torchbooks, 1957), 97.

truth. Even the accumulation of all human knowledge only scratches the surface of the world right around us. The more scholars learn, the more they discover they have more to learn. Human beings are doomed to struggle with an incurable finiteness.

But as serious as this problem is, a more severe complication looms ahead: sin. The Bible teaches that humans are blinded by sin. Some apologists call this the *noetic effects of sin*. This phrase denotes the negative consequences human sin has on the knowing process (Isa. 6:9–10; Zech. 7:11–12; Matt. 13:10–13; 2 Cor. 4:4). In fact, reason in the negative sense is often described as a kind of outright rebellion against God (Job 21:14; Isa. 59:1–15; Rom. 1:18–25; Eph. 4:18; 2 Pet. 3:5). In these cases, reason functions as a master; it is rationalization, not rationality. It is the use of the mind as a weapon to fend off the Hound of Heaven. Here the Holy Spirit must break through to a hardened heart protected by a bulwark of artful rationalization.

Faith and Reason Related

I conceive of faith and reason relating in roughly this way: Biblical faith is the whole soul committed to God in Christ. It is essentially a stance of personal trust in, loyalty to, and reliance on God. As such it requires an act of willing. But it also engages all dimensions of a human person, including reasoning. When it functions as a servant (rather than as a master, like autonomous reason), reason is the God-created function of understanding the truth content of the Christian gospel and of God's world.[26] Because reasoning grasps and justifies the message that describes the right object of faith, it is an important dimension of the larger life of faith. How then do faith and reason connect?

One view of this relation leads to a blind alley. In this view, all persons must begin their reasoning with faith. Since reason does not generate first premises, faith must create these initial principles. According to this view, therefore, everyone (even an atheist) needs faith to jump start reason.

Defending this claim begins with the observation that all arguments need premises. Suppose I assume this principle:

---

26. See William Lane Craig's discussion of Luther's distinction between the magisterial (i.e., master) and ministerial (i.e., servant) uses of reason. *Apologetics: An Introduction* (Chicago: Moody, 1984), 21.

(4) Everything one believes must be supported by an argument.

Now principle (4) means real trouble. It leads directly to an infinite regress, an unending chain, of prior arguments. If I believe p, (4) requires me to know some q from which I can infer p. If I believe q, (4) requires me to know some r from which I can infer q. If I believe r. . . . This process will very quickly get tiresome. If (4) is right and I need an argument for everything I know, then I will never know p *or anything else either*. This is why "the giving of reasons must come to an end."[27] "If there is any knowledge at all then there must be some source of knowledge other than argumentation."[28] Since the chain of reasoning must begin somewhere, this view rightly claims that if I know anything at all, I must know some things without reasoning.

But here the trouble begins: those who take this view want to say that whatever I know without reasoning (i.e., those first premises of thought) I should accept by faith. But if this is right, then everyone, including atheists, uses faith. Madalyn Murray O'Hair, who has no biblical faith, still knows her first principles by faith. This view, which attributes faith to everyone, is exactly what incensed Calvin. Calvin's intuitions on this point were exactly correct.

The difficulty with this view, of course, is that it implies the notion of faith as "knowledge one accepts without evidence." From my point of view, this is simply not the best definition of *faith*. I agree that some things are known without prior argument. But I consider it misleading to say that these things are known *by faith*. Philosophers have other, more appropriate ways of speaking about beliefs not built on arguments. (Some such beliefs are called properly basic beliefs, and I will discuss them later.)

We need a different way to relate faith and reason. It is this: faith and reason operate reciprocally. The whole of life influences the reasoning function. What I *want* to believe for emotional or financial or political reasons will affect what I *do* believe. Thus, a commitment of faith does enhance one's understanding of God. At the same time, however, no one can exercise a commitment of faith to an object about whom *no knowledge at all* is available. Minimal knowledge precedes the exercise of saving faith. But faith makes possible a fuller

27. Ludwig Wittgenstein, *Blue and Brown Books* (New York: Harper and Row, Harper Torchbooks, 1960 [dictated 1933–35]), 143.
28. George I. Mavrodes, *Belief in God: A Study in the Epistemology of Religion* (New York: Random House, 1970), 49.

understanding and acceptance of God's truth. And richer knowledge in turn can deepen faith. In this mutually enriching way, saving faith and reason complement each other, developing reciprocally in the life of a growing Christian.[29]

Notice that this sketch of faith and reason has moved away from traditional meanings. I did not follow the classic definition of *faith* as knowing through special revelation and *reason* as knowing through natural revelation. Instead I believe it is better to incorporate both special and natural revelation in all rational assessments. Both faith and reason (in their traditional senses) are part of a larger network of Christian truth claims that confront a person and force her to make rational evaluations. As God draws her to assess Christian claims positively, she may take further steps of personal allegiance to the One who is revealed by that network of beliefs.

This is saving faith. Saving faith is the broader concept because it incorporates all dimensions of the person. Jesus commanded his followers to love God with heart, soul, strength, and mind (Luke 10:27). That God exists and humans should respond to him are truths about which a potential believer must make a minimal, reasoned assessment. The person may then respond in trust, as the Holy Spirit enables, to the God those truth claims reveal. Having responded with embryonic faith, the believer then comes to know more richly, both intellectually and personally, the Object of his faith. In roughly this way, saving faith and reason function reciprocally.

Paul suggests the best illustration of this process in Ephesians 5. Here he compares the relation of the believer to Christ with the relation of bride to groom. When a man and a woman first meet, they begin by sharing their backgrounds. He was born in Toledo. She was born in Kansas, on a farm. He loves jazz. She enjoys jazz, but she studied classical piano in college. Chopin really excites her aesthetic passions.

Now as this process continues, it moves beyond the mere transfer of information. Though they are overtly exchanging information about themselves, they are actually weaving a relationship with tiny strands of implicit commitment. The small talk is the context in which relationship is woven. As the cloth gains texture and strength, opportunities for a series of gradually deepening explicit commitments

---

29. David L. Wolfe, *Epistemology: The Justification of Belief*, Contours of Christian Philosophy (Downers Grove: InterVarsity, 1982), 71.

present themselves. Finally, a total, whole-soul commitment becomes possible. If the lovers choose to, such commitment actually happens:

"Will you marry me?"

"Yes!"

The reciprocity of knowing about (reason) and knowing personally (faith) climaxes in the total commitment of the wedding vow. This beautifully pictures a person gradually moving toward God. Initial comprehension enables timid commitment; tentative commitment evokes interest and understanding; deeper understanding leads to fuller allegiance. If this process is not interrupted, the magical experience leads to a deep, satisfying relationship of faith in God. And a person can experience the very thing for which God created him.

The reciprocity of faith (whole soul commitment) and reason (the understanding aspect of that commitment) in the courtship of a woman and a man mirrors the complementary relationship between faith and reason in a relationship with God. For this reason, knowing God is a human act full of intellectual fiber. Yet it is not a purely intellectual process. For the believer, the stance of faith aids the act of knowing, and knowing undergirds trust. As Elton Trueblood stated, "armchair religion is really no religion at all."[30]

The Holy Spirit permeates this process. He works to overcome the blinding effects of sin and to lead a person toward openness to the Christian message. The role of a sensitive apologist is to defend the truth that the Holy Spirit then drives home to a needy heart and mind. As minimal Christian truth initially sinks in and is intellectually acknowledged, the Holy Spirit persuades a person to respond to the Person the truth reveals. When response comes, understanding is deepened. Another step of deeper reliance is possible. And the process of growth continues.

Summary

Christian thinkers have not reached unanimity on the faith and reason issue. Orthodox believers have accepted three of the views I sketched. (Kant's emphasis on reason alone strikes traditional Christians as fundamentally wrong-headed.)

30. D. Elton Trueblood, *Philosophy of Religion* (New York: Harper and Bros., 1957), 22.

Part (not the whole) of this problem is semantic. Both *reason* and *faith* contain ambiguous elements. Thus an important part of the solution to this tangle is clarifying uses of these words.

The three words connected with reason all have a double sense. The first emphasizes specific ideas that can be compatible or incompatible with Christian teaching. The second highlights the (relatively) neutral process of human understanding and evaluation.

The word *faith* also has a double meaning. It could mean *believing that*, a more intellectual operation involving knowing about God through revelation, or *believing in*, which is saving faith, a more holistic, personal act.

From a biblical starting point, faith is best defined as the whole soul commitment of the self to God as revealed in Christ. This act requires action of the will and involves the whole person, including intellect.

Reason is best seen as the God-given function of understanding and assessing the truth about God and his creation in a minimal yet possibly correct way.

But though human reasoning is important, so is the powerful warning that humans readily turn their capacities—intellectual and otherwise—against the Creator. Thus in seeking to understand whatever I can of God, I must exercise both courage and humility.

Faith and reason function reciprocally. Each positive assessment of Christian truth makes possible a deeper step of faith. And deeper faith enhances Christian understanding.

Before we discuss an apologetic method consistent with this view of faith and reason, however, we will review two very important contemporary movements. Complete with its view of faith and reason, the first of these two, a movement called Reformed epistemology, will provide some of the materials for building dialogical apologetics. One of its main agenda items is assessing the question, To what degree do central religious beliefs require independent evidence? What kind of support must we have for belief?

2

Philosophy in Calvin's Heritage

"Studying medicine must raise fascinating ethical questions," I said enthusiastically. Medicine engages interesting, but perplexing moral problems, and I anticipated thinking through some of those issues as a graduate student in philosophy.

"We don't need ethicists in medicine," retorted my friend. "Science gives us all the answers we need. Philosophy and ethics are irrelevant in medicine. Treating patients is entirely a matter of scientific fact and medical technique."

"In fact," he stated emphatically, "everything we know about the world we learn by observation and experimentation. We cannot achieve knowledge without first finding the relevant evidence. Those who hold unscientific beliefs are superstitious and gullible. They are susceptible to myths and fairy tales."

I felt stunned. Gary Thompson seemed very sure of himself. He had graduated from college one year before me and now had a year's worth of medical school lectures and attitudes stuffed in his brain. Still a bit naive, I stood on the threshold of graduate work in philosophy and ethics, the very subjects Gary had so knowingly declared irrelevant. I recognized as important his pursuit of medicine. Would my chosen career in philosophy count for nothing?

As I reflected on this conversation, Gary's self-assured pronouncements made me wonder about a related, but wider question: Must everything anyone believes be proved by sensory observation? I wondered what he thought about his Christian beliefs, convictions about truth revealed in the Bible, for example. Surely some of these are not founded on scientific evidence. Shell-shocked by Gary's barrage, I did not have the resources to press the point. I soon learned, however, that Gary represented a position that today is thoroughly and rightly discredited.

Currents in Religious Epistemology

Christian philosophers are today the talk of the epistemological town. In the last twenty years, a coterie of Christians has been developing a new perspective in epistemology (the theory of knowing) that seriously undermines the general position Gary represented. This new perspective is called Reformed epistemology. Reformed epistemologists are not, as Alvin Plantinga (a leading exponent) once quipped, those who used to be epistemologists and now see the light. Reformed epistemologists are part of a philosophical movement that stands self-consciously in the tradition of John Calvin's Reformed theology.

Evidentialism

An important item on Reformed epistemology's agenda is rebutting a mentality very much like Gary's. The villain is an Enlightenment based position called *evidentialism*. Reformed epistemologists argue that "the Enlightenment conception of rationality and its estimations of the rationality of religious belief are as mistaken as they are influential."[1] Evidentialism partakes of the Enlightenment spirit, the spirit of autonomous reason, when it asserts that in the absence of sufficient evidence, a believer in God is irrational in that belief. Philosophers commonly point to W. K. Clifford's (1845–1879) essay, "The Ethics of Belief," as the shining example of evidentialism.[2]

Clifford began with a story about a wealthy ship owner. The ship was not well built in the first place, has often needed repair, and is now old and shabby. Its seaworthiness is in grave doubt. Yet it has served adequately for its entire life, and, to its credit, it is still afloat. As the crew prepares the ship for a journey to take hopeful emigrants to a new land, doubts nag the ship owner. He wonders whether he should have his vessel refitted despite the great expense. He convinces himself, however, that the ship is seaworthy, for she has survived many long journeys and ferocious storms. So he entrusts the emigrants to Providence and sends the ship to sea. When the ship goes

---

1. Kelly James Clark, *Return to Reason: A Critique of Enlightenment Evidentialism and a Defense of Reason and Belief in God* (Grand Rapids: Eerdmans, 1990), 5. Return to Reason is a very competent introduction to Reformed epistemology.

2. W. K. Clifford, "The Ethics of Belief," in *Lectures and Essays*, ed. Leslie Stephen and Frederick Pollock, 2d ed. (London and New York: Macmillan, 1886), 339–63.

down in mid-ocean, he collects his insurance money and says nothing.

Here is Clifford's interpretation: the ship owner is guilty of the deaths of the ship's crew and passengers. Given the available evidence, he had no right to believe his ship was seaworthy. He had acquired this belief not through honest investigation but through ignoring his doubts. Consequently, he was morally wrong in holding to and acting on his belief. Had the ship not gone down, the man still would have been guilty of believing wrongly. The only difference is that he would not have murdered the passengers and crew. With respect to his guilt, whether or not the ship went down is irrelevant. The only issue is whether the ship owner had the right to believe as he did given the evidence before him.[3]

One premise undergirding Clifford's story affirms a close connection between belief and action. Since beliefs and actions are inseparable, Clifford argued for achieving certainty of belief. Those who act without being certain will harm themselves and others. Believing without sufficient evidence breeds gullible citizens; this in turn aids and abets liars and cheats. Even those who are not among society's elite can erode the social fabric. Thus those who believe on insufficient evidence reinforce the human tendency to believe without adequate testing and cause society to "sink back into savagery."

Clearly, Clifford thought that believing with improper evidence was moral failure, not just intellectual error. This is obvious from a number of his statements. He argued that the privileges of power should be gained only through properly investigated knowledge. When it is based on unsupported belief, power is stolen. Clifford claimed that a belief is unjustified if one learns it as a child and continues to hold it as an adult only by virtue of suppressing doubts: the life of anyone who does this is "one long sin against mankind." In summary, in a parody on the ancient test of orthodoxy, Clifford concluded, "it is wrong always, everywhere, and for any one, to believe anything upon insufficient evidence."[4]

Clifford's program sets very high requirements for knowledge. The implications for religious knowing are severe. Very briefly, evidentialism implies something like this: before religious claims can be

---

3. Ibid., 339–41.
4. Ibid., 342–46. The famous criteria for orthodoxy: that which was believed "everywhere, always, and by all" is orthodox. Vincent of Lérins, a mid fifth-century monk, first used this test.

rationally or epistemologically correct or count as genuine knowledge, they must be grounded in sufficient evidence. But religious beliefs never are (or will be) grounded in such evidence (or so evidentialist skeptics typically argue). Consequently, religious convictions are not (or never could be) justified and should not be believed.

This negative implication of Clifford's perspective for religious knowledge is echoed in contemporary writers. The title of Antony Flew's book, *The Presumption of Atheism*, makes the point clear: in case of *no evidence for* the religious view, *presume* the nonreligious view.[5] Michael Scriven put it bluntly: "we need not have a proof that God does not exist in order to justify atheism. Atheism is obligatory in the absence of any evidence for God's existence."[6] In sum, belief in God must be supported by sufficient evidence. If it is not, one is duty bound to disbelieve.

In theory, then, evidentialism commends neutrality with respect to beliefs that are not sufficiently supported by evidence. If two interpretations of a situation were available, but neither had sufficient evidence, one ought (in a moral sense) to disbelieve them both. The implication for religious knowledge, however, is not neutral but negative. If belief in God's existence cannot be demonstrated by sufficient evidence, then one ought to disbelieve.

Put another way, belief in God is "guilty until proven innocent." But since disbelief in God is presumed (as Flew's title suggests), atheism is "innocent until proven guilty." If evidence does not prove one way or the other whether God exists, one is duty bound to embrace atheism. Atheism, or at least agnosticism, is the epistemological default setting. A tie goes to the runner—and agnosticism is the runner!

William James's Critique

Before laying out the responses typically given by Reformed epistemologists, we should first note briefly the critique offered by the American pragmatist philosopher William James (1842–1910). In a classic essay, "The Will to Believe," James directly combatted the evidentialists' claims. He argued that in certain carefully defined in-

---

5. Antony Flew, *The Presumption of Atheism and Other Philosophical Essays on God, Freedom and Immortality* (New York: Barnes and Noble, 1976), 22–23.
6. Michael Scriven, *Primary Philosophy* (New York: McGraw-Hill, 1966), 103.

stances, one may still be entitled to hold some beliefs even when they are not fully supported by evidence.[7]

James's fundamental claim is that the requirement that all beliefs must be grounded in evidence is overly restrictive and sometimes inappropriate. This is true because life presents different kinds of options. (An option is a choice between two competing hypotheses). Options may be *living* or *dead*. A live option is between two hypotheses that one might really choose. A dead option is not. (E.g., the choice between becoming a Christian and becoming a Druid is a dead option for most people today.) Options may be *forced* or *avoidable*. And they may be *momentous* or *trivial*. A *genuine* option is living, forced, and momentous. It offers choices one might really make, it cannot be avoided, and it is very important. Any option that is either dead, avoidable, or trivial is *nongenuine*.

Contrary to evidentialism, James argued that beliefs can be supported either by intellectual or by passional (i.e., volitional) demands. (According to evidentialism, only intellectual evidence can rightly support beliefs.) But in James's view, even scientific beliefs are at times influenced by passional, volitional factors. He offered this illustration: if telepathy were possible, the canons of biology would change significantly, rendering biologists unable to carry on their profession without radical revision. So biologists who are committed to their discipline resist believing in telepathy despite not having investigated it intellectually. But if belief in telepathy could somehow help their discipline, they would alter their strategy and accept it. As this illustration suggests, pure intellect does not always determine beliefs even in science.

James argued that when pure intellect cannot conclusively decide *nongenuine* options, one should simply suspend judgment. If I am unsure about whether President Zachary Taylor was murdered by arsenic, I can simply wait for more evidence to come in or for a more comprehensive theory to develop. I lose nothing in waiting. But in the case of *genuine* options, I must choose (the option is unavoidable) even when the evidence is indefinite. In that case, the passion or volition may rightly take the lead: "*Our passional nature not only law-*

7. "Faith and the Right to Believe," a lecture title, captures James's view better than "The Will to Believe." *The Writings of William James*, ed. John McDermott (New York: Random House, 1967), 735–37. In *Pragmatism*, James says that he should have called his famous essay "The Right to Believe."

fully may, but must, decide an option between propositions, whenever it is a genuine option that cannot by its nature be decided on intellectual grounds."[8]

Questions of a personal, moral, or religious nature occasionally present genuine options that are intellectually undecidable, said James. In these cases, humans must make decisions before all the evidence is in; indeed it sometimes seems likely the evidence will never arrive. Now if the main goal were to avoid being duped, one ought to sit back and wait. One could assume that anything worth believing would surely have irrefutable evidence to support it. But James argued that it would be surprising if truth were so neatly attuned to human intellectual abilities that one could with absolute assurance find truth and avoid error by taking this timid, skeptical attitude. "In the great boarding-house of nature, the cakes and the butter and the syrup seldom come out so even and leave the plates so clean."[9]

Genuine but intellectually undecidable options require one of two strategies. On the one hand, one can choose to disbelieve and risk losing truth in hopes of avoiding error. This is the evidentialist stance. In this first way, no one will believe error because no one will believe anything. But such skepticism is dangerous. It carries with it a unique sort of peril, but it is perilous nonetheless: if no one ever believes, then no one will ever believe the truth.

On the other hand, one can choose to believe and risk error in hopes of gaining truth. In this second way, one might come to believe in error. But James believed worse things could happen. "Our errors are surely not such awfully solemn things," he wrote. "In a world where we are so certain to incur them in spite of all our caution, a certain lightness of heart seems healthier than this excessive nervousness on their behalf."[10] Metaphorically speaking, the knight may choose to go to battle and risk some wounds, or shirk the battle to avoid all wounds and never gain the victory. Though victory is never assured, it can come only to those who take the chance and face the dangers.

What shall we think of James's position? Initially, his argument may seem unsatisfying for any who think, as I do, that we can find

---

8. William James, "The Will to Believe," in *The Will to Believe and Other Essays* (New York: Longman's, Green, 1896), 11.
9. Ibid., 22.
10. Ibid., 19.

proper reasons for believing in God.[11] But even so, James makes several helpful points. First, suppose for the moment that the reasons for faith were inconclusive and the decision to trust in God was entirely undecidable intellectually. If James is right, it still would not follow that one ought to become agnostic. The epistemological default position is not atheism or even agnosticism. Indeed, the evidentialist "displays an attitude not of reasonable caution but of cramped miserliness."[12]

Second, one cannot not decide. The religious question forces itself upon human persons; everyone chooses which fork in the road she will travel. Christians have regularly noted this fact. Once in a while atheists do, too. Scriven chides his readers: "Agnosticism as a position is interesting and debatable; agnosticism as the absence of a position is simply a sign of the absence of intellectual activity or capacity."[13]

And finally, every position involves some risk. The stance of faith is not the only perilous one. As Pascal's famous wager implies, agnosticism involves danger, too. It is dangerous in a different and potentially more disastrous way: agnosticism guarantees that a person will lose all truth—some of which may be vitally important. In the end, argued James, it is irrational to accept agnostic truth-seeking principles that completely rule out certain sorts of truth that might be critical. Whether or not one accepts those rules, "we *act*, taking our life in our hands."[14]

Reformed Epistemology

The Enlightenment mentality and its rules of evidence still affect modern culture. People commonly think they need facts to support everything they believe. Like Sergeant Friday on *Dragnet*, they say, "Just give us the facts, ma'am." A common reflex reaction is to suspend be-

11. C. Stephen Evans argues that James developed subjectivist arguments for faith because he limited knowledge to science. *Subjectivity and Religious Belief: An Historical, Critical Study* (Grand Rapids: Christian University Press, 1978), 203–6. As I shall argue in chapter 3, this view of knowledge is too restrictive.

12. Rod Sykes, "Soft Rationalism," *International Journal for the Philosophy of Religion* 8 (1977): 58.

13. Scriven, *Primary Philosophy*, 107.

14. James, "Will to Believe," 30.

lief unless it is supported by scientific facts. Accepting this mentality and conceding that the facts cannot prove Christianity, some Christians, like John the car salesman, retreat to dogmatism: "I can't prove it so I just accept it by faith." The critical feature of James's essay is his insistence that Enlightenment agnostics should not write the rulebook of knowledge. Reformed epistemology shares this spirit.

Classical Foundationalism

Like James, Reformed epistemologists in general and Alvin Plantinga in particular[15] reject the evidentialist approach to religious knowledge and evidence. But they offer a critique of evidentialism quite different from what appears in James's "The Will to Believe." They employ a two-step strategy. Step one is arguing that evidentialism depends on a long tradition in epistemology called *classical foundationalism*. Step two is showing the bankruptcy of classical foundationalism. The argument is simple: if evidentialism depends on classical foundationalism and classical foundationalism is defective, then evidentialism is unwarranted.

Classical foundationalism is a strict form of *foundationalism*. Foundationalism is the view that we should construct knowledge in sequential stages. Building knowledge is like erecting a house. A builder must start at the bottom and move upward so that the foundation grounds the first story and the lower stories support those above. In this way, absolutely solid foundations hold the whole structure up. Similarly, one should construct knowledge by first laying a very secure, undoubtable foundation and then building other truths on that base. In both cases, everything depends on the solidity of the footings. A cracked foundation spells disaster both in house building and in knowledge building.[16]

Beliefs that are part of a foundation are called *basic beliefs*. They form the grounding for all other beliefs. The question is, What sorts

15. We shall follow Plantinga's thought most closely. Other well-known defenders of Reformed epistemology include William Alston, Nicholas Wolterstorff, and George Mavrodes.

16. Plantinga states it more formally in this way: every person has a set of beliefs plus a series of logical connections that together form her noetic structure. In foundationalism, "every noetic structure has a foundation; and a proposition is rational for S, or known by S, or certain for S, only if it stands in the appropriate relation to the foundation of S's noetic structure." "Is Belief in God Rational?" in *Rationality and Religious Belief*, C. F. Delaney (Notre Dame: University of Notre Dame Press, 1979), 12.

of beliefs are *legitimately* basic? A legitimately basic belief is *properly* basic; it is a belief that is *appropriately* part of a foundation.[17] It is rational or epistemologically correct to believe properly basic beliefs without evidence; we need not argue for them. Given these definitions, Reformed epistemologists discuss this important issue: Is belief in God properly basic? Can belief in God legitimately be in the foundation? Or must a person support such belief with evidence in order to be rational?

As I mentioned above, classical foundationalism is a specific kind of foundationalism. Classical foundationalism is distinguished by the way it specifies what sorts of beliefs are legitimately placed in the foundation (i.e., what beliefs can be properly basic). According to Plantinga, to make their footing sure, ancient and medieval defenders of classical foundationalism allowed as foundational only statements that are self-evident or "evident to the senses." (A statement is self-evident if it is immediately obvious upon understanding it. The philosopher René Descartes thought that "nothing comes from nothing" is self-evident.)[18]

For modern advocates of classical foundationalism, foundational statements must be self-evident or incorrigible. (Incorrigible propositions cannot be corrected. "I feel a headache" is incorrigible.) Here is the key: by specifying these very strict requirements, classical foundationalism permits only a few very secure propositions in the foundation. In this way, classical foundationalism defenders hope to render knowledge absolutely sure.

An excellent example of a classical foundationalism strategy is the work of Descartes (1596–1650). As everyone learns in Introduction to Philosophy class, Descartes built his epistemology on a worst-case scenario: What could he know, he wondered, if a powerful demon systematically deceived him? He decided that even in that worst of all possible epistemological worlds, he could at least know he was doubting. Of this he was absolutely sure: the most powerful and malicious demon imaginable could not cause him to doubt that he was doubting. Now if he was doubting, he could be certain he was thinking; and if he was thinking, he could be sure he existed.

This conclusion, of course, is Descartes's famous *cogito ergo sum* ("I think, therefore I am"). By this procedure, Descartes thought he

17. Almost everyone acknowledges that some beliefs must be properly basic. As I pointed out in chapter 1, all giving of reasons must end somewhere. See pp. 22–23.
18. Alvin Plantinga, "Is Belief in God Properly Basic?" *Nous* 15 (1981): 44.

poured an undoubtable footing for his philosophical home: "I exist" is properly basic. It provides an absolutely secure, unquestionable foundation upon which to build knowledge. From this meager start, Descartes sought to prove the existence of God and the reliability of the senses. (He used deductive inferences, hoping to transmit the absolute certainty of his premises to his conclusions.) For our purposes, what is important is not the success or failure of his enterprise, but the shape of his foundationalist method: start with completely secure premises and infer deductively the rest of human knowledge. This Cartesian method promises certainty in knowledge.

Notice in Descartes's foundationalist epistemology the "guilty until proven innocent" principle that evidentialists employ. Clifford's claim that "it is wrong always, everywhere, and for any one, to believe anything upon insufficient evidence," mirrors the Cartesian method of doubt. These men advised taking a worst-case scenario approach. Accept only what is undoubtable or what can be established by sufficient evidence. Build knowledge on that secure foundation. Do not risk believing something that might turn out to be erroneous. Better to risk losing the truth than to hazard committing an error.[19]

Classical foundationalism has been pervasive in Western philosophy. That point is rarely debated. Nor do philosophers discussing this issue expend much energy showing that evidentialism does in fact assume classical foundationalism. For example, Plantinga says simply, "insofar as the evidentialist objection is rooted in classical foundationalism, it is poorly rooted indeed: and so far as I know, no one had developed and articulated any other reason for supposing that belief in God is not properly basic."[20]

Classical foundationalism has been widespread among Christian thinkers as well. Just as critics of Christian knowledge have assumed it in their attack, so advocates have presupposed it in their defense. Thus Christians have felt compelled to reach very specific standards before their beliefs could count as *knowledge*. Thomas Aquinas, for instance, did not use the word *knowledge* for what we apprehend through revelation. One *believes* what revelation says; one does not *know* it. Knowledge must be rooted in what is self-evident. The Trinity is not so rooted. Thus the Trinity cannot be known. Assumptions of the same sort, others have argued, also lie behind the views of other Christian philosophers.

19. Clark, *Return to Reason*, 146.
20. Plantinga, "Is Belief in God Properly Basic?" 44.

Many have noticed, however, that this all or nothing approach creates a dilemma for theology.[21] The two extremes between which people feel compelled to choose are *rationalism* and *fideism*. *Rationalism* in this generic sense includes perspectives that emphasize demonstrating all knowledge claims with certainty. Rationalism exhibits great confidence in epistemology; it tends to make bold claims for the results of arguments and natural theology. Ironically, rationalistic Christians share with Enlightenment skeptics this high view of human rationality. These Christians disagree with the agnostics, of course, in thinking that human reason properly exercised leads toward God, not away from him.

In contrast, *fideism* generally denotes views that place little confidence in rational argument. Fideists emphasize believing even without evidence. Fideism is a stance that has very little confidence (or none at all) in the ability of human reason to come to knowledge of God outside of special revelation. Obviously, therefore, fideism shies away from natural theology.

The word *fideism* has a nasty connotation, however, so most people do not like to be classed as fideists. Because of their distaste for the word, many authors define the word so it does not apply to them. Thus, one can find a variety of suggested definitions for the word. Broadly, however, I use the word *fideism* for views that deny we can gain knowledge of God through human argumentation.

Since classical foundationalism requires that knowledge meet high standards, assuming classical foundationalism permits little middle ground between rationalism and fideism. Taking classical foundationalism as a presupposition forces one either to argue that natural theology proves God's existence or to admit that the evidence is not demonstrative. Choosing the former leads to rationalism. Selecting the latter entails admitting that apologetic arguments do not absolutely prove the faith and are therefore (given classical foundationalism) of little use. (The "guilty until proven innocent" principle of evidentialism implies that one should not put stock in anything less than a conclusive argument.) Accepting the rules of classical founda-

21. Arthur F. Holmes, *Contours of a World View*, Studies in a Christian World View (Grand Rapids: Eerdmans, 1983), 138–41. Jerry H. Gill traces a parallel dichotomy between positivist and existentialist views on religious knowledge. Part of the problem here is assuming an uncrossable gulf between facts and values. This creates a pervasive intellectual schizophrenia. *The Possibility of Religious Knowledge* (Grand Rapids: Eerdmans, 1971), 13–15.

tionalism and admitting that arguments are not absolutely compelling leads toward fideism. In this way, assuming classical foundationalism forces people to extremes.

Contemporary apologetic writing by evangelicals has until recently generally presumed classical foundationalism. Thus while some claim apologetic arguments are powerful, others think apologetics does little outside the Holy Spirit's initial conviction. Without discussing this in detail, simply notice for now that classical foundationalism forces apologetics into the "all or nothing" dilemma. Either God's existence is conclusively provable or it is not. If it is, one is propelled to rationalism. But if not, religious knowledge is impossible outside revelation, and one is nudged toward fideism and the claim that natural theology is apologetically pointless.

Secular intellectuals today generally believe that conclusive proof for God (the sort that classical foundationalism demands) is not forthcoming. Given this, many unbelievers conclude that apologetics is ineffective and cannot achieve its purpose. Apologetics today must be done with this sociological fact clearly in mind: the majority of intellectuals do not think the case for Christianity is airtight. If one claims apologetics is successful if and only if it presents an airtight case (i.e., if one assumes classical foundationalism), then the probability of failure is high.

In sum, classical foundationalism has had a powerful influence in history, forcing theologians and Christian philosophers to presuppose that their convictions count as knowledge if and only if they pass the most stringent of tests. Reformed epistemology defender Nicholas Wolterstorff claims that this has served to "confuse and intimidate" Christian thinkers. In his analysis, Christians should rid their thinking of classical foundationalism: "Only if the sting of foundationalism is plucked will the infection subside."[22]

Critique of Classical Foundationalism

If classical foundationalism causes such serious infection, Christians must find the necessary surgical instruments, pluck the stinger, and lance the wound. Reformed epistemologists seek to do just this by formulating two major lines of argument against classical founda-

22. Nicholas Wolterstorff, *Reason within the Bounds of Religion*, 2d ed. (Grand Rapids: Eerdmans, 1984), 34.

tionalism. The common theme of these arguments is this: The rules of rational etiquette drawn up by classical foundationalism are so restrictive that they eliminate many beliefs humans do normally and correctly accept as knowledge.

Christians develop this theme in two ways. First, classical foundationalism rationally self-defeats. Self-defeat occurs when a statement purports to say, do, or be what it asserts to be impossible. For instance, I once opened a fortune cookie that said, "Never trust a fortune cookie." Or consider this universal claim:

(5) All universal statements are false.

(5) is a universal statement, so it fails its own rule. It is self-defeating and thus false. Sometimes apologists get carried away with this principle, as in this case:

(6) There are absolutely no moral absolutes.

I have often heard Christians claim that (6) is self-defeating, and that therefore moral relativism is false. But this argument surely does not carry the day. Since (6) is not itself a moral absolute, it does not self-destruct. It is not self-referential; it does not include itself among the sentences about which it speaks. It is like saying, "I cannot speak a word of English" *in Japanese*, in contrast to saying it in English. The Japanese utterance is perfectly in order.

Now consider the general statement:

(7) For any statement S, S is true if and only if it meets criterion C.

If (7) meets C, it is a true statement, and everything is fine on this score. If (7) fails C, then it is false. For in this case, (7) purports to be a true statement that fails C. But this is exactly what (7) denies is possible; no statement, *(7) included*, can be a true statement that fails C. So (7) either meets C, or it is false.

Like (5), classical foundationalism is self-defeating in that it does not live up to its own standards. It has not met and likely cannot meet its own criteria for proper basicality, for it is neither self-evident, "evident to the senses," nor incorrigible. Neither can it be built on or inferred from properly basic premises. So classical foundationalism is self-defeating or "self-referentially incoherent" and therefore false.[23]

Second, classical foundationalism not only destroys itself, it also eliminates many other clearly acceptable knowledge claims. Many properly basic beliefs are unwarranted if classical foundationalism were correct. Reformed epistemologists discuss a number of different kinds of such beliefs. Their purpose in so doing is to show that the swath cut by classical foundationalism is too wide. Classical foundationalism destroys everything in its path.

For example, classical foundationalism eliminates as properly basic the belief that other persons or minds exist. A long debate in philosophy swirls around this issue: How do I know other minds exist? Certainly everyone acts on the belief that other minds do exist. When I talk to my friend about J. S. Bach, for instance, I do so on the conviction that my friend (and Bach, too, for that matter) exists outside my mind. And I am surely rational in doing so.

But does belief in other minds meet the criteria of classical foundationalism? Well, no. It is not properly basic (since it is not self-evident, evident to the senses, or incorrigible). And it is hard to see how we could deduce the existence of other minds from other properly basic beliefs. This suggests a simple argument:

If classical foundationalism is right, then I am not justified in believing in other minds.
But I am justified in so believing.
So classical foundationalism must be defective.

In a word, classical foundationalism eliminates too many perfectly acceptable beliefs.

The same sort of argument applies to other kinds of beliefs, for example, memory beliefs. I remember taking my two boys to a baseball game on July 11. The Twins defeated the Red Sox, 7–3. I am certainly justified in believing this is so, but I cannot *prove* it according to the requirements of classical foundationalism. (I could look up the newspaper account for July 12 to show the Twins did win, 7–3, but that still would not prove that we three took in the game.)

---

23. Alvin Plantinga, "Reason and Belief in God," in *Faith and Rationality: Reason and Belief in God*, ed. Alvin Plantinga and Nicholas Wolterstorff (Notre Dame: University of Notre Dame Press, 1983), 59–61.

This suggests that we can generalize the simple argument above in this way:

If classical foundationalism is right, then I am not justified in believing B.

But I am justified in believing B.

So classical foundationalism must be defective.

In this argument, B could stand for a variety of beliefs. Any one of them could suffice to show classical foundationalism defective. In addition to the belief in other minds and in memory beliefs, Plantinga suggests the belief that physical objects endure through time or that the world has existed for more than five minutes. These and many others are all appropriately believed, yet not acceptable by classical foundationalist standards. So there must be something wrong with classical foundationalism.[24]

Given these two lines of argument, the conclusion is a challenge: "the next move is up to the evidentialist objector." If he wishes to eliminate belief in God as rational, the evidentialist must create a criterion to identify properly basic statements. But to make the argument work, the evidentialist's criterion must do several things: First, it must meet its own requirements (i.e., it cannot be self-defeating). Second, it must rule out belief in God as properly basic. Third, it must offer some reason to think it is true.[25]

Reformed epistemologists believe rightly that this challenge will not likely be met. The classical foundationalism-based evidentialist critique of God is mortally wounded. A continued insistence on classical foundationalism-based objections to theistic belief amounts to "intellectual imperialism."[26]

Reformed Epistemology's Positive Claims

Evidentialism is hemorrhaging. The critiques leveled against classical foundationalism-based evidentialism are devastating. But from a theistic viewpoint, the arguments against it are defensive. They only show that the classical foundationalism-based evidentialist objection

24. Ibid.
25. Ibid., 62–63.
26. Plantinga, "Is Belief in God Rational?" 26.

against God does not carry the day. They do not positively prove God's existence. Just as the baseball team cannot score runs when it is in the field, so an apologist cannot show positively that God exists by using the defensive arguments I have been discussing. What does Reformed epistemology do on this score?

Positively, Reformed epistemologists claim that theists are rational to ground belief in God in their experiences of him. To put this another way, Reformed epistemologists hold that belief in God is properly basic. This means the Christian's conviction that God exists does not need arguments or evidence to back it up. That conviction is rationally appropriate even when the Christian cannot produce such evidence. I can know God exists just as I can know other minds exist. This is one thesis of Plantinga's landmark book, *God and Other Minds*. Just as I am rational to believe in other minds even though I cannot prove they exist to the satisfaction of classical foundationalism, so, by analogy, I am rational to believe in God.

Evidentialism, with its strict rules, is just not relevant in personal knowing with the love and intimacy this demands. In fact, the unrelenting pursuit of objective evidence may be detrimental to the very qualities that make personal knowing what it is. In this vein, C. S. Lewis argued,

> There are times when we can do all that a fellow creature needs if only he will trust us. In getting a dog out of a trap, in extracting a thorn from a child's finger, in teaching a boy to swim or rescuing one who can't, in getting a frightened beginner over a nasty place on a mountain, the one fatal obstacle may be their distrust. We are asking them to trust us in the teeth of their senses, their imagination, and their intelligence.[27]

Just so, it may be rationally acceptable to believe in God without evidence.

This does not imply, however, that belief in God is groundless or baseless or arbitrary. Notice that Plantinga distinguishes *evidence* from *grounds*. *Evidence* is what apologists look for in theistic proofs (i.e., arguments for God like the one based on design in the universe). Evidence involves putting together a formal argument in which several statements are related by correct logical structure.

27. C. S. Lewis, "On Obstinacy in Belief," in *They Asked for a Paper* (London: G. Bles, 1962), 191.

But *grounds* could be more straightforward than evidence. Direct experience provides grounds to justify belief even without argumentation. For example, take the case of perceptual beliefs. If I see before me a traffic signal lighted red, I will come to believe that a red traffic light is signaling me to stop. That experience by itself legitimately grounds and justifies my belief. If I am wise, I will guide my actions by this belief!

Plantinga thinks the same is true of God: my experience of God appropriately grounds my belief in his existence. Evidentialists, on the other hand, assume that belief in God is rational only if it is the conclusion of an argument. But Reformed epistemologists hold that I am within the guidelines of rational etiquette to believe that God exists on the ground, for instance, that he answered my prayer. Just as I am right to believe my wife exists because I talked to her this morning, so I am rational to believe God exists because he responds to my prayer. A believer does not need evidence, in the sense of a formal argument, to back up belief of this sort.

How can I know without argument that the red light is telling me to stop or that my wife exists? Following the suggestions of a philosopher named Thomas Reid,[28] Reformed epistemologists affirm that human knowing uses several belief-forming mechanisms. The ability to reason, of course, is one of these mechanisms, but it is neither the only one nor the main one. The list of mechanisms includes the senses and the memory. Reid calls this constellation of cooperating mechanisms, taken together, *common sense*. Common sense enables one to ground many beliefs.

Plantinga combined these Reidian observations with Calvin's teaching that God reveals himself lavishly in nature and creates all humans with a propensity to take in and accept that abundant revelation. So Plantinga wrote, "God has so created us that we have a tendency or disposition to see his hand in the world about us."[29] Theologically speaking, God so constituted the human mind that the inclination to believe that he exists is triggered under certain conditions. Believers come to know God exists just as my tendency to believe my wife really exists is triggered when we discuss the day's events over coffee.

In sum, believing in my wife's existence and in God's is appropri-

---

28. Thomas Reid, *An Inquiry into the Human Mind, on the Principles of Common Sense*, 6th ed. (Edinburgh: Bell and Bradfute, 1810).
29. Plantinga, "Is Belief in God Properly Basic?" 46.

ate under certain conditions even without external evidence. One writer puts the issue this way: Reformed epistemology claims that "religious experience plays an *independent role* in the justification of religious beliefs; it does not require a prior *argument* showing that such experience is reliable."[30] If someone says this strategy sounds acceptable in the case of traffic lights and daffodils, but not in the case of belief in God, Reformed epistemologists will suggest that he may still be marching to the drumbeat of classical foundationalism. And it should be clear by now what they think of that drum.

This means that one major objection to Reformed epistemology misses the point. This is known as the Great Pumpkin Objection.[31] If an experience legitimately grounds a belief and if Linus and I experience the Great Pumpkin next Halloween, does not Reformed epistemology imply that we might be rational in believing in the existence of the Great Pumpkin? Can just anything count as rational belief? Put another way, does it seem that too many false beliefs could pass the tests that some Reformed epistemologists advocate? While classical foundationalism is too restrictive in ruling *out* clearly justified beliefs, maybe Reformed epistemology is too liberal because it rules *in* clearly unjustified beliefs—like Linus's belief in the Great Pumpkin. Maybe we should demand evidence for all beliefs after all.

In response, the major point is that the Great Pumpkin Objection misses the distinction between grounds and evidence. But a couple of other things are relevant. First, Plantinga's work is still in process, and he has not yet fully responded to this problem. He is now working on a book on epistemological warrant.[32] Presumably this work will spell out more fully his criteria for rational belief. In other works (such as the weighty volume *Epistemic Justification* by William Alston), other Reformed epistemologists are making considerable headway in addressing a variety of these complex issues.[33]

Second, Plantinga argues minimally that the criteria for assessing the grounds of properly basic beliefs will be arrived at inductively. That is, one should first look at clear cases of justified belief and work

---

30. Michael L. Peterson et al., *Reason and Religious Belief: An Introduction to the Philosophy of Religion* (New York: Oxford, 1991), 130.

31. Plantinga, "Reason and Belief in God," 74–87.

32. Two volumes of *Warrant* are out. The crucial third volume is promised soon.

33. William P. Alston, *Epistemic Justification: Essays in the Theory of Knowledge* (Ithaca, N.Y.: Cornell University Press, 1989).

from them rather than pontificating broad general principles that apply universally.[34] His point is *not* that we cannot distinguish justified and unjustified claims. Rather, it is that no one is likely to find one general rule that will draw this distinction simply and cleanly in all cases. Given the difficulty philosophers have had in finding just such a universal principle, Plantinga's suggestion seems correct.

A related objection (or perhaps another form of the same objection) charges Reformed epistemology with being fideistic. If, in order to be rational or epistemologically proper, belief in God need not be grounded in arguments, then a Christian is free just to believe God exists. This is fideism, says the objector. Reformed epistemology holds that belief in God does not need such arguments, and so Reformed epistemology must be fideistic.[35]

This question is not settled. At a professional meeting, I once heard a leading exponent of Reformed epistemology half-jokingly speak of his own view as "fideism—what Al Plantinga calls Reformed epistemology." But others defend Reformed epistemology against the charge, noting, for example, that Plantinga is very well known for his defense of the ontological argument. Indeed, Plantinga has offered two dozen theistic arguments that he considers sound.[36] And he has admitted that arguments like these can confirm God's existence for some believers and prepare the way to faith for some unbelievers.[37]

The slipperiness of the word *fideism* makes the point hard to pin down. In my view, the best way to see the matter places rationalism and fideism at the poles of a continuum. Various views can be plotted at different points along the continuum. (As I have argued, only an assumption of classical foundationalism eliminates middle ground and forces a choice between strong rationalism and fideism.) If this is right, then Reformed epistemology should be plotted closer to fideism than evidentialism is. But this fact does not automatically imply that Reformed epistemology is a full-blown fideism.

The central positive point made in Reformed epistemology is that belief in God is rational even without evidence. The word *rational*

34. Plantinga, "Is Belief in God Properly Basic?" 49–50.

35. William J. Abraham, *An Introduction to the Philosophy of Religion* (Englewood Cliffs, N.J.: Prentice-Hall, 1985), 88–97.

36. Clark, *Return to Reason*, 156; cf. Peterson, *Reason and Religious Belief*, 131; Plantinga, "Reason and Belief in God," 87–91.

37. Alvin Plantinga, "The Reformed Objection Revisited," *Christian Scholar's Review* 12 (1983): 58.

here does not mean true. *Rational* here implies a kind of epistemological permission. It is *not irrational* to believe in God on the ground of experience. So Reformed epistemologists do not claim that a belief's being rational shows its truth; rather it means the belief is *possibly* true. If theistic belief were not rational, then it would be false. Since it is rational, it is possibly true.[38] Thus, evidentialist rules do not conclusively rule out belief in God. They do not show belief in God to be defective just because it is not supported by arguments. Reformed epistemology's strategy here is primarily defensive.

Other Epistemological Options

The discussion so far has emphasized the dominant understanding of religious knowledge in Western intellectual history. Classical foundationalism-based evidentialism says that belief in God must be proved by evidence or propositional arguments if it is to be rationally acceptable (and thus grounding belief in God in experience is illegitimate). Evidentialists come in two varieties. Religious evidentialists say God can be proved in this way; agnostic evidentialists say not. A major agenda item for Reformed epistemology is the critique (in my view successful) of classical foundationalism-based evidentialism. In the wake of evidentialism's demise, what alternatives are still available?

Coherentism

One major option is *coherentism* (sometimes called contextualism or holism). As the name implies, coherentism depends heavily on the principle of coherence. Briefly, I will argue that this principle is an essential feature of all human thought. But while coherence as a principle is important, coherentism as a system is too limited. Why is this so?

The coherence principle is a logical guideline that tests statements by comparing them to other propositions already believed or known. Coherence judges the truth of beliefs by assessing whether they fit logically with the rest of a person's judgments.

38. William Lane Craig, *Apologetics: An Introduction* (Chicago: Moody, 1984), 17; George I. Mavrodes, "Jerusalem and Athens Revisted," in *Faith and Rationality*, ed. Plantinga and Wolterstorff, 195–96.

Sometimes people equate coherence with logical consistency, which means a lack of contradiction within a set of propositions. For example, consider these statements:

(8) John Williams plays the bassoon in the Minnesota Orchestra.

(9) Not all swans are white.

(10) All swans are white.

Statements (8) and (9) are not logically contradictory; they *could* both be true. But (9) and (10) do contradict logically; they *cannot* both be true. So a set of statements made up of (8) and (9) is logically consistent while the set made up of (9) and (10) is not. That (8) and (9) are consistent tells me they both *may* be true; but either or both could be false. That (9) and (10) are inconsistent tells me that *one must* be false, but it does not tell me which one actually is false. Logical consistency is a good negative test, then, for it helps eliminate false statements. But it does not by itself identify true ones.

Generally, however, coherence means something more than consistency. Coherence means a positive relation between or connectedness of several statements to each other. In this sense, (8) and (9) are not coherent because they do not positively relate to each other. But (8) does cohere with something like

(11) John Williams plays the bassoon very well.

Assuming that only very good instrumentalists become members of the Minnesota Orchestra, (8) and (11) fit together nicely and so are coherent.

The principle of coherence is generally contrasted with the principle of correspondence. Though correspondence is hotly debated, in general it means that one assesses the truth status of statements by comparing them to the real world revealed through sensory observations. In general, therefore, coherence is a more rational principle, while correspondence is more empirical.

Coherentism is any epistemological stance that takes coherence in some sense to be both necessary and sufficient as a test for truth. Many other forms of epistemology use the coherence principle, saying it is *necessary* for knowledge. But coherentism is distinct in affirming that coherence is a *sufficient* test. Coherentism, therefore, essentially rejects correspondence as necessary to warranting knowing.

Foundationalism sees knowledge as a building with certain ideas in the foundation and others built on top as part of the first or second floors. A very different model portrays coherentism. According to coherentism, knowledge is like a ship at sea. What allows a steel plate to float is not its being grounded in a foundation on the sea floor, but rather its being welded securely to the other plates in the ship. Beliefs are known to be true not because they sit on top of other beliefs but because they hang together.

This model may seem to lead to circularity. Foundationalists believe that if foundational belief A grounds belief B, then B cannot legitimately ground A. (Evidence *cannot* move in both directions.) But with a coherentist ship, all the plates are welded to others, so any plate can be the first plate. Plate A supports plate B; plate B supports plate A. (Evidence *can* move both ways.) Now this amounts to circularity, but coherentists usually admit it. They agree with Elton Trueblood: all reasoning is circular, but circularity is acceptable so long as the circle is large enough. Put enough plates in the ship, weld them securely together, and the ship will float.[39]

Coherentism is not common among Christian apologists. Empirical observations organized by scientific methods have produced impressive results. Thus modern people tend not to see coherence as *sufficient* for knowledge even if it is very important. Wheaton College philosopher Arthur Holmes committed himself to coherentism.[40] But judging by the rest of his writings, he gives some weight to observations. Thus he apparently holds a weak form of coherentism. Rationalist Gordon Clark, who is my relative neither biologically nor philosophically, was undoubtedly the strongest proponent of coherentism among Christian apologists in this century.[41]

Soft Rationalism

Despite the coherentist option, I will seek a more empirically oriented perspective. *Coherence* is surely *necessary* to knowledge. But

---

39. D. Elton Trueblood, *Philosophy of Religion* (New York: Harper and Bros., 1957), 53.

40. Holmes, *Contours of a World View*, 51–52.

41. See the overview of Clark's epistemology by Ronald Nash, "Gordon Clark's Theory of Knowledge," in *The Philosophy of Gordon H. Clark: A Festschrift*, ed. Ronald Nash (Philadelphia: Presbyterian and Reformed, 1968), 125–75.

coherentism, which affirms the *sufficiency* of coherence, is too unbalanced. Both the unprecedented success of science and the way people do actually learn about their world seem to require that experience play a more important role in epistemology. Coherentism cannot account for certain kinds of knowledge that are properly basic. An epistemological underpinning for dialogical apologetics, therefore, must take account of the demise of classical foundationalism as well as the obvious relevance of empirical data.

Classical foundationalism and Reformed epistemology join forces (surprisingly) to reject coherentism. This leaves, in addition to evidentialism, two major options that we will be able to discuss, Reformed epistemology and what I will call soft rationalism. Unlike coherentism (which renounces all foundations), the other three positions are all foundationalist. The major issue that divides them is the *size* of the foundation. They debate the question, What sorts of beliefs can legitimately be placed in the foundation? What beliefs may one rationally accept without building arguments?

Classical foundationalism has the narrowest foundation because its rules for properly basic beliefs are so restrictive. Classical foundationalism is like a pyramid on its point—a small foundation holds up a large structure. By contrast, Reformed epistemology puts the pyramid on its bottom—a large foundation holds up a smaller structure. Reformed epistemology allows many more beliefs (though not all beliefs indiscriminately) into the foundation. Obviously, belief in the existence of God is the key idea Reformed epistemology places in the foundation.

The third view, soft rationalism, lies between classical foundationalism and Reformed epistemology on the continuum between rationalism and fideism. Since it agrees that classical foundationalism is false, soft rationalism sees a bigger foundation than classical foundationalism. But soft rationalism also questions the strategy of placing belief in God in the foundation. That is, it questions whether it is enough to say that belief in God is properly basic. Soft rationalists suggest that people use evidence to discriminate among competing religious claims, all of which depend on experience. Soft rationalism is perhaps like a square—its foundation is bigger than classical foundationalism's, but smaller than Reformed epistemology's.

Parenthetically, with its strong emphasis on accepting without evidence, fideism can be seen as a foundationalism with the widest foundation of all. Virtually anything can be part of the foundation. But that is just the problem; fideism is simply too generous. It allows too many beliefs to be acceptable. Since it cannot discriminate true and false beliefs, it does fall prey to the Great Pumpkin Objection. Now fideism does have a big plus: it is invulnerable to rational attack. But this advantage is more than offset by a critical liability: a fideist cannot argue rationally for her position.

In sum, on the continuum between rationalism and fideism lie classical foundationalism-based evidentialism (a type of hard rationalism), soft rationalism, and Reformed epistemology. Classical foundationalism-based evidentialism in particular and hard rationalism in general are unwarranted. Fideism is defective. Coherentism is flawed as well. It does not account for certain things we know directly. Thus two major options, Reformed epistemology and soft rationalism, remain for our discussion of the epistemological underpinning of dialogical apologetics.[42]

Summary

Clifford (evidentialism) asserted that belief in God is epistemologically defective unless it is supported by formal arguments. An experience of God cannot legitimately ground belief in God.

According to James, evidentialism is faulty because, in hopes of avoiding all errors, it eliminates the very possibility of finding truth. Belief in God should not be "guilty until proven innocent."

Plantinga (and other Reformed epistemologists) see evidentialism based in classical foundationalism and rebut the evidentialist challenge to religious belief by showing that classical foundationalism is self-defeating.

Following Calvin and Reid, Reformed epistemologists argue that many beliefs (e.g., memory beliefs) are acceptable without argumentation. These beliefs are legitimately grounded in experience.

42. The positions I include here do not exhaust the possibilities. For example, between Enlightenment rationalism and soft rationalism are views (like Aquinas's) that have a larger foundation than Clifford, but a smaller one than does soft rationalism. For a balanced explication of Aquinas's position, see Norman L. Geisler, *Thomas Aquinas: An Evangelical Appraisal* (Grand Rapids: Baker, 1991), 57–90. For a good source that illustrates various epistemological options, see R. Douglas Geivett and Brendan Sweetman, eds., *Contemporary Perspectives on Religious Epistemology* (New York: Oxford University Press, 1992).

Similarly, belief in God is rightly grounded in experience (i.e., it is properly basic).

Coherentism, which judges truth by looking at the fit between statements, does not give sufficient weight to beliefs generated directly in experience. Coherentism is not the best form of religious epistemology.

Soft rationalism recognizes the bankruptcy of classical foundationalism, but still argues that finding knowledge about God requires the use of evidence. This view lies between evidentialism and Reformed epistemology on the continuum between rationalism and fideism.

This discussion leaves two major options, Reformed epistemology and soft rationalism, as possibilities for the basis of dialogical apologetics.

In addition to these currents in religious epistemology, a second movement that can provide relevant materials for dialogical apologetics is philosophy of science. While science itself has enjoyed respect in Western culture for many years, philosophy of science is relatively young. Yet some of its ideas (e.g., the phrase *paradigm shift*) have found their way into common parlance. The facet of this field most important for this study focuses on the question, How do scientists actually arrive at warranted scientific conclusions? We will also consider a second question: Can scientific procedures fruitfully illuminate religious epistemology?

3

The Challenge of Science

"My head really hurts and I feel terrible," Tyler complained at supper.

"Why do you hurt so much, Tyler?" We felt our nine-year-old son's forehead for signs of fever and listened as he explained that while roughhousing with some children, he had hit his head hard on a concrete floor.

"Could it be a concussion?" Mom and Dad communicated silently. Mom pulled out a medical encyclopedia. Under "concussion" it listed these symptoms: extreme headache, dizziness, short breathing, blurred vision, memory loss, and vomiting. I asked him to read a line from his Hardy Boys book. No problem. Mom asked him his birthday, what he had for lunch, and where we went for vacation last year. No problem. I checked Tyler's pupils, but I wasn't sure how to interpret what I saw. Still his head throbbed. We put him to bed.

"Do you think Tyler could have the flu?" I wondered out loud.

Suddenly he began breathing with short, staccato breaths and became nauseous. We called the clinic. The nurse read the same symptoms of concussion from a list in a similar medical encyclopedia.

"If he vomits two or three times, bring him in. In the meantime, continue to observe him," he told us. After two more trips to the bathroom, at 2:30 A.M., we took our son to the clinic. The physician found nothing wrong. The vomiting and extreme pain continued, however, so the doctor ordered a CAT scan. If there were any bleeding, swelling, or fracture in that skull, he wanted to find it. To our relief, the report proved negative.

After receiving liquid intravenously for several hours, Tyler came home. He awakened at noon with a fever. He felt achy and fluish. Within a day, however, he was back on his feet, recovering, as children sometimes do, almost in a snap.

What could explain what happened? Did Tyler have a concussion or the flu? Or both? The evidence was mixed. At first it favored one explanation; later it leaned a different way. Looked at one way, certain facts made sense, but others did not. Viewed a different way, new facts became understandable, but others became inexplicable. I faced that day an uncertain choice between rival interpretations. Similarly, the processes scientists use to arrive at explanations of the world sometimes force choices between rival perspectives. A proper view of science will take this into account.

Philosophy of Science

A developing field called philosophy of science seeks to do just that. As a kind of philosophy, this discipline is an analysis of science at work. Philosophers and historians of science do not do science. They study scientists and how they do science. They discuss these questions, among others: Do the results scientists produce describe the real world or are they useful fictions? Do scientists support their claims by rational principles primarily, or are they more influenced by sociological and psychological factors? Though philosophers of science share a common goal (to ascertain the metaphysical and epistemological status of scientific claims), fierce debates on these issues continue to rage.

The Metaphysics of Science

"Yes, Virginia, there is a Santa Claus." These famous words once reassured a little girl that the story about the jolly old elf was true indeed. Virginia assumed, I am sure, that if she were to travel to the North Pole, she could see her benefactor with her own eyes, tug on his white beard, and pat his ample belly. But those who know more than Virginia realize that Santa Claus only exists "in our hearts" when we experience the "spirit of Christmas"—the spirit of love, giving, and good cheer.

Some philosophers of science do not believe scientific explanations describe a real world in Virginia's sense of the word. They opt for a position called *antirealism*. In this view, scientific theories do not *copy* the world, they merely help humans *cope* with it. Science *manipulates* the environment; it does not *describe* it. In contrast, many people assume science does picture the real world. This view is called *naive realism*. Its sophisticated cousin, *critical realism*, says that scientific theories map the world so that, as science progresses, its theories become more refined and more precise. Critical realism admits that science never mirrors the world exactly. But like other maps, scientific theories do correspond meaningfully to an objective world.

Why discuss philosophy of science in a book on apologetics? Because it has important implications for epistemology. As Henry Veatch observed, "the greatest seeming stumbling block in the way of religion [and apologetics] has long been, and still continues to be, modern science."[1] I hope both to debunk extravagant claims to the absoluteness of scientific conclusions and to tease out principles that will help apologists warrant their Christian beliefs. But I have paused here to note the furor of the realist versus antirealist debate, for it will teach careful apologists something of great value.

Science is an intimidating authority in this culture. The reigning prejudice among nonscientists is that only science possesses respectability. Only scientific ideas are really true and put one in touch with solid reality. Thus because religious ideas are not scientific, they are mythological—one who believes them may feel better, but they do not represent reality. But not all experts share this prejudice. The heated debate between critical realist and antirealist should suggest that the "Science is real, but religion is myth" thesis is itself very much up for debate.

The structures of knowledge in science and religion have more in common than often thought. Now I am not calling religion respectable because it *really is scientific* after all. This move sets up science as the ideal and then grants legitimacy to religious knowledge only when it placates the canons of science. Instead, both scientific and religious thinking are human attempts to understand the world. As such they reflect acceptable modes of knowing. Indeed, as Wolterstorff suggests, "science and ordinary life can be viewed as on a continuum with respect to the presence of theories and with respect to the actions performed on those theories. . . . science [is] different only in degree from ordinary life."[2]

1. Henry Veatch, "A Neglected Avenue in Contemporary Religious Apologetics," *Religious Studies* 13 (1977): 30.

2. Nicholas Wolterstorff, *Reason within the Bounds of Religion*, 2d ed. (Grand Rapids: Eerdmans, 1984), 65; cf. Francis Schaeffer, *The God Who Is There: Speaking Historic Christianity into the Twentieth Century* (Downers Grove: InterVarsity, 1968), 109.

Two Approaches to Philosophy of Science

Not only do philosophers of science argue over their subject (the metaphysics and epistemology of science), they debate their method as well. The two major choices are a philosophical approach and a historical one. The first method develops its view of science by starting with broader theories of knowledge. It looks outside the practice of science itself to general views about human knowing. On this basis it constructs an idealized view of science. Thus it earns the designation *external philosophy of science*. External philosophy of science uses its ideal view of science to evaluate actual scientific work. It tends not to use actual scientific work to prompt an understanding of scientific methods.

A classic example of this "top down" method is Aristotle. The great Greek developed his concept of science in the *Posterior Analytics*. But his discussion took no account of the work he actually did as a practicing biologist![3] In spite of Aristotle's genius, this move is flawed. Indeed, recent decades have witnessed a shift toward the historical approach. In this method, researchers study how scientists actually do their work. The way successful scientists reason should guide philosophy of science. Leaders in this shift include Stephen Toulmin, Michael Polanyi, Ernan McMullin, and Thomas Kuhn.

The phrase *internal philosophy of science* describes the method that emphasizes the history of science. On this view, philosophers assume science is working correctly and does not need external validation. They observe science at work and then allow an understanding of science to grow out of those observations. This "down up" approach is more inductive than deductive. For internal philosophy of science, history is not just illustrative (as it can be for external philosophy of science). History actually provides the data from which philosophers should draw a theory of scientific knowing.

Note that internal philosophy of science (the historical approach) exhibits a striking similarity to Reformed epistemology on at least one point: good epistemology begins with the fact that humans do know something. No one need start with Descartes's methodological doubt or Clifford's miserly evidentialist rules. These lead to skepticism not

3. Ernan McMullin, "The History and Philosophy of Science: A Taxonomy," in *Historical and Philosophical Perspectives of Science*, ed. Roger Stuewer, Minnesota Studies in the Philosophy of Science (Minneapolis: University of Minnesota, 1970), 24.

only in religion but even in science. Epistemology should begin with the patently obvious: humans possess genuine knowledge about the world, even if that knowledge is imperfect. Apologists can work inductively from that premise to construct an epistemology—an understanding of human understanding.

Empirical Approaches

If the first dominant question for philosophy of science is metaphysical, the second is epistemological. The realism versus antirealism debate swirls around disagreement over the metaphysical status of scientific pronouncements. A different conflict revolves around the epistemological *warrant* for these claims. Here the issue is: Are scientific pronouncements controlled by rational principles or are they dominated by subjective influences? First we will discuss several views, dominant in early philosophy of science, that are similar to evidentialism in their defense of rational science. These strong forms of empiricism are now as thoroughly discredited as evidentialism.

Inductivism

Perhaps the earliest modern philosophy of science is the inductivism associated with Francis Bacon (1561–1626). Bacon held that scientists form hypotheses by observing the patterns that arise from the data. The scientist begins with a *tabula rasa* (his mind is a blank slate) and allows the facts to form a preliminary thesis. Next he tests this thesis against other observations to see if it holds generally. Similar in spirit to Sergeant Friday's naive evidentialism, Bacon's inductivism sees the scientist allowing the meanings to emerge on their own initiative from the facts.

All philosophers of science today recognize the weaknesses of this view. Fundamentally, inductivism fails to recognize the active role scientists play in forming theories. Hypotheses result not only from the researchers' observations but also from their creative imagination and synthetic model-building. Scientists do not follow any direct, predetermined route from data to theory. Their theories must posit new categories and novel entities and relationships that cannot be observed directly. "Science, in short, is at the same time a process of discovery and a venture in human imagination."[4]

The classic story of August Kekulé illustrates the point. The great chemist struggled mightily to find the molecular structure of benzene. His many failures greatly frustrated him. Then one evening, dozing by a crackling fire, he dreamt of frolicking atoms and snakes. One of the dancing snakes created a circle by biting its own tail. Upon awakening, with that picture as his clue, Kekulé worked into the night to identify the ring-like structure of benzene. This famous story illustrates the now universally recognized principle that without scientists' creativity, facts alone do not produce theories.

Confirmationism

According to another view of science, researchers follow these rational steps:

Collect the relevant data.

By creative imagination, propose a general theory (a working *hypothesis*) that appears to explain the data.

Predict (by *deduction*) the particular experimental or observational results implied in the hypothesis.

Perform experiments or record observations to see whether the predicted results actually occur.

A match between the predicted results and the observed results supports the proposed theory. This so-called *hypothetico-deductive* model of science dominated the philosophy of science scene into the 1960s.

One view of what happens here is confirmationism, and Rudolf Carnap articulated one of its forms.[5] In practice, according to confirmationism, the deductions from a general hypothesis are not precise. Rather they are suggestive; they present a range of possible predictions. In fact, the number of possible observational outcomes is nearly infinite. Thus a hypothesis is never verified definitively. Rather, the

4. Ian G. Barbour, *Religion in an Age of Science*, The Gifford Lectures, 1989–91, 2 vols. (San Francisco: Harper, 1990), 1:44.

5. Rudolf Carnap, *Philosophical Foundations of Physics* (New York: Basic, 1966).

gradual accumulation of positive results increases the probability of a hypothesis being correct. A single negative result, however, shows the general hypothesis wrong and forces its abandonment. In confirmationism, the combination of a large number of positive confirmations and no disconfirmations justifies a theory as probably true.

The classic Enlightenment vision of absolutely proven knowledge has retreated. In science, the pullback has involved several phases. Carnap's perspective can be read as one stage in that retreat; it is a move from the ideal of proven knowledge back to the concept of probable knowledge.[6] But many have argued that the ridge of probability (where Carnap sought to rally his troops and halt the evacuation) is indefensible. For one thing, confirmationism commits a fundamental logical error, a fallacy called *affirming the consequent*. (In the following syllogism, B is the consequent that is affirmed. A is called the antecedent.) Any good logic text will show the flaw in this argument form:

If A, then B.
B.
Therefore, A.

Sometimes a person carelessly confuses this form with a different one:

If A, then B.
A.
Therefore, B.

This latter form is valid. To illustrate the difference, consider an example. (In this example, A stands for "John earned 124 credits with a 3.5 average," and B stands for "John graduated from college.")

If John earned 124 credits with a 3.5 average, then he graduated from college.
John graduated from college.
Therefore, John earned 124 credits with a 3.5 average.

6. Imre Lakatos, "Falsification and the Methodology of Scientific Research Programmes," in *Criticism and the Growth of Knowledge*, ed. Imre Lakatos and Alan Musgrave, Proceedings of the International Colloquium in the Philosophy of Science, 4 (London: Cambridge University Press, 1970), 93–95.

Obviously, this is fallacious. Maybe John's average was 2.7 or he earned 128 credits. But if "John earned 124 credits with a 3.5 average" is the second premise, then "John graduated from college" follows as the conclusion. That argument form is valid.

Confirmationism makes this same error, for its basic form affirms the consequent:

If Hypothesis H is true, then Prediction P will follow.
P.
Therefore, H is true.

Further, confirmationism is also wrong about the effect of failed predictions. Hypothesis H is actually connected with and tested in the context of a number of auxiliary hypotheses assumed to be true. Now consider what a failed prediction really does:

If H and Auxiliary Hypothesis A, then P.
Not P.
Therefore, either not H or not A.

This is a valid argument. Its conclusion is that either H or A is false— or possibly both are. ("Not H or not A" means only that H and A cannot both be true; either one or both is false.) Thus the argument allows that if P does not occur, maybe A is the problem and H could be true after all. That is, a single disconfirmation of P (or even quite a number of disconfirmations) does not necessarily falsify H. It might lead scientists to revamp A instead of disqualifying H. Contrary to confirmationism, a single negative experimental result does not always negate a theory.

Falsificationism

Another view may be interpreted as a further retreat from the ideal of absolutely proven knowledge. Karl Popper presented a form of the hypothetico-deductive model in *The Logic of Scientific Discovery* and *Conjectures and Refutations*.[7] To be precise, Popper's agenda was not primarily the question, When is a theory true? Instead, he ad-

---

7. Karl Popper, *The Logic of Scientific Discovery* (New York: Basic, 1959); *Conjectures and Refutations: The Growth of Scientific Knowledge* (New York: Basic, 1963).

dressed the problem, When is a theory scientific? He was most interested in drawing the line between true science and pseudo-science. But his view implies certain responses on the matter of warranting scientific claims. According to Popper's view, called falsificationism, science weeds out false theories, permitting the fittest theories to survive as possibly true.

As a youth, Popper felt attracted to Marxism, psychoanalysis, and Alfred Adler's individual psychology. Observations seemed to confirm each of these theories. Yet the methods they employed seemed suspicious. Confirmations were too easy to find; true believers readily produced ample verification for their pet views. Thus Popper sought a way to distinguish these questionable hypotheses from truly scientific theories like Einstein's. The difference, he concluded, is this: in science, confirming evidence counts only when it grows out of determined efforts to falsify, to prove false, a theory. This prevents one finding only what is sought, picking out the facts that fit with the preconceived theory and ignoring the rest.

Unlike pseudo-science, good scientific hypotheses are risky. They predict the unexpected. They do not rummage about looking for confirmations and ignoring the disconfirmations. They risk being proved false. They are scientific by virtue of being refutable or falsifiable. Unfalsifiable theories—those that no counterevidence could ever falsify—are unscientific. The mark of true science is testability, and testability means falsifiability. The experimenter's job, therefore, is "to wrest interpretable facts from an unyielding Nature who knows so well how to meet our theories with a decisive *No*—or with an inaudible *Yes*."[8]

If nature does say yes even after vigorous attempts at falsification, a theory is said to be *corroborated*. This does not mean for Popper that the theory has been confirmed or verified. It means it has been tested rigorously and has passed all tests. Having passed a battery of exams, a hypothesis is *possibly* true (but not *probably* true as confirmationism says). Falsifiable theories that are proven false are clearly false. Falsifiable theories that are *not* proven false are possibly true. Unfalsifiable theories are simply not scientific whether or not some facts confirm them.

Why did Popper refuse to accept as *probably* true a theory that passes the grade? Why is it only *possibly* true? Popper was impressed with the virtual impossibility of comparing a large theory with the

8. Herman Weyl, quoted in Popper, *Logic of Scientific Discovery*, 280.

world as a whole. He reasoned that the total number of observational results a scientist could derive from a certain theory far exceeds the number of predictions he could actually test. The examination of a theory in one small place and at one brief time does not justify saying the theory is probably true everywhere and always. A theory's passing a few tests does not guarantee it can pass all or even most of the nearly infinite number of possible tests.

The problem here is something like the fallacy of special pleading. One who commits this fallacy looks for positive evidence (ignoring the negative evidence) and extrapolates too quickly to a general theory. For example, after a career of plying the deep, cold waters of the North Sea, an old fisherman made a startling pronouncement: no fish less than four inches in girth swims the North Sea. Who could doubt his credentials? He had caught millions of fish in that sea and none was smaller than four inches. The logical error came to light only later: the fisherman used nets with four-inch holes. Though he had much confirmation, he wrongly generalized from only part of the evidence to a wrong conclusion.

For reasons like these, falsificationism says science must rest content with tentatively accepted, corroborated theses. Popper believed scientists have no ground for saying even that one theory is more probable than another. Carnap saw theories as *equally unprovable*, and so he settled for probability. Popper argued they are *equally improbable*, so he opted for mere possibility. This then constitutes a further retreat from the Enlightenment ideal of absolute knowledge.

Like confirmationism, however, falsificationism is flawed. Both see science as a fight between a theory and the facts. But as in my attempt to explain Tyler's symptoms, science is more often a fight between two theories over experimental results. Further, falsificationism is wrongly interested only in decisive refutations of scientific theories. But history shows that positive results can be important scientifically. Suppose Hypothesis A competes with Hypothesis B in light of experimental evidence. Assume the evidence confirms A and falsifies B. Falsificationism says only the falsifying evidence against B matters. Yet in this case, both negative and positive results are significant.[9]

Confirmation and falsification *as principles* both function validly in the knowing process. Confirmation helps justify singular statements. If I cannot remember whether the restaurant my wife and I plan to eat at is on 12th Avenue or 21st Avenue I confirm the address

9. Lakatos, "Falsification and Methodology," 115.

by looking it up in the telephone book. Falsification helps negate universal statements.[10] If I am convinced all New Yorkers drive like maniacs, experience with New York drivers who are sane should gradually modify my belief. Though confirmation and falsification are legitimate principles, the empiricist systems built on them do not adequately describe how scientists actually do their work.

Holistic Approaches

Many object that these strongly empiricist approaches derive their views of science from general theories of knowledge; that is, they represent the approach of external philosophy of science. As the previous criticisms suggest, history shows that the empirical views do not reflect actual scientific practice any more than Aristotle did. Since the 1960s, philosophers have exhibited more interest in internal philosophy of science that begins with the history of science. This shift in focus has accompanied fundamental changes in the dominant views of how science works. Recently, philosophy of science has seen the rise of views that relativize science by emphasizing contextual, sociological, and even psychological factors in scientific theory formation.

A Sociological View

Perhaps the best known of the new philosophies of science is Thomas Kuhn's. In writing about *The Structure of Scientific Revolutions*, Kuhn caused a revolution of a different sort. In the first line, he wrote: "History, if viewed as a repository for more than anecdote or chronology, could produce a decisive transformation in the image of science by which we are now possessed."[11] This fundamental change of method propelled Kuhn's response to naive forms of falsificationism. Kuhn saw science not as proving theories by following epistemological *rules* but as choosing among competing theories under the influence of sociological factors and the guidance of epistemological *values*.

Kuhn's central concept is the *paradigm*. Broadly, a paradigm is an

10. Keith E. Yandell, *Christianity and Philosophy* (Leicester: Inter-Varsity; Grand Rapids: Eerdmans, 1984), 167.

11. Thomas S. Kuhn, *The Structure of Scientific Revolutions*, 2d ed. (Chicago: University of Chicago Press, 1970 [first edition 1962]), 1.

ordered set of beliefs, values, and methods shared by a particular community.[12] It is a self-contained holistic perspective, a total view of things, not just an unorganized accumulation of facts. The paradigm tells its adherents what to believe about the world and how to communicate their beliefs. It includes *values*, guidelines for judging the success of attempts at problem solving. Values are the general criteria (not specific rules) scientists use to judge theories When they approach new problems by following the strategies that worked before, scientists learn to solve new puzzles.[13]

Armed with these concepts, Kuhn saw the history of science as a story of the rise and fall of competing paradigms. All science operates in the context of a paradigm; that is, the reigning complex of beliefs, values, and methods is the matrix in which scientific progress occurs. Most of the time, scientists work to extend and defend the current paradigm. Rarely do scientists work to develop new macroscopic theories. At times they even resist novelty. They usually focus on puzzle solving, on fleshing out answers to the microscopic questions that arise *within* a paradigm, rather than on paradigm testing, on assessing the adequacy of the perspective itself. Kuhn called this necessary phase of consolidation and elucidation *normal science*.[14]

But the elaboration of a paradigm inevitably uncovers *anomalies*, rogue observations that contradict the predicted results of the paradigm. Anomalies, like proverbial square pegs in round holes, do not fit the theory. Scientists use one of several strategies to eliminate anomalies. They may look for theoretical or experimental errors. Or they may create auxiliary hypotheses to explain the rogue facts away. At times these strategies save the reigning paradigm; at other times they do not. If the anomalies continue to mount and stubbornly resist interpretation, they erode confidence in the paradigm and throw science into a phase called a *crisis state*.

In a crisis state, a scientific discipline breaks down, and the unanimous support for the reigning paradigm crumbles. As time passes, the paradigm may catch a second wind, finally finding a suitable way to incorporate the anomalies. But sometimes, in order to explain the data, scientists will propose a new paradigm, complete with a new set of assumptions and rules. If the new paradigm handles the anomalies

12. Kuhn admits to using *paradigm* in two senses. More narrowly, it can mean a concrete solution to a specific riddle during normal science. Ibid., 175.

13. Ibid., 182–85.

14. Ibid., 24.

more successfully, it may replace the old and become the new champ. This shift is called a *scientific revolution*.

Kuhn described scientific revolutions as "non-cumulative developmental episodes" during which a paradigm shift occurs.[15] For an individual, the paradigm switch is not a gradual, one-step-at-a-time change. It is a "gestalt switch" that happens as a whole. For instance, one who looks at the duck-rabbit figure tends to see either the duck or the rabbit. A switch from seeing one animal to seeing the other happens all at once. In that change of perspective, the picture suddenly looks completely different. So it is with a paradigm shift. After a revolution, a scientific discipline returns to a period of normal science, and scientists work to flesh out the new paradigm.

This raises the critical question: How do scientists know which paradigm to adopt? Kuhn identified five values to which scientists appeal in making judgments about competing paradigms:

Accuracy: agreement with existing observations.

Consistency: consonance with itself and other accepted theories.

Scope: applicability to observations or theories beyond what it is intended to explain.

Simplicity: tendency to bring order to otherwise confused or disconnected phenomena.

Fruitfulness: ability to illuminate previously undisclosed phenomena or relationships.

These criteria are *values* that influence theoretic decisions, not *rules* that *determine* them. The transfer of loyalty during scientific revolution from one paradigm to another cannot be explained by objective factors alone. It is more like conversion or choice. Kuhn believed that sociological factors strongly influence scientists. Why is this so?

The new paradigm provides a new lens through which a community of scientists sees the facts in new and different patterns. But the new patterns are so distinctive that paradigms are *incommensurate*. This means that scientists cannot compare different paradigms. They are not calibrated on the same system; they have no common denominator, no common scale. They are like Macintosh and IBM. Since paradigms are incommensurate, scientists face several problems in assessing them. In general, no one complete comparative procedure

15. Ibid., 92.

applies to all paradigms. Scientists have not agreed on a set of rules by which to decide which paradigm is best or most true.

Because paradigms are incommensurate, the evaluation of paradigms is neither simple nor routine. For one thing, scientists can apply the values to specific questions only in rather imprecise ways. For another, the values sometimes give conflicting signals. Maybe simplicity will favor one theory when consistency points to another. Finally, different scientists (especially those with differing paradigm commitments) may attach different levels of importance to each criterion.

This last point is especially troublesome. Since paradigm commitments influence the application of values, researchers have no neutral perspective from which to choose between paradigms. Those who advocate one paradigm may not accept all the presuppositions critical to the defense of another. Thus the "competition between paradigms is not the sort of battle that can be resolved by proofs."[16] This apparently leads to circularity, since an advocate of a particular perspective always follows the rules that are part of the fabric of her own paradigm. Kuhn's conclusion? "Each group uses its own paradigm to argue in that paradigm's defense."[17]

An upstart paradigm needs early supporters who accept the new gestalt only because of its potential. Often these are younger persons who have no vested interest in the old paradigm. They willingly adopt the new paradigm before it is substantiated. As more people work with the new paradigm, it may gradually capture the allegiance of the entire scientific discipline: "There is no single argument that can or should persuade them all. Rather than a single group conversion, what occurs is an increasing shift in the distribution of professional allegiances."[18]

Statements like this have led critics to charge Kuhn with relativism and irrationalism. Kuhn's claim, however, was that science is not guided by pure, objective principles *alone*. On the other hand, neither is science a purely subjective matter. He argued that a newly suggested paradigm must ultimately fulfill its early promise. If it does not, the early supporters who struck out without evidence may turn out to have been misled. Kuhn therefore rejected the conclusion that paradigm choice follows mere scientific fashion or personal preference.

16. Ibid., 148.
17. Ibid., 94.
18. Ibid., 158.

In a postscript to the second edition of *Scientific Revolutions* (1970), Kuhn clarified his views on the incommensurability thesis. In his thinking, it does not entail that communication over paradigm borders is impossible. Nor does it imply that theory choices are merely personal, subjective, or irrational. He emphasized that objective factors do not explain scientific decision-making *by themselves*. But this does not entail relativism. As science develops, newer theories do a better job of solving the puzzles nature bequeaths to the scientific community. In comparing two theories about certain phenomena, an observer can identify the theory that comes later in the evolution of science. Objective criteria pinpoint the better puzzle solver every time. Thus, Kuhn argued, both subjective and objective factors help explain paradigm shifts.

Assessments and Alternatives

Practitioners of many disciplines have co-opted Kuhn's notion of the paradigm shift. Indeed, it illuminates the experience of seeking to explain the world. When I interpreted Tyler's headache and nausea as concussion, I could not explain why he had a fever. This forced a paradigm shift of sorts. But when I worked on the assumption he had the flu, I could not account for the short, staccato breathing. So I concluded he had a slight concussion that coincidentally overlapped a bout with the flu. While it is improbable that concussion and flu would happen at just the same time, this is the best theory I have. Now this Kuhnian interpretation of my reasoning process seems quite plausible. Yet some critics still think Kuhn places too much emphasis on the effect of sociological factors on theory decisions.

Kuhn's revolutionary theorizing has been assessed as overly relativistic.[19] For example, Maurice Mandelbaum argued that Kuhn accepts an unwarranted form of conceptual relativism. According to conceptual relativism, people view the world through intellectual frameworks or conceptual grids inherited from a cultural background. These grids dictate factual judgments; they manipulate the facts. Thus all human understanding is relative to an individual's cognitive principles and categories. Conceptual relativists believe these intellectual frameworks are not rationally defensible. Humans have no way to decide between different grids because all rational assess-

19. See Basil Mitchell, *The Justification of Religious Belief* (New York: Seabury/Crossroad, 1973), 84.

ment presupposes the grids. Thus all human understanding is culture bound.

Mandelbaum's major complaint against such conceptual relativism is what he calls the "self-excepting fallacy." Conceptual relativists forget that their own arguments and observations are undercut by the same pervasive relativism they use to sabotage all other arguments. They apply generalizations (e.g., "All knowledge is culture-bound") to others' views, but not to their own. If they are consistent, conceptual relativists face a dilemma. If their view were true, it could not be defended from anything like an objective perspective. But if an objective argument is possible (as the relativists' dogged defense of relativism seems to assume), this would show that their position could not be true.

In Mandelbaum's view, Kuhn held that scientists cannot defend intellectual grids. This led Kuhn to exaggerate the context-dependency of facts. To prove facts depend on paradigms, he appealed to reversible figures like the duck-rabbit figure. Looked at in one way, this figure looks like a duck; in another it appears to be a rabbit. The evidence is inconclusive. If all observations were this ambiguous, the choice between different conceptual grids could not be decided by facts. But this ambiguity is not typical of normal observation. In fact, the duck-rabbit figure is interesting precisely because it is so unusual! Most observations are not this ambiguous.

Consider this illustration. The great Hindu thinker Shankara speaks of everyday observation as *illusory*—like seeing a coiled rope as though it were a snake. Now people do confuse visual objects. At times they think wrongly that a rope is a snake or a snake is a rope. In these cases (like reversible figures), the confusion seems irresolvable. But at other times, on closer examination, the ambiguity is cleared up. In such cases, where one is obviously looking at a coiled rope, it is absurd to think one could just as easily see it as a snake. Having eliminated the ambiguity, the figure is no longer reversible; it no longer looks equally like a snake or a rope. The ambiguity of the duck-rabbit figure is not typical of all perception.[20]

Although Kuhn made much of the context-dependency of scientists' judgments about facts, Mandelbaum noted that Kuhn also used language that seems to refer to the world as it is. If Kuhn adopted conceptual relativism, Mandelbaum argued, he was inconsistent to

20. Maurice Mandelbaum, "Subjective, Objective, and Conceptual Relativisms," *The Monist* 62 (1979): 415.

use such language. If conceptual relativism were right, he should not appeal to facts about the world as it is. But since he does appeal to such facts, he should not be committed to conceptual relativism.[21] This is precisely the sort of criticism Kuhn reacted to in the second edition of *Scientific Revolutions*. Kuhn argued there that theory choices are affected both by factual observations and by paradigm commitments.

Whether Mandelbaum was right in ascribing conceptual relativism to Kuhn or not, his criticism does highlight an important tension. Kuhn argued strongly that paradigm decisions are influenced by sociological factors (saying, e.g., that the competition between paradigms is decided by professional allegiances). But he also stated that these choices can be judged by objective factors (claiming, e.g., that later theories stand out over earlier ones on objective grounds). Is this balance or inconsistency? This is a difficult judgment.

On the spectrum of views, some theorists, among them David Bloor and Barry Barnes, emphasize Kuhn's subjective themes. They believe that the standards of science are virtually determined by sociopolitical forces. They therefore support a strong relativism or conventionalism, outdistancing Kuhn by giving even more weight to social factors in theory choice. Other theorists stress the more objective side, however, and imply that full-blown conventionalism is untenable. For instance, Imre Lakatos developed a view of science that sees scientific progress in terms of a series of scientific theories. Science achieves real progress when a new theory improves on the previous one by explaining more empirical content.

Lakatos developed an approach in which he explored the methodology of scientific research programs. A research program is a series of experiments. The theoretical base includes a *hard core* that the research program seeks to develop and *auxiliary hypotheses* that form a protective belt around the hard core, insulating it from anomalies. Actual scientific testing is generally aimed at the protective belt. As these auxiliary hypotheses are refined and adjusted and the theory develops in its ability to account for data, the research program leads to scientific progress.

Progress in dealing with anomalies, however, cannot be made by simply playing with key definitions. Eliminating problems by manipulating concepts semantically amounts to sustaining the program through ad hoc maneuvers. This is regressive, not progressive. In-

21. Ibid., 419–20.

stead, the research program seeks to develop new auxiliary hypotheses that actually incorporate more data. If this fails, scientists should abandon an untenable hard core when it cannot promote better explanations. In spite of the protective action of the auxiliary theories, therefore, objective observations can decide when one hard core is superior to another.

This view preserves a greater thread of continuity among successive theories than does Kuhn's notion of paradigm shifts.[22] For Lakatos, the change from one perspective to another, in other words, is more evolutionary and less revolutionary. This highlights a difference of emphasis between Kuhn and Lakatos. For Kuhn, the major force in the paradigm shift is the sociological dimension (although he does recognize the relevance of facts). For Lakatos, the warrants for theory choice are dominantly logical and empirical (although scientists do make personal decisions about which hypothesis to adopt). Abandoning a hard core is still primarily an objective matter. Lakatos wrote, *"experience still remains, in an important sense, the 'impartial arbiter' of scientific controversy."*[23]

The position Lakatos developed draws on several other views. Like empiricism, this approach gives observation a primary role in developing scientific knowledge. But unlike the strong empiricist accounts, it is chastened in recognizing that research and learning are affected by other factors. Like Kant's, this position sees the human mind taking an active role in the knowing process. The mind does not act like a passive sponge merely soaking up data about its surroundings. Like Kuhn's, this view sees the importance of personal decisions and preexisting perspectives in science. Humans are neither neutral recording machines nor creative fiction writers.

Thus Lakatos differs from Kuhn in several ways:

Although he recognizes personal factors in theory decisions, Lakatos has a more firmly objective thrust than Kuhn. His objective criterion is the demonstrated ability of a research program to incorporate novel, unexpected facts.

Lakatos also elaborates fruitfully the distinction between central and peripheral claims, between hard core and auxiliary hypotheses.

22. Harold I. Brown, *Perception, Theory and Commitment: The New Philosophy of Science* (Chicago: Precedent Publishing, 1977), 166–67.
23. Lakatos, "Falsification and Methodology," 131.

Lakatos allows that rival research programs can coexist for a time. A discipline need not be homogeneously committed to only one paradigm at a time.

Development in science is more evolutionary than revolutionary in Lakatos's theory. New perspectives incorporate much material from previous points of view.

For reasons like these, theologians have adapted Lakatos's philosophy of science for theology. Similarly, I will use some of his insights to help in developing an epistemology for dialogical apologetics.[24]

Science and World Views

The common, naive view sees science and religion as completely distinct. Science points to *real* reality; religion discusses *spiritual* realities (i.e., real only to the individual). Science produces true knowledge; religion traffics in myth. So goes a view that prevails on the street, in the press, and on campus. This opinion is not absent from the parish. The new internal philosophy of science is making it clear, however, that science is not as absolute, exacting, and cut-and-dried as the prevailing view holds. Science is more indefinite. Yet science is a valuable model of knowing. Though science and religion obviously differ, significant parallels between scientific and religious thinking can fruitfully guide the development of apologetic method.

The relation of science to religion is incredibly complex. Some think immediately about warfare between the geocentric and heliocentric models of the solar system, between concepts of natural law and miracle claims, or between creational and evolutionary perspectives. These prominent episodes support the *conflict view*: science and religion fight like mortal enemies.

But two perspectives on the relation of science to religion posit less conflict. Some people favor the separation of these two fields believing they are about entirely different things. Like a water polo team from Perth, Australia, and the Garden Club of New Brighton, Minnesota, each follows its own rules in its own arena. They never conflict because they never come into contact. In one version, science

24. For example, Barbour, *Religion in an Age of Science*, 1:62; Nancey Murphy, "Acceptability Criteria for Work in Theology and Science," *Zygon* 22 (1987): 279–97.

takes over the task of describing the world as it is, but religion concentrates on unverifiable values. Such claims describe a *compartmental view*: science and religion remain isolated in their own distinct domains.

Popper's campaign to draw a line of demarcation between science and pseudoscience represents a compartmental view. His real agenda was not to demonstrate how science warrants its claims, but to define clearly which enterprises count as science and which do not. The positivist corollary often attached to this move is that science is somehow epistemologically right while other claims to truth are not. But internal philosophy of science has significantly eroded confidence both in the sharpness of this line and in the positivist corollary. On the second point, one philosopher even accepted Popper's line of demarcation, and then argued that the epistemological rightness lies, not on the scientific side, but on the religious side of that line![25]

A third approach opts for the compatibility of science and religion. I believe that the structures of reasoning in the two fields are more similar than is generally thought, especially at their inner core. Though specifics differ, these differences hide basic similarities in their fundamental rationality.[26] Religious thinking is more like the humanities than science is, but both scientific and religious thinking are rational exercises performed by human persons.[27] This is the *complementary view*: despite important differences in the object of study and the method of thought, parallels in thinking processes do exist.

This claim that science and religion are closer in thinking process than popularly thought could only come in the wake of the demise of the Enlightenment spirit. The hope for an absolutely proven knowledge that fueled evidentialism and early philosophy of science alike has been thoroughly dashed. One important discovery of philosophy of science is that like world view thinking, science operates holistically. W. V. O. Quine made this point: reasoning processes involve

---

25. Veatch, "Neglected Avenue in Contemporary Religious Apologetics," 48.

26. See John Polkinghorne, *One World: The Interaction of Science and Theology* (Princeton: Princeton University Press, 1986), 6–42; Patrick Sherry, *Spirit, Saints, and Immortality* (Albany: State University of New York Press, 1984), 31–50.

27. Science can be more readily quantified than religion. Yet "scientific passions are no mere psychological by-product, but have a logical function that contributes an indispensable element to science." Michael Polanyi, *Personal Knowledge: Towards a Post-Critical Philosophy* (Chicago: University of Chicago Press, 1958), 134; cf. Willem B. Drees, *Beyond the Big Bang: Quantum Cosmologies and God* (LaSalle, Ill.: Open Court, 1990), 155–57.

clarifying, extending, testing, and adjusting *networks* of belief. Philosophy of science has come to accept that science too tests, not individual hypotheses one by one, but whole organized complexes of beliefs.

Quine pictures knowledge like a spider web. (Contrast this with the foundation and the ship models discussed in chapter 2.) At the web's edge, the strands provide strength if they are affixed to the branches of a tree. The outer reaches of a web of belief, in other words, must have solid connection to facts. But in the core of the web, the strands gain strength by being tied together. Though they are not directly verified, these inner beliefs play the role of holding the outer strands together. When an outer strand is cut (i.e., an observational belief is falsified), the whole web, even at the core, comes under new strains and must adjust to new pressures. Like a spider web of beliefs, a paradigm functions as a coordinated set.[28]

For instance, Galileo's claims about craters on the surface of the moon confronted the traditional view that celestial bodies are perfect crystal spheres. His assertions depend on theories about optics that lie behind the telescope. Galileo's critics could have questioned these optical theories rather than their own views about the moon (though in fact they did not). Negative results do not always cause researchers to jettison a central theory. Initially, at least, they overcome difficulties caused by negative experimental results by altering peripheral beliefs, not by abandoning central theories. Scientists usually augment their hypotheses in some way in order to preserve the system of thought that guides their work.

Christian theism, similarly, is a web of beliefs. In this respect, a religious world view is like a scientific paradigm.[29] To designate broad theoretical constructs like these, I will use the phrase *point of view*. A point of view is any broad set of coherently interlocking beliefs, whether a scientific model (e.g., geocentrism) or a religious world view (e.g., Islam). Some adopt Kuhn's word *paradigm* for such large-scale sets of ideas. But *paradigm* may connote a conceptual relativism that rules out rational choices between points of view. So I choose the neutral phrase *point of view*. Vocabulary choice should not prejudge

28. W. V. O. Quine, "Two Dogmas of Empiricism," *Philosophical Review* 60 (1951): 39–40.

29. Mitchell, *Justification of Religious Belief*, 134; Arthur F. Holmes, *Contours of a World View*, Studies in a Christian World View (Grand Rapids: Eerdmans, 1983), 44.

whether rational choices between competing points of view (religious or scientific) are possible.

Of course, theism is much more than a web of ideas. Theism guides believers' personal living, not just their professional research. In this way, some may want to redraw the line between religious world views and scientific paradigms. The former give values for living; the latter describe the world. But scientific points of view do guide living. Scientific points of view explaining the mechanisms of pollution, for instance, may describe a real world, but they also direct daily living. Surely different sorts of webs, including scientific ones, can both be about the world and still function to guide life. Indeed, only antirealists willingly follow points of view they consider to be disconnected from a real world.

The theistic point of view has hard core and auxiliary hypotheses. Its hard core includes beliefs that a creator God exists, humans are the creatures of this God, and humans' lives and destinies are wrapped up with their creator. The *Christian* theistic point of view adds to this core the belief in Jesus Christ as the Son of God and the one through whom any person can come into relation with the Creator. These are nonnegotiables.

But many auxiliary hypotheses with varying degrees of probability flesh out this fundamental Christian vision.[30] Christians adjust these outer belt beliefs to new evidence in order to protect the hard core. Suppose, for example, that *how* God creates is part of the protective belt while *that* God creates is in the hard core. Under the influence of geology and biology, theists have clearly altered their views on the precise nature of God's creative activity. Now some may see this as making concessions to the enemy. But in fact, this maneuver protects the hard core even while it allows the theistic vision to incorporate more data about the world. In this way it brings progress.

Theological conversion involves something like a paradigm shift. The change from an atheistic perspective on the whole of life to a theistic one (or vice versa) is a point of view shift. Of course, we must note some provisos. This point of view shift usually occurs in the life of a single person, not in a whole community (although in some places, mass conversion to a new religion is culturally feasible and has actually occurred). Note that by using *point of view shift* (instead of

30. See Alvin Plantinga, "When Faith and Reason Clash: Evolution and the Bible," *Christian Scholars Review* 21 (1991): 15.

paradigm shift), we avoid any implication that theological conversion is influenced only by sociological factors and not by rational ones.

Further, note that *philosophical* conversion is not the same as *spiritual* conversion. The former is an intellectual matter, the latter a faith issue. Someone may adopt the theistic point of view philosophically (either bringing it to apologetic dialogue or accepting it as a result of dialogue), but this may not be spiritual conversion in the sense of personal trust and loyalty toward God. Given the view of faith and reason I sketched out, a minimal grasp of the Christian world view logically accompanies any commitment of faith. Yet faith may not automatically follow from this intellectual point of view change. The task of apologetics is to promote philosophical point of view shifts toward Christian theism and in this way to set the stage for faith, that is, for spiritual conversion.

Conversation across world view lines is not easy. If I converse with someone who shares a Christian theistic vision, I cannot assume naively that the person is a fellow Christian *spiritually*. Of course, this person is a fellow Christian *philosophically*. In this case, conversants will share a common set of key terms, rules of evidence, and sources of evidence for the discussion. For instance, a nonChristian who accepts the Bible as true shares a key epistemological premise of the Christian vision. But talking across point of view boundaries is, if anything, more difficult in religion than in science. Dialogue partners tend to talk past each other, not to each other. They often disagree about the questions, let alone about the answers.

Apologetics is very interested in the reasoned defense of the Christian theistic point of view. For this reason, the extent to which a point of view shift can be decided on objective grounds in science is directly relevant to world view decisions in apologetics. If the point of view shift *in science* could not be decided or guided objectively, then objectively grounded world view choices or philosophical conversions seem a fantasy. This conclusion would propel one toward fideism, the idea that people choose religious world views by faith. Obviously, such a conclusion has far-reaching implications for apologetics.

Summary

The burgeoning field of philosophy of science shows that the results of science are not as secure as many people think. Historical approaches reveal that actual scientific reasoning is quite rich and varied.

Inductivism fails to describe science adequately, for it sees the mind as passive. In science, as in other fields, the human mind does not passively receive knowledge but actively engages its subject.

Confirmationism, with its emphasis on probability, represents a retreat from the Enlightenment vision of absolute knowledge. Though it recognizes the active role of the mind, it commits the fallacy of affirming the consequent.

In a further retreat, falsificationism opts for possible knowledge. But like confirmationism, it errs in applying scientific testing to individual statements rather than to sets of propositions.

New approaches in philosophy of science have placed more emphasis on the intrusion of subjective factors into scientific reasoning. The best known of these is Kuhn's sociological approach that stresses the effect on paradigm shifts of personal allegiances within scientific communities.

Although he defended himself against this charge, Kuhn's perspective is too relativistic. He overstated both the ambiguous nature of evidence and the effect of paradigms on evidence.

Lakatos spelled out a position that gives more weight to objectivity while making several improvements on Kuhn (e.g., distinguishing clearly between core and peripheral beliefs).

Quine argued that scientific ideas fit into networks of belief. Testing means assessing the webs, not isolated hypotheses. Religious world views also must be tested holistically.

Conceiving of the Christian theistic vision as a point of view is fruitful. Apologetic conversations sometimes soar; other times they crash and burn. Part of the problem is that they involve talking across point of view boundaries.

Two contemporary movements shed light on the apologetic task. They are Reformed epistemology (with its critique of evidentialism) and philosophy of science (with its criticism of strong empiricism). By showing that the Enlightenment quest for absolute knowledge has floundered, these movements come to complementary conclusions. They have discredited two strong Enlightenment beliefs, the irrationality of religious knowledge and the supremacy of the knowledge available in science. In light of these developments, what sort of epistemology should apologists follow? We turn now to address this question: How can one build a case for the Christian theistic vision?

4

The Question of Questions

"'When *I* use a word,' Humpty Dumpty said in a rather scornful tone, 'it means just what I choose it to mean, neither more nor less.'

"'The question is,' said Alice, 'whether you *can* make words mean different things.'

"'The question is,' said Humpty Dumpty, 'which is to be master—that's all.'"

Traveling *Through the Looking Glass* into Wonderland brings certain risks. Those who dare to make the journey find themselves playing—with words—by a different set of rules. Of course, this is part of the fun. Like all good children's books, *Through the Looking Glass* simultaneously delights its younger audience and prevents parental drowsiness by entertaining adults with quips that go over the childrens' heads. The conversation between Alice and Humpty Dumpty raises a profound question: Could words mean in Wonderland something entirely other than what they mean elsewhere?

Obviously, Humpty thinks they can. He believes that in Wonderland he has the power to make new and different rules. He insists that those who would live comfortably in Wonderland must shed the linguistic habits of the real world. Alice keeps resisting Humpty's conclusion, trying always to be sensible about things. But in Wonderland, only Wonderland rules will work. Alice never quite gets the hang of it.

Conceptual Schemes

Stepping into Wonderland with its own set of rules is like stepping into a different conceptual scheme. A conceptual scheme is any large-scale point of view like a paradigm or world view. Conceptual schemers (those who particularly like to speak of conceptual schemes)

76

are usually relativistic. They argue that schemes are incommensurable. According to conceptual relativism, one can step through the looking glass, as it were, into utterly different conceptual lands where the old rules no longer apply in any sense. Like Alice, a person must simply accept new procedures to live comfortably in the new scheme.

But conceptual schemers are like Humpty Dumpty who forgot one thing: though he can make words follow his own rules if he likes, when he communicates with others (i.e., when he *tells* others about his rules instead of *using* them), he must follow everyone's rules. This suggests that although points of view influence all perceptions, experience, and communication, the case for an utter relativism of conceptual schemes is flawed.

The Nature of Conceptual Schemes

Metaphysics includes the attempt to clarify, articulate, extend, and justify world views. As total interpretations of life, world views are the broadest points of view, and they provide the cognitive context in which humans live. They are all-inclusive sets of ideas that enable a person or community to make sense of life's experiences. A person makes sense of a novel idea by relating it to the furniture of his world view, situating the idea in his intellectual living room.

A world view effectively guides metaphysical thinking by using control beliefs. Data beliefs are beliefs about specific observations. But control beliefs are regulators that guide the development and defense of a world view. Control beliefs incorporate new data beliefs into a world view. For example, orthodox Christians have this control belief: God is the uncreated creator of all. If some new idea is proposed, they will ask, Does this compromise the Christian view of God? If it does, then the idea will be rejected. If not, the view of God will help integrate the new idea into the existing structure of belief.

As with scientific paradigms, one critical question in apologetics revolves around the possibility of choosing rationally between world views. To put this another way, Do control beliefs dictate how data beliefs will be interpreted, or can data beliefs help decide which set of control beliefs to accept? For instance, the Mormons believe God is a male creature who grew into godhood. Thus because they are guided by different central beliefs about God, the Mormon and the Christian will make sense of the world in different ways. The question is,

Can data help make the choice between the Christian view and the Mormon one?

Conceptual relativists claim that data beliefs are putty in the hands of control beliefs. Data beliefs, in other words, cannot decide world views. To make their case, they emphasize several ideas. Data do not completely determine a theory, for data are contaminated by theories. The expectations of researchers, for example, affect data collection. For the relativist, these ideas suggest the impossibility of rational choices between grids. Because these conceptual schemes cannot be adjudicated on neutral grounds, they are said to be incommensurable.

Now admittedly data cannot completely demonstrate a theory, since theories do contaminate facts. Indeed, new theories often enable researchers to see things they would not otherwise look for. For instance, pictures of positrons appeared in cloud chamber photos for years, but physicists ignored them as anomalies. When a theory suggested that they look for positrons, however, physicists suddenly recognized the evidence that was there all along. In a sense, researchers could not see what they were not looking for. Perhaps "I'll believe it when I see it" should be augmented by "I'll see it when I believe it."

This evidence leads some to claim that there are no facts, only "interprefacts." Facts are not mirror images of the world, but partially the result of the observer's theorizing. Volts, meters, seconds, and tons do not exist in the brute world of nature. Researchers bring these to the world. They use categories, their intellectual cubbyholes, to organize their experiences of the world just as the mail carrier uses a hundred little cubby holes to sort the mail. Given all this, it seems obvious that the mind actively shapes understandings. Inductivists who believe in raw data, who deny the theory-laden character of facts, fall prey to the "dogma of the immaculate perception."[1]

Conceptual Relativism in Religion

Conventionalists in philosophy of science believe that scientific paradigms cannot be defended rationally. If this is argued seriously in science, it is defended even more stoutly in religion. Given the more subjective character of religion, the alleged incompetence of humans to decide among religious points of view will exceed the supposed in-

1. Holmes Rolston III, *Science and Religion* (New York: Random House, 1987), 3–10.

ability to choose among scientific ones. Indeed, the general tenor of the current age reflects relativist premises like these. Regrettably, the writings of many significant philosophers and theologians converge on the conclusion that no rational interparadigm choice is possible.[2]

R. M. Hare provided a well-known example. In a classic dialogue among three thinkers, Hare concocted the idea of a *blik*, an unfalsifiable perspective. (*Blick* is the German noun meaning *look, view*, or *glance*.) Hare agreed with David Hume:

> differences between *bliks* . . . cannot be settled by observation. . . . That was why, having performed the interesting experiment of doubting the ordinary man's *blik* . . . and showing that no proof could be given to make us adopt one *blik* rather than another, [Hume] turned to backgammon to take his mind off the problem.[3]

In this three-way conversation, Hare took issue with both skeptic Antony Flew and theist Basil Mitchell. Representing an evidentialist point of view, Flew claimed that theistic belief needs, but cannot generate, a rational defense. Advocating a mild form of rationalism (in which he acknowledges the partial ambiguity of the evidence), Mitchell argued that theism can be defended. But Hare resolutely supported a fideism in which different points of view are indefensible. *Bliks* may be different, but they are not rationally better or worse.

To illustrate his view, Hare told this story. A lunatic believes all Oxford dons are plotting to murder him. Hoping to dissuade him, the lunatic's friends introduce him to many gentle dons. But the lunatic sees the dons' mild manners as part of the plot. No amount of evidence can change the lunatic's mind and convince him the dons pose no threat. The friends have one *blik*: they believe the dons are gentle. The lunatic has another *blik*: he believes the dons are maniacal. They are at an impasse, and no evidence can resolve their dilemma.

Hare's story perfectly illustrates the modern prejudice: science is rational and absolute judgments about competing theories are possible; but religion is personal and so reasoned judgments are impossible. I have already argued in chapter 3 that this claim for science is

2. Ludwig Wittgenstein, D. Z. Phillips, Brian Braithwaite, and John Hick represent philosophy; Karl Barth, Reinhold Niebuhr, and Paul Tillich represent theology.

3. R. M. Hare, in "Theology and Falsification," by Antony Flew, R. M. Hare, and Basil Mitchell, in *New Essays in Philosophical Theology*, ed. Antony Flew and Alasdair MacIntyre (London: SCM, 1955), 101.

exaggerated. Is there reason to challenge the second claim about religion as well? Or does the fideism of Hare, rooted in conceptual relativism, carry the day? What about perspectives that see point of view choices controlled by subjective factors to the exclusion of objective ones?

A Critique of Conceptual Relativism

Conceptual relativism and its theological cousin, fideism, deserve to be questioned. In his critique of Kuhn, Mandelbaum offered two reasons for rejecting conceptual relativism. First, it commits the self-excepting fallacy. Conceptual relativists who claim all arguments work only within paradigms cannot explain how their own arguments (in defense of conceptual relativism) can apply universally. Second, it exaggerates the paradigm dependency of facts by emphasizing vivid but atypical examples of ambiguous perception like the duck-rabbit figure. Perhaps the most telling criticism of conceptual relativism, however, is this: the very notion of utterly unrelatable conceptual schemes is rationally incoherent.

Everyone acknowledges today that theories contaminate facts. The only question is what is to be inferred from this. Conceptual relativists believe it proves that points of view are incommensurable. From this they conclude that the choice between world views, paradigms, or conceptual schemes is not rationally decidable. But is this right?

It is important to pin down the sense in which intellectual frameworks are said to be incommensurable. Kuhn used this word to mean that we cannot assess cognitive grids in a pure, neutral manner. Facts do not completely decide paradigm choices. Such choices are difficult and complex. Yet Kuhn admitted that one can identify better paradigms and eliminate inferior ones. I call this milder view *meek incommensurability*. Others, however, use the word to mean that intellectual grids have nothing whatsoever in common. In this stronger sense, incommensurable systems literally cannot be compared in any way. I call this view *strict incommensurability*.

If conceptual relativists mean that different world views, paradigms, or conceptual grids are *strictly* incommensurable, they will have a difficult time proving it. Keith Yandell argues that two strictly incommensurable schemes will have to be about two different objects. Presumably, if two schemes were about two entirely unconnected objects, they could themselves be unrelated. But if they were about the same object and they each reflected the object with some degree of accuracy, they could hardly be *strictly* incommensurable. Since world views all describe the same reality, it seems very unlikely they could ever be strictly incommensurable. World views, after all, are about the universe, and there is only one universe.[4]

In a classic essay, Donald Davidson argues that the very idea of radically different conceptual schemes is incoherent. No one could ever show that some system of belief differs radically from his own. For me to understand that my intellectual grid is utterly unique to me requires that I understand the other conceptual scheme thoroughly enough to know it is radically different than mine. But if the two schemes are commensurate enough for me to compare them, then they arc not really *entirely* unique. The notion of radically different schemes that could be compared and seen as *utterly* unrelated is incoherent.[5] The very concept of strictly incommensurate schemes makes no sense.

It is coherent, however, to speak of difference of belief. Davidson's argument does not eliminate them. This notion makes sense, however, only because one can plot different viewpoints on a "common coordinate system."[6] We can grasp the very concept of different languages because ideas in one can be translated into the other. Humans share enough commonness of thought to enable this translatability. Translatability falsifies the strict incommensurability claim. Thus *relatively* different points of view are possible. But conceptual relativism both overstates the paradigm-dependency of facts and exaggerates the degree of difference in perspectives.

Davidson names Kuhn as a proponent of the conceptual relativism he rejects. Other thinkers he so identifies are Paul Feyerabend and Benjamin Lee Whorf. Whorf bolsters his case for conceptual relativism by telling about the metaphysics that lies behind the Hopi language. It is so alien to Western modes of thought, says Whorf, that Hopi and English cannot "be calibrated." Hopi and English allegedly presuppose two utterly different, irreconcilable grids.

Davidson observes, however, that Whorf "uses English to convey

4. Keith Yandell, *Christianity and Philosophy* (Grand Rapids: Eerdmans, 1984), 140–48.

5. Donald Davidson, "On the Very Idea of a Conceptual Scheme," *Proceedings and Addresses of the American Philosophical Association* 47 (1973–74): 5–20.

6. Ibid., 6.

the contents of sample Hopi sentences. [Similarly] Kuhn is brilliant at saying what things were like before the revolution using—what else?—our postrevolutionary idiom."[7] Like Humpty Dumpty, who explains Wonderland language in normal language, Whorf betrays his own thesis by doing the allegedly impossible: in order to build a defense for his view, he explains in English the supposedly inexplicable (because strictly incommensurable) Hopi metaphysics. Whorf should have realized that while humans can adjust some of the rules of thought, they cannot change them all. "One cannot have a game in which every card is a joker."[8]

All this leaves three major options:

Facts determine schemes because neutrality in theory choice and undoubtable knowledge are possible. Enlightenment evidentialism, classical foundationalism, naive inductivism, and hypothetico-deductive philosophy of science generally share this assumption. In apologetics, this view is rationalistic.

Facts are at the mercy of conceptual schemes so no rational choice between paradigms is possible. Conceptual relativism, with its corollary, strict incommensurability, takes this perspective. In religion, this option tends to fideism.

Facts are influenced by perspectives, yet facts and reasons can help determine the rational merits of competing points of view. This view acknowledges differences of point of view but rejects strict incommensurability and conceptual relativism.

The spirit of Enlightenment rationalism in all of its forms has lost its wind. Conceptual relativism shoots off its own foot in self-defeat whenever it seeks to mount a defense. As a basis for dialogical apologetics, I shall now turn to this third option, a view some have called *soft rationalism*. Soft rationalism stands between Reformed epistemology and Enlightenment evidentialism (or hard rationalism) on the continuum from fideism to rationalism.[9] This epistemology takes to the deep water at the middle of the stream, but it avoids the error of those who "keep too close for comfort to either the fideistic or the ra-

7. Ibid.

8. Maurice Wiles, "The Reasonableness of Christianity," in *The Rationality of Religious Belief: Essays in Honour of Basil Mitchell,* ed. William J. Abraham and Steven W. Holtzer (Oxford: Clarendon, 1987), 46.

9. See pp. 48–50.

tionalistic bank—or, perhaps I should say, seem to keep for comfort too close to one of the two banks."[10]

The Strategy of Soft Rationalism

The basic assumptions embedded in Humpty Dumpty's Wonderland language and in the King's English have something in common. That is why everyone understands Humpty even when he tries to change some of the rules. This shows that these two grids are not entirely incommensurable. But it does not show how to go about choosing between them. So how does one identify the best world view?

World View Criteria

Can general rational principles be used to assess world views? Consider this illustration: If a particular bull gets the blue ribbon at the Iowa State Fair, the judges have assessed that bull's size, shape, and general appearance according to some standard. (I have no idea what those standards are, but surely the judges do.) Like bull judging at the fair, world view judging requires proper criteria. Value judgments compare whatever is being judged to some standard.

Criteria for judging arise from the enterprise at hand. The purpose of raising beef cattle is to earn a living selling the meat. So market conditions will influence the judges. Are consumers worried about cholesterol? Then today's blue ribbon cattle will be leaner than their forebears. Similarly, the task of assessing the truth value of world views gives rise to the relevant criteria. Since the purpose of a world view is to provide a total interpretation of the world, philosophers have discovered and employed criteria to evaluate success in achieving that goal. The question here is not whether raising beef cattle or developing world views is preferable. Assuming the value of finding a true world view, the destination shapes appropriate criteria.[11]

But why would anyone want to develop a total explanation of the world? Not everyone cares about the bulls at the Iowa State Fair. "That just isn't my thing," the city slicker from Des Moines might say. Human beings have an itch for adequate explanation of the world, a

10. Wiles, "Reasonableness of Christianity," 41–42.
11. See David Wolfe, *Epistemology: The Justification of Belief,* Contours of Christian Philosophy (Downers Grove: InterVarsity, 1982), 45–50.

curiosity that propels reflection. They need to scratch this itch by developing a world view that incorporates relevant data, is simple enough to grasp, and is unified and harmonious.[12] Now some people have little natural curiosity. But compelling life experiences, especially tragic ones, often force world view reflection. The search for an adequate total explanation arises from the human need to cope with the environment intellectually—especially when that environment creates stress in some way.

Several points of view I have already discussed argue against inter-world view criteria. Conceptual relativism (along with its theological cousin, fideism) implies that criteria exist only *within* schemes, not *between* them. On the one hand, *some* criteria surely are world view dependent; they operate only within a world view. Conformity to the Bible, for example, is an intra-world view standard. It is perfectly legitimate in its place as a control belief within the Christian point of view, but it is not universally applicable. On the other hand, the bankruptcy of conceptual relativism argues that *not all* criteria are world view dependent. To the extent that different world views seek the same general goal (viz., developing an adequate total explanation of the world), they are subject to similar criteria.

If some inter-world view criteria do exist, does this imply that some standards arise from outside all world views? I think not. Evaluative principles do not drop in from the stratosphere beyond all world views. Such a privileged status might be welcomed, but it seems unlikely. We derive criteria inductively by observing how humans actually reason.[13] "The criteria do not stand *outside* all systems of belief. They are rather trans-systemic in that they are *imbedded* in all systems of belief committed to the project of 'making sense out of total experience.'"[14]

Rational Principles

The word *reason* denotes the human function of using rational criteria to evaluate ideas. I tried to straighten out several confusions in chapter 1. I noted there two important points. First, *reason* is ambiguous. It can mean *autonomous reason*, the haughty human at-

12. Frederick Ferré, *Basic Modern Philosophy of Religion* (New York: Charles Scribner's Sons, 1967), 392.

13. Alvin Plantinga, "Is Belief in God Properly Basic?" *Nous* 15 (1981): 49–51.

14. Wolfe, *Epistemology*, 60.

tempt to build a world view without recourse to God. Or it can mean the relatively neutral human function of assessing evidence and arguments. In this discussion, I will use *reason* in this latter sense. Second, reason in its neutral sense is a tool for building a house, not a foundation on which to build the house. Thus the claim, "I base my belief on reason," makes no sense. Reason in this sense *assesses* knowledge claims; it does not *generate* them. It is like the judicial branch that interprets the law, not the legislative branch that creates law.

Reason in its neutral sense includes at least three kinds of principles. First, reason involves the use of basic logical laws like identity (a = a) and noncontradiction (a ≠ ~a). The laws of logic emerge in any attempt at meaningful explanation. Thus these laws assess *meaningfulness*. Statements or systems of thought that do not pass these laws are not false so much as they are rationally meaningless. Now some technical discussions challenge the universal applicability of these fundamental laws. But no attempt at knowledge successfully suspends them in the long run. Even radical views that resist normal rational modes of thought (like Zen) cannot evade them permanently.[15] Since world views are attempts at meaningful explanation, they should conform to basic logical laws like noncontradiction. Whether a particular world view has successfully done so may be debated. But no one doubts that world views *ought* to do so.

Second, reason includes the use of systemic criteria. The job of systemic criteria is to appraise the *truth* of a system of thought (including points of view). Again, these criteria are imbedded in rational systems of explanation. Thus they do not *produce* systems of thought; instead they *judge* them. They are not seeds from which systems grow, but search lights by which they are evaluated. What sorts of search lights are there? Classically, philosophers have used two general categories of standards. One class assesses the relationships between the important ideas inside a point of view. The other class judges the connections of important claims to the world. Generally, the first group operates rationally, and the second empirically. David Wolfe identifies four: consistency and coherence (the rational criteria) plus comprehensiveness and congruity (the empirical criteria).[16]

Consistency means that ideas do not contradict each other. *Coherence* requires that the ideas have a positive fit, a real unity with

15. See David K. Clark and Norman L. Geisler, *Apologetics in the New Age: A Christian Critique of Pantheism* (Grand Rapids: Baker, 1990), 174–76.
16. Wolfe, *Epistemology*, 50–55.

each other. "Christians believe in prayer" and "The earth has only one moon" are consistent because they are not logically contradictory. To show their positive relation, however, would require a broader net of statements to tie them together.[17] *Comprehensiveness* demands that a system of thought incorporate broad ranges of experience; it should "gobble up" experience. *Congruence* requires that a world view fit human experience. The match must exhibit elegance and appropriateness; the facts should not get distorted when they are squeezed into the point of view's categories.

Different lists, of course, are possible. Basil Mitchell suggests "consistency, coherence, simplicity, elegance, explanatory power, [and] fertility" as appropriate criteria.[18] Ian Barbour proposes agreement with the data, coherence, scope, and fertility.[19] Essentially these lists are variations on a theme. Classically, since world views are systems of thought, they have been evaluated by the two categories of standards: the rational and the empirical. A world view worth accepting must face the music, conceptually speaking, by fitting together with itself and by connecting to the world. A philosophy of life that does this explains total experience and in so doing helps to scratch the intellectual itch all persons feel.

Third, reason involves the use of general rules of evidence. Like the rules of evidence in a court of law, these rules are not themselves evidence. Rather they guide the process of deciding the *admissibility of evidence*. In Swinburne's words, one "must have, in order to infer from things experienced to things not experienced, inductive principles which are independent of experience." He calls these "primary inductive principles." An example is the principle of credulity: when something seems to someone to be true, it probably is, unless there are some special disqualifying circumstances.[20] Humans use this kind of principle regularly even if not consciously.

Note that the principle of credulity is on the same order as Clifford's evidentialist principle (never believe anything upon insufficient evidence). Of course, the principle of credulity differs from the miser-

17. See the discussion of coherence and coherentism in chapter 2, pp. 46–48.

18. Basil Mitchell, *The Justification of Religious Belief* (New York: Seabury/Crossroad, 1973), 95.

19. Ian G. Barbour, *Religion in an Age of Science*, The Gifford Lectures, 1989–91, 2 vols. (San Francisco: Harper, 1990), 34; see also Frederick Ferré, *Language, Logic and God* (New York: Harper and Row, 1961), 162–65; Richard Swinburne, *The Existence of God* (Oxford: Clarendon, 1979), 51–69.

20. Swinburne, *Existence of God*, 254–71.

ly evidentialist principle both because it is more generous and because it is truer to the way we really think. But the two rules are on the same level in that neither is *evidence* per se. Both are *guidelines* for dealing with evidence.

Assessing evidence means bringing to bear (at least subconsciously) rational guidelines somewhat like one of these. Such principles are control beliefs, and they function as central strands in any web of rational belief. Some of these principles are world view dependent, in which case they gain legitimacy by being a critical part of a successful rational system. But others, like the principle of credulity, apply broadly to all systems. Again, since world views seek to incorporate evidence, they must use principles like these. In sum, rational standards, including laws of logic, systemic criteria, and rules of evidence, are applicable to world view assessment.

A Cumulative Case Approach

A central tenet of soft rationalism is its appeal to the cumulative effect of many areas of evidence. Since a world view should explain the total experience of the world, a good world view will do a credible job in many areas. A football team that scores 42 points a game is not a good football team if its defense gives up 52 points a game. As Elton Trueblood writes, "since no single line of evidence is ever adequate, our security lies in the phenomenon of convergence." The "cable is far stronger than a single wire."[21] Similarly, G. K. Chesterton says his reason for believing is "an enormous accumulation of small but unanimous facts."[22] Joseph Butler argued that "probable proofs, by being added, not only increase the evidence, but multiply it."[23] Many theologians, philosophers of religion, and apologists have adopted a cumulative approach.[24]

The cumulative approach is not new. But its appeal is greater today in light of internal philosophy of science, which teaches that even science must deal with evidence holistically. W. V. O. Quine wrote, "our statements about the external world face the tribunal of sense

21. D. Elton Trueblood, *Philosophy of Religion* (New York: Harper and Bros., 1957), 74–76.

22. G. K. Chesterton, *Orthodoxy* (New York: John Lane, 1909), 263.

23. Joseph Butler, *The Analogy of Religion to the Constitution and Course of Nature* 2.7 (London: Religious Tract Society, 1881), 284–85.

24. Including Charles Hartshorne, F. R. Tennant, Richard Swinburne, Basil Mitchell, and C. S. Lewis.

experience not individually but only as a corporate body."[25] Scientific theories are like Quine's webs of belief. New evidence directly affects the edge of the web. The middle of the web is relatively remote from evidence and functions to coordinate the edges and tie the whole together. World views do much the same.

Critics of the cumulative case approach disagree with Butler's claim that adding probable proofs multiplies evidential weight. For example, Flew argues that since each probable proof is *individually* inconclusive, the argument *as a whole* must fail. The sum can be no greater than the parts: "if one leaky bucket will not hold water that is no reason to think that ten can."[26] But Flew's illustration (not argument) would, if it proved anything at all, prove too much. He failed to recognize that science works cumulatively as well. If Flew's ten leaky buckets demolish apologetics, they destroy science as well. Insisting on a conclusive proof for everything one believes is a vestige of evidentialism.

The Best Explanation

Soft rationalism appeals not to one definitive line of argument in isolation, but to various areas of evidence. This makes sense given that world views deal with the big, panoramic picture, not with the postage stamp-sized areas that researchers in highly specialized disciplines investigate. The task of world views, after all, is to explain one's *total* experience of the world, not just some aspects of the world. Soft rationalism, therefore, follows this general principle: *the world view that most naturally explains wide ranges of evidence is the best.*

Because of this macroscopic feature, certain areas of evidence will augment others.[27] Among others, these areas of evidence include:

25. W. V. O. Quine, "Two Dogmas of Empiricism," *Philosophical Review* 60 (1951): 38.

26. Antony Flew, *God and Philosophy* (New York: Dell; Delta, 1966), 63; cf. Michael Scriven, *Primary Philosophy* (New York: McGraw-Hill, 1966), 107–10.

27. The cosmological argument (which points to a necessary but not a personal cause of the universe) and the teleological argument (which suggests a personal but not a necessary cause) can reinforce each other. C. Stephen Evans, *Philosophy of Religion*, Contours of Christian Philosophy (Downers Grove: InterVarsity, 1985), 67–68; Mitchell, *Justification of Religious Belief*, 39–40.

Cosmology: the existence of a universe that is not eternal; its order and structure, especially its capacity to sustain life.[28]

Anthropology: the existence of humans with incredible potential for thought, creativity, and beauty; their thirst for ultimate meanings.

Ethics: the nearly universal experience among humans of obligation to others and of outrage at injustice, cruelty, and undeserved human suffering.

Religious experience: the nearly universal human desire for self-transcendence and connection to a higher reality; the sense of duty to this higher reality.

History: the life of Jesus, his character, teachings, and works, especially his miracles and resurrection.

The cumulative case approach posits the Christian world view as the best explanation for this network of evidence.[29]

It may seem initially that one could easily find many other options for explaining these ranges of evidence. But in the whole history of human thought, only a limited number of world view candidates have emerged (although variations on basic themes are legion). Given the limited number of alternatives, therefore, a world view epistemology can defend one position by arguing against another. The critical issue, of course, is to state the alternatives as completely and fairly as possible. If this proviso is met, then a case for theism will include critiques of naturalism, pantheism, and dualism. Though theism has its rough spots, many have returned to theism and to Christianity after finding that the alternatives have greater difficulties.[30]

In arguing for theism as the best explanation for total human experience, I do not claim the case is airtight. Building a case is art, not science. Apologists weave a rational cloth with many tiny threads,

28. The so-called anthropic principle underscores how incredibly improbable it is that the combination of very precise cosmic conditions necessary to sustain life as we know it could develop simultaneously without the guidance of intelligence. See John Leslie, "Anthropic Principle, World Ensemble, Design," *American Philosophical Quarterly* 19 (1982): 141–51.

29. Swinburne, *Existence of God*, 131–32. In a similar move, Arthur F. Holmes speaks of defending a world view by pointing to universal laws of logic, value areas, action spheres, categories of thought, and basic beliefs. *Contours of a World View*, Studies in a Christian World View (Grand Rapids: Eerdmans, 1983), 52.

30. John Baillie, *Invitation to Pilgrimage* (New York: Charles Scribner's Sons, 1942), 15.

meeting objections here, pointing to evidence there. Such an argument achieves only probability. But a cumulative case argument for one of a limited number of alternatives does have a certain strength: the conclusion does not stand or fall with any one point. All the apologetic eggs are not in one evidential basket. If new evidence shows one piece of the total fabric (e.g., the claim that the universe was formed in 4004 B.C.) is flawed, the web of belief adjusts and the argument can be mended.

Some may want something more secure. They may argue that if absolute proof is unavailable, skepticism is a better alternative. But those who want to build arguments to defend skepticism show that they do not consistently believe skepticism. If skepticism were really right, any argument either for it or against it would be equally ineffective. It may be that skepticism is correct. But if it is, any attempt to prove it is as misguided as any endeavor to refute it. One can never *know* that skepticism is true. Adopting it leads to stress because defending it places one in an intellectual double bind—which is why David Hume chose to relieve the stress not with argument but with dining and backgammon.[31]

In philosophy of science, the view that scientific theories are not objectively provable may be rooted, not in internal philosophy of science (the observation of the history of science), but in external philosophy of science (a general skepticism about all human knowing). But an extensive skepticism like this undermines not only scientific theories, but philosophy of science theories as well. If general skepticism is right and *scientific theories about the world* are denied a rational defense, how can skepticism, a *philosophic theory about scientific theories*, be rationally defensible? Although the Enlightenment vision of absolute knowledge is dead, I believe objectivity is possible in both science and apologetics.

Sources of Knowledge

The soft rationalism described so far is a general strategy for mounting a world view defense. It needs data with which to work, however, for it does not *create* evidence; it is a way to *coordinate* evidence.

31. J. R. Lucas, "Reason Restored," in *The Rationality of Religious Belief*, ed. William Abraham and Steven Holtzer (Oxford: Clarendon, 1987), 73–74; Richard Swinburne, *Faith and Reason* (Oxford: Clarendon, 1981), 90–91.

If the principles and strategy discussed so far provide a structure, but the structure needs content, where does an apologist get the content? Soft rationalism says humans acquire knowledge by appealing to the totality of their experience. Thus to defend a world view, one must draw evidence from a variety of sources.

Experience

Constructing a view of life involves sorting out experiences. But once again an ambiguous word muddies the waters, for *experience*, too, is used in several ways. First, someone with experience has done a certain task many times and is now an expert. An experienced chief executive has developed skill; trial and error have led to a gradual refinement of technique. But this is not the relevant sense here. Second, *experience* can mean feeling the world via the senses. In this sense, experience is a rough equivalent of sensory experience or perception. It produces facts or observations about the world that flesh out a world view. I will discuss sensory experience below.

Experience can also refer to a nonsensory experience of things like love of family, betrayal by a trusted friend, or the peace of God that passes understanding. These involve something more than perceptual experience. To relate sensory and nonsensory experience, one model posits four interpenetrating and simultaneous dimensions of experience: physical, moral, personal, and religious.[32] This raises the question, Can experiencing God (say, having God answer a prayer, or feeling guilty before God for wrong behaviors) ground a belief in God? This is exactly what Reformed epistemologists have claimed as legitimate grounding for belief in God.

Like Reformed epistemologists, Christian mystics ground their belief in God on experience. Empiricists, however, reject mystics' claims that direct experience of God requires no external confirmation. Evidentialists assert that any experience needs external testing before its deliverances can be trusted. They argue that sense perception has appropriate testing procedures while nonsensory experience does not. They think this counts against direct encounters with God. In contrast, the mystics think sensory experience is defective precisely because it carries no inner certification and must therefore rely on artificial, external tests. Both are wrong. Mystics' writings show that

32. Jerry H. Gill, *The Possibility of Religious Knowledge* (Grand Rapids: Eerdmans, 1971), 119–20.

they use testing procedures just as empiricists do. Humans assess both perceptual and sensory experience by connecting them to their larger webs of belief.[33]

Where does all this lead? Here is a concrete way to get at this question: When the angel told Joseph to take Mary and her newborn to Egypt to escape Herod, did Joseph need confirming evidence to prove he was in fact being addressed by an angel? Or was he right to take the experience at face value, pack up his family, and go? If Joseph had followed Clifford's advice, he likely would have been working out his rational argument just as Herod's minions arrived at the front door. So it seems right that he took the experience at face value. But what about a Mormon who believes that a burning in the heart confirms the Book of Mormon as God's revelation? Is he right to accept that experience as an appropriate ground for his belief?

These two examples lead to the heart of the difference between Reformed epistemology and soft rationalism. Defenders of Reformed epistemology are willing to say religious experience is by itself an appropriate ground for religious belief. My knowledge of God is perfectly in order epistemologically speaking if I believe he exists on the ground that he answers my prayer. Confirming evidence may be available, but it is unnecessary. Reformed epistemology says that theistic belief is properly grounded if it is grounded in an experience of God. But soft rationalists believe Reformed epistemology is too meek. While they agree that Clifford is much too harsh, they say he overstates what is basically a correct point: we should confirm a claimed experience of God by connecting it to a wider web of belief.[34]

Here is the reason: because prior beliefs can contaminate experience, religious experiences can yield conflicting results. Generally, when several experiences produce opposing signals, other facets of a web of belief help one discriminate among experiences. Usually one looks for confirming evidence. This evidence does not *replace* experience, but it does help *refine* and evaluate it.[35] Thus when a Mormon believes the Holy Spirit confirms the Book of Mormon and a Christian believes the same about the Bible, the impasse pushes the Christian to use other dimensions of his thought to break the deadlock.

33. Clark and Geisler, *Apologetics in the New Age*, 159–74.
34. Swinburne, *Faith and Reason*, 79.
35. Stephen Wykstra, "Toward a Sensible Evidentialism: On the Notion of 'Needing Evidence,'" in *Philosophy of Religion: Selected Readings*, ed. William L. Rowe and William J. Wainwright, 2d ed. (San Diego: Harcourt Brace Jovanovich, 1989), 434–37.

While experience does confirm a world view, therefore, it does so as one facet of a larger enterprise (viz., of finding the best explanation of one's total experience). An experience of God's working in my life is part of my reason for continuing to believe he exists. In fact, *in any specific situation*, I am perfectly right to take an experience of God at face value. I need not develop a rational argument every time I experience God before I can be justified in acting on that experience. When the angel visited Joseph, he was right to head for Egypt ASAP. Joseph interpreted the angelic visitation as he did, however, because he was already a believer. Knowing that an angelic visitation is possible was part of his broader framework of beliefs.

Evidence

As conceptual commitments and expectations contaminate experience, so they influence empirical observation. Conceptual relativists overemphasize this point. They claim that world views and conceptual grids completely control what facts a person observes. If this is so, then the facts cannot be decisive in choices between points of view. For this reason, relativists finger other factors—sociological, cultural, or psychological—as the molders of point of view decisions.

Certainly conceptual grids sometimes hold great power over individuals. Ideologies can grip the human mind, causing the *content* of belief to be dominated by its *perspective*. An ideology is "a theory grown arrogant, too hard to be softened by experience."[36] Ideologues overextend their generalizations, applying their theories simplistically in areas where they do not really fit and so running roughshod over the evidence. Listen to a Freudian psychoanalyst who later saw the light: "My Party education had equipped my mind with such elaborate shock-absorbing buffers and elastic defenses that everything seen and heard became automatically transformed to fit the preconceived pattern."[37]

The power of conceptual grids means that human judgments are as complex as they are important. But though some facts are particularly vulnerable to total domination by paradigms, many facts are not. The claim that different conceptual grids cannot agree as to what constitutes fact is true to a point but sometimes exaggerated. Hard core theories do have resilience, and their outer belts can protect the

36. Rolston, *Science and Religion*, 11.
37. Arthur Koestler, quoted in ibid.

hard core to some degree, but facts can at times help one identify better hard cores and eliminate false ones. Facts are not putty in the hands of theories. Even though people make individual judgments about evidence, they cannot manipulate the evidence freely.

For example, adult male identical twins told their story on a television talk show last summer. One was homosexual and the other heterosexual. Because the audience members operated with the assumption that sexual orientation is determined by heredity, they could hardly wait to find out how these genetically identical persons could be so different. When the homosexual twin said he knows many identical twins with opposite sexual orientations, the audience audibly gasped. His claim (I cannot verify its truth) had struck hard at their theory. Some people will discount the homosexual twin's claim; it is not politically correct. Yet it can be tested and, if true, would deal a crippling blow to the audience's hard core theory.

World views, metaphorically speaking, are more like a pair of glasses than a pair of eyes.[38] For instance, my eyes are permanently color blind. I see colors my own way. I wish I could see things as others see them, but I cannot. If a world view were like my eyes, I would be trapped. I could not step out to see things from another's point of view. But glasses are impermanent; I can take them on and off. Similarly, since a world view is like glasses, I can take off my world view and try on someone else's. I can consider what it would be like to see the world another way. If I am willing and I work at it (no one said it would be easy), I can enter into a Mormon's perspective and begin to see things from inside his point of view.

Two Other Considerations

The areas I have discussed so far reflect the two traditional tests for truth, coherence and correspondence. Truth is assessed by its rational structure (how the strands in a web of belief fit each other) and its empirical connections (how the strands connect to the branches). Two other areas will flesh out this discussion of soft rationalism. The first of these, assessing an idea by its results, is a third test for truth in addition to coherence and correspondence. The second, knowledge

38. Norman Geisler, "Some Philosophical Perspectives on Missionary Dialogue," in *Theology and Mission*, ed. David J. Hesselgrave (Grand Rapids: Baker, 1978), 247.

based on authority, is a source of content usually (and erroneously) thought to be found only in religious epistemology.

Results

Today a third major test for truth has gained prominence: pragmatism. Pragmatism is found even in philosophy of science. It is emphasized by some who reject a realist view of science. The pragmatic test assesses ideas or systems of thought by evaluating their consequences. A scientific theory is acceptable, say some antirealists, if it helps humans manipulate their environment. Antirealists abandon any thought that the theory corresponds to reality (that it reflects the way things *really* are) in favor of a what's-in-it-for-us view.

Soft rationalism does consider the pragmatic aspects of theories. An evaluation of the results of a hypothesis is appropriately part of a total judgment. The problem is this: a pragmatic appraisal cannot stand alone; pragmatism is parasitic on other forms of assessment. Suppose theory T brings about result R. This does not help me decide whether to accept T unless I have a prior evaluation of R. Pragmatic considerations establish that T produces R, but they do not show whether R is good or beneficial. Evaluating R depends on another source of knowledge. For this reason, pragmatism is an important part of a total world view evaluation, but it cannot be the only part of that assessment.

Suppose, for example, someone develops a technique for teaching four-year-olds to read. Suppose further that after field testing, it turns out this method helps children read better their whole lives, but it also severely diminishes the childrens' musical ability. The pragmatic test shows that the experimental teaching technique produces heightened reading and lowered musical skills. But it cannot determine whether that tradeoff is good—whether reading is more important than music. Other considerations must lead to that judgment.

Now someone may defend the view that teaching four-year-olds to read in this way is good because it will have a positive effect on the economy in twenty years when the children graduate from college. This too is a pragmatic move. And so it runs into the same problem. A pragmatic test will not show whether it is good to have an improved economy twenty years from now at the expense of musical ability. Other kinds of arguments must do that. Thus pragmatic considerations are part of an evaluation for a world view, but they cannot be the whole. They can at best form one aspect of a cumulative case argument.

Authority

Religious people have long depended on another kind of warrant for their beliefs, namely, authority. They accept the word of religious teachers and leaders about things they cannot evaluate for themselves. If Clifford's miserly rule is right, of course, this technique is fatally flawed. Each person ought to be able to formulate the evidence for his own beliefs. But this seems unrealistic. Clifford's grudging evidentialist spirit is the culprit. People use authority to warrant beliefs every day, and, when they do not have contrary evidence, it seems entirely right that they should do so.

Believing something on authority means at root taking someone else's word for it. As one of his "primary inductive principles," Swinburne formulates the principle of testimony: "other things being equal, if someone tells you that *p*, then probably *p*." Humans naturally and properly believe testimony. They routinely accept the word of others, and not just in fuzzy-minded enterprises like theology. No one could do science unless she accepted enormous amounts of knowledge on the say-so of the scientific community. It is simply impossible for any one scientist to verify personally even a fraction of what she knows. One could seek confirmation of some things accepted on authority, but only by accepting other things on authority.[39] Scientists stand on the shoulders of their predecessors, both in and out of the lab.

In this context, the common phrase *take it by faith* makes sense. I argued in chapter 1 that some identify two ways of knowing. The first is knowing on the basis of evidence (which is better). The second, when no evidence is available, requires "taking it by faith" (which is not very good, but at times the best one can do). I see two major problems with this. First, it turns faith into a kind of knowing that lacks intellectual credentials (as distinct from the New Testament sense of *faith* as a kind of personal allegiance and relationship). Second, it encourages people to say about the Christian faith, "There's no evidence for the faith, but don't doubt—just take it by faith." I have seen this lazy evasion of tough issues actually erode confidence in God's truth.

39. Swinburne, *Faith and Reason*, 41–43.

Although it is often misused, the phrase *take it by faith* does have a legitimate sense. It means to accept the testimony of a trustworthy witness. Because a person has faith (i.e., he has a personal trust, loyalty, or allegiance to someone), he accepts what she says at face value even though he cannot independently assess the truth of her claim. For example, should I believe heaven awaits those who trust in God? How could I know? Well, I can take it by faith. That is, someone I trust, Jesus Christ, has told me heaven is coming. So I have no *direct* evidence for heaven, but I do have good *indirect* evidence, the word of Jesus himself.

Knowing in this way introduces certain dangers. It is certainly unacceptable to have a circle of authorities where each authority quotes the one next to him all the way around the circle. This leads to group-think. In group-think, members of a clique all begin to think alike. Then the clique members gain security in their beliefs by citing the unanimity of opinion they see within their group. This procedure promotes ideology and fosters a false sense of security. Not everyone can warrant his beliefs by the say-so of others. Someone in the group should be in a position to know, by some means other than authority, whatever the community takes on authority.[40] Thus religious communities should nurture "a band of scholars and critics who explore the depths and horizons of the faith and report back on their findings."[41]

Authority-based knowledge has other risks. What makes a good authority? The two primary qualities are reliability and expertise. This means humans must make judgments about the moral character and the intellectual acumen of their authorities. Such personal judgments are sometimes wrong. For this reason, con men can take advantage: "The ducks who come to the call 'Dilly, dilly, come and be killed' have confidence in the farmer's wife, and she wrings their necks for their pains."[42] Yet, as James argued against the evidentialists, far better to risk error in hopes of finding truth than to risk losing the truth for fear of error. Though trusting authority involves dangers, so do the alternatives.

Knowledge based on authority requires personal decisions. But so

40. Wykstra, "Sensible Evidentialism," 430.

41. William Abraham, "Cumulative Case Arguments for Christian Theism," in *The Rationality of Religious Belief*, ed. Abraham and Holtzer, 36.

42. C. S. Lewis, "On Obstinacy in Belief," in *They Asked for a Paper* (London: G. Bles, 1962), 194.

do all forms of knowledge. Critics are wrong to believe that accepting authority necessitates sacrificing the mind. In one sense, some do abdicate their personal responsibility for their beliefs in favor of an unquestioned authority figure. But they have still made a judgment, however poor it is, about which authority to believe. Indeed, all people at some time or other make rational assessments about competing claims to authority. Thus just as experience, evidence, and pragmatism can give conflicting signals among which individuals must choose, so accepting authority requires reasoned personal judgments. In the final analysis, all persons take responsibility to discriminate among various claims to truth.

This suggests a very important point: all knowledge is person-centered.[43] Coming to know is not a function of computer-like minds but of persons who make reasoned judgments. If I load fifty Macintosh computers with the same program, plug in the same information, and hit the same button, I will get fifty copies of the same result. If I express the gospel of Jesus to fifty people, I will get fifty results. Judging the effectiveness of an apologetic argument, therefore, means assessing the consequence of the argument for a particular person. Proving something is proving something *to someone*. "There is no epistemic significance *in vacuo*; some person must be involved."[44]

What aspects of a person influence knowledge? In a word, all of them. What a person already believes is relevant because it is the network of beliefs against which new information is processed. The mental skills a person possesses are important. Not all people can understand all arguments, let alone accept them. But other dimensions of a person's life are relevant, too. If accepting the conclusion of an apologetic argument will create strain in persons' marriages, employment status, social relationships, or political allegiances, they will assess the argument in light of those implications. Knowing is a function of persons, not of brains.

43. Kelly James Clark, *Return to Reason: A Critique of Enlightenment Evidentialism and a Defense of Reason and Belief in God* (Grand Rapids: Eerdmans, 1990), 42; C. Stephen Evans, *Subjectivity and Religious Belief: An Historical, Critical Study* (Grand Rapids: Christian University Press, 1978), 202; Gill, *Possibility of Religious Knowledge*, 140; Holmes, *All Truth Is God's Truth* (Grand Rapids: Eerdmans, 1977), 103.

44. George I. Mavrodes, *Belief in God: A Study in the Epistemology of Religion* (New York: Random House, 1970), 28–33.

This means that a particular argument may not carry the day in all cases. Some arguments will carry weight for certain persons, but not for others. Some reasoning will possess evidential force at certain times in a person's life and not at others.

Now some will find this assertion unsettling. They will think that if the arguments for the Christian faith are not universally powerful, they should be discarded. But is an effective apologetic really rendered worthless just because it fails to convince every single Muslim in the world? I think a different perspective is better: "Why . . . should not each of us make use of his own knowledge, and extend it by argument if he can, even if it happens not to be universally shared? It would seem foolish for anyone else to construe another's ignorance as a limit upon his own intellectual life."[45]

What I have said does not imply the relativity of truth. Truth and knowledge are very different things. *Truth* describes statements that accurately reflect objective states of affairs. Truth is not subject to correction or improvement. But *knowledge* describes some person's grasp of truth. That a statement is true says nothing about whether any human knows it. God grasps truth exhaustively; truth and God's knowledge are coextensive. But most truth is not humanly known. What is humanly known is known imperfectly. So Christians err when they think that the absoluteness of truth entails the absoluteness of human knowledge. (Similarly, relativists err when they think that the relativity of human knowledge implies the relativity of truth.) While truth is absolute, the human grasp of truth—human knowledge—is relative.

If human knowledge is relative to persons, the implications for apologetics are enormous. Apologists cannot present a single set of arguments and expect all persons to find them convincing. Practically, this does not happen, and I have tried to suggest theoretically why it does not. Apologetics, then, should be reconceived. It should not be understood as an attempt to develop a perfect system of assertion and argument that will prove the faith once and for all. Rather, it is a strategy for presenting, in the course of a unique discussion with a particular audience, the sort of case that makes sense to those persons. In other words, apologetics is the reasoned defense of the Christian faith in the context of personal dialogue.

45. Ibid., 47.

Summary

Conceptual relativists, both in philosophy of science and in religion, argue that humans cannot choose one intellectual grid or conceptual paradigm as rationally superior to others.

It makes no sense, however, to speak of two conceptual grids that are so different that they cannot be correlated in any way. Different grids may be somewhat different, but they are not strictly incommensurable.

When relativists try to prove their point by explaining examples of radically different paradigms, their success in getting others to see what the two different points of view are saying shows that the two are not radically different, but only relatively so.

Evidence is influenced by perspectives, yet the facts are not so dominated by these perspectives as to rule out rational choices between paradigms.

Since world views all seek the same goal (viz., a total explanation of life), they can be assessed rationally by using criteria embedded in all world views. Some of these criteria are rational while others are empirical.

Using these criteria, we can defend a world view by using a cumulative case argument that asks which of several alternative world views does the best job of explaining all the evidence.

Reason provides the *form* of argumentation while experience, evidence, pragmatic results, and authority provide the *content* a world view ought to explain.

Unlike truth, which is absolute, all human knowledge (i.e., the apprehension of truth) is person-relative. Apologetic practice must take into account the person to whom an argument is offered. Apologetics must be audience specific.

Apologetics is best defined as the art of the reasoned defense of the Christian faith in the context of personal dialogue.

I have sketched a middle-of-the-road view on how humans can choose world views. This view, sometimes called soft rationalism, accepts the demise of absolutist claims to knowledge. These include classical foundationalism and evidentialism in philosophy and strong forms of empiricism in science. They also include hard rationalism in theology and apologetics. But soft rationalism does not slide all the way into conceptual relativism, into conventionalism in philosophy of science, or into fideism in religion. It insists that humans can use rational procedures in choosing world views. It remains now to sharpen the focus on apologetics: What sort of apologetic strategy is appropriate in light of the current epistemological scene?

5

Apologetics as Dialogue

I am corresponding with an atheist whom I have never personally met. He is the cousin of an acquaintance. I began writing him when this acquaintance told me he had written all he could in defense of his faith and not found success in converting his cousin to Christianity.

William Nelson and I have exchanged several letters. He admits that in the past he has been touched by religious experiences while among Christians. These experiences once meant a great deal to Will. But they also confused him. He had similar experiences while among several different groups, and these groups do not always agree with each other. This eroded his confidence that experiences like these could lead him to truth. For the last few years, Will has been working in mundane jobs and spending time thinking philosophically about Christianity and religion, trying to sort out the significance of his life.

I think that short of a miracle, Will is confirmed in his atheism. (Of course, this is true of any unbeliever: short of a miracle, no one will believe.) But my inklings about the firmness of Will's atheism do pose a dilemma. I could spend my time doing other things, for it is beginning to look as though Will has decided not to believe. This leads me to ask, Do I participate in dialogue with non-Christians simply in hopes that they will believe? If it seems that they will not so believe, should I drop them like proverbial hot potatoes? What is the point of apologetic dialogue?

Christians who live in American culture too often view relationships purely pragmatically: Successful apologetics brings an unbeliever to faith. For those with this preoccupation, the only issue becomes: What is the right way (i.e., the most effective way) to reach this end? Now dialogical apologetics is in one sense an attempt to find a more effective way. But dialogical apologetics means renouncing a fixation with mere results. It is instead a service-oriented apologetic, an others-focused method, that recognizes other values—honest dialogue and genuine relationship—for their own sakes.

Apologetic Alternatives

Among apologetic systems evangelicals advocate, dialogical apologetics is entirely unique in its stress on dialogue that is based on audience sensitivity and orientation. Dialogical apologetics is also somewhat distinctive in that it recognizes both strengths and weaknesses in other traditional apologetic approaches. Each of the major apologetic methods advanced among evangelical Christians today includes epistemological underpinnings that are partly right. But each also exaggerates its strong points in relation to other facets of a balanced apologetic. Dialogical apologetics recognizes and incorporates the strengths found in four traditional apologetic alternatives.

Existential Apologetics

Existential approaches to apologetics stress the uniqueness and convicting appeal of Christian experience. The work of God in the heart, the existential encounter with Christ, or the still, small voice of the Spirit convinces an unbeliever of Christian truth. Writers like Blaise Pascal (1623–1662), Søren Kierkegaard (1813–1855), and Karl Barth (1886–1968) take this general view. So have many anonymous mystics and pietists throughout Christian history. Their testimony points to the overwhelming force of God's Spirit as he breaks in upon the searching soul. Often a single dramatic experience gives a believer a life-long assurance of God's presence.

Given the strong emphasis on the experiential dimension, existential apologetics plays down or even rejects outright any rational defense of the faith. Natural theology and theistic arguments do more harm than good. God is hidden in his eternality, and the human mind is too puny ever to grasp his being. Tension and paradox plague the best human attempts to understand an infinite God. What is worse, the noetic effects of sin magnify this problem.[1] Given the utter inability of the human mind to grasp God, knowledge of the divine being depends entirely on God's decision to speak to the human heart.

---

1. *Noetic effects of sin* refers to the mental blindness caused by contamination of the mind by the pollution of sin.

Despite its strengths, this view is not without its critics. The difficulty with existential approaches, with their stress on Christian experience, parallels a point I made about Reformed epistemology. Reformed epistemology and existentialism agree that an experience can by itself legitimately ground belief in God. An experience of God's Spirit needs no rational augmentation. But this raises again this problem: Could a non-Christian legitimately ground his religious views in personal experience?

This problem is not easily resolved, for it can lead to question-begging procedures. If someone says, "I know my experience is true because it is an experience of the *one true God*," she argues in a circle. She says in effect, "My experience is legitimate because it is of the true God; I know my God is the one true God because I have experienced him." Like pounding the pulpit, this adds bombast, but little evidential weight.

An existential apologetic insists that experience stands on its own and that rational assessment operates only within world views. (In other words, rationality elucidates a world view for those who have already adopted it.) But if all arguments are world view dependent, then that includes arguments intended to distinguish deceptive experiences from legitimate ones. Without a strategy to identify which experiences really do reveal God, a person must either adopt fideism or admit the legitimacy of non-Christian religious experiences. Neither of these conclusions is attractive. It is better to acknowledge the practical need for augmenting (not replacing) Christian experience with broader reasoned assessments as part of a holistic defense of the faith.

Yet existential apologetics possesses important strengths. First, existentialism posts a prominent warning sign against dry rationalism. Now this sign may at times contribute to a dangerous anti-intellectualism. Apologists are rightly reminded, however, that it is the cool, refreshing winds of the Spirit that in the end convince the heart. Second, experiences of God do carry some argumentative weight. If all who earnestly sought God through Christ's word failed to find the promised living water, the case for Christianity would be sorely weakened. The testimonies of believers who become aware of God's presence in the midst of hardship can be part of a total apologetic case.

Presuppositional Apologetics

Presuppositional apologetics emphasizes special revelation as the starting point for apologetics. Both parties in an apologetic encounter must assume that biblical revelation gives the only framework within which people can correctly interpret evidence. Without this presupposition, an unbeliever is shut off from all truth. This approach is rooted historically in the Augustinian and Calvinistic tradition. It builds on the writings of the Dutch theologian Abraham Kuyper (1837–1920). In this century, apologists Cornelius Van Til and E. J. Carnell, as well as evangelist Francis Schaeffer, have elaborated this view. Interestingly, because they have the same intellectual grandparents, Reformed epistemology and presuppositionalism are cousins.

Presuppositionalism stresses a strongly negative assessment of human rationality. Following Calvin, it sees sin as the primary cause of spiritual blindness. Because of the noetic effects of sin, non-Christians do not share the Christian world view. For this reason, they cannot understand the world as it truly is. Although God shed his light throughout nature, human minds darkened in sin cannot see it. Van Til expresses this theme using the *no common ground* thesis. According to this, believers and unbelievers have no common intellectual ground, no common cognitive commitments or understandings. God's grace must first confront an unbeliever, convicting the heart of Christian truth. Only then can he pursue knowledge.

Presuppositionalism, especially in its firmer Van Tillian form, faces a dilemma. If the Christian and non-Christian have *no* common ground—no common point of view, rational principles, or experiential facts—*at all*, then the apologist has no raw materials for building an argument. Even criticizing another person's view must fail, for such an argument presupposes at a minimum that the unbeliever acknowledges some correct principles for world view evaluating. But the *no common ground* thesis presumably denies that this is possible. Thus presuppositionalism tends toward fideism.[2]

Consequently, the dilemma is this: If a presuppositionalist wants to avoid fideism, she will connect with her dialogue partner by building some sort of argument. But if she presents an argument, then she abandons (or at the very least erodes) the *no common ground* thesis. Any argument must depend on something, at least one fact or one rational criterion, in common.

Milder forms of presuppositionalism like Schaeffer's take this second route. Schaeffer argues roughly in this manner: If one assumes the Christian world view, then life makes more sense and is

---

2. Whether it actually is fideism depends on precise definitions. Definitive answers on this are probably impossible and perhaps unimportant.

more livable than before. Only the Christian presupposition *makes sense* of facts like: humans crave purpose in life; they live as though rationality and morality are real. But these things make no sense, they are fish out of water, given an atheistic world view. A life built on an atheistic presupposition is livable only when it plunders the Christian world view for its values. The Christian assumption, therefore, makes life humane, livable, and meaningful both socially and individually.

This milder presuppositionalism acknowledges that a non-Christian has enough acumen both to recognize that world views should make sense and to understand what *makes sense* means. It assumes that unbelievers already understand and accept some primary inductive principle like this: world views that make sense of human life and experience are better than those that do not. This must be common ground with Christian truth.[3] In contrast, one who says an unbeliever must first accept the Christian world view *en toto* before the unbeliever can understand even this primary inductive principle (i.e., one who denies common ground to the bitter end) flirts with fideism.

This discussion highlights two important strengths in presuppositionalism, especially in its milder forms. First, this method is correct in stressing the impact of a world view on a person's apprehension of truth. This fits with the results of holistic philosophy of science. Facts do not always speak for themselves. Observers must attune themselves to nature to receive its broadcast. Second, spiritual blinkers also influence human knowledge. Presuppositionalism rightly recognizes the noetic effects of sin. But note: an apologist must not too quickly dismiss others by saying, "He doesn't see things my way. Wow, is he ever blind!" This attitude prevents one from attending carefully to others' words, attitudes, and beliefs.

Evidential Apologetics

Evidential apologetics (not to be equated with Clifford's evidentialism) stresses the accumulation of biblical and historical evidence. It uses an array of facts, both scientific and historical, to defend the central claims of Christianity. William Paley's (1743–1805) *Natural Theology*, a classic example of arguing for a creator from design in the creation, represents this view. Many who today use the phrase

3. It is common because it is implied in all thinking about the world—it is a criterion of thought embedded in any world view enterprise.

Christian evidences follow evidential apologetics. Perhaps the two best known evangelicals advocating this approach today are historian and lawyer John Warwick Montgomery and popular evangelist Josh McDowell. McDowell's *Evidence that Demands a Verdict*, a never-ending compilation of quotes and facts, is quintessentially evidentialist.

In contrast to existential and presuppositional apologetics, evidential apologetics views human reasoning more positively. The human person can adequately grasp knowledge about God despite being hampered by finiteness and sin. The case evidential apologetics builds for Christianity gradually gains force as a person confronts its accumulated weight. Like Paley, evidential apologists often cite examples of design in nature as proof of an intelligent and creative God. One favorite, for instance, is the evidence for an intelligent Creator provided by the intricate structures of the human eye. Historical arguments based on the resurrection of Jesus and the fulfillment of biblical prophecy are also popular.

Because of its greater confidence in reason, evidential apologetics is more rationalistic than the first two views. Naive evidentialists often make extravagant claims for their arguments, believing that facts speak unambiguously for themselves. The influence of points of view on interpretations of fact is lost on most evidentialists. For example, some think wrongly that a historical argument for the resurrection of Jesus clinches the case for Christianity. But a Jew could admit that Jesus rose from the dead without being convinced of Christianity.[4] Similarly, an atheist could acknowledge that Jesus' body came out the tomb but interpret the event as a yet-unexplained anomaly.

Yet the insistence of evidential apologists on a defense connected to objectively checkable evidence is a strength. Though facts do not prove a point of view in a simple, straightforward way, a person can rationally judge world views in part by assessing their capacity to explain his total experience of the world. This total experience, of course, includes scientific evidence, historical data, and personal experience. The evidence evidentialists appeal to must be augmented by a broader, holistic, world view based argument. But the emphasis on incorporating objective facts, insofar as that is possible, is correct. It is part of a cumulative apologetic case.

4. Jewish scholar Pinchas Lapide acknowledges Christ's resurrection, but he limits its saving power to a small band of disciples. *The Resurrection of Jesus: A Jewish Perspective*, trans. Wilhelm Linss (Minneapolis: Augsburg, 1983), 85–93.

Classical Apologetics

Classical apologetics emphasizes a two-phase defense. Phase one employs natural theology in defense of theism as the best world view. Phase two uses several lines of argument, including especially historical evidence, to confirm Christianity as the best form of theism. The best known advocate of this method is C. S. Lewis. Proponents writing today include popular speaker and author R. C. Sproul and prominent apologist Norman L. Geisler. Several rising stars in apologetics, William Lane Craig and J. P. Moreland, represent mild forms of the classical view in that each uses both theistic argumentation and historical evidence to defend the Christian faith.

Given that it uses theistic argument, classical apologetics exhibits a confidence in human reasoning. But unlike the evidentialist view, this apologetic method recognizes the effect of a point of view on the evidence. Classical apologetics correctly emphasizes that world views provide the context in which facts form patterns of evidence. Evidential apologists act as though evidence alone is adequate. They point to cases where appeals to historical evidence have proved convincing. But they forget that this happens in cultures where the audience already assumes a general theism. A historical argument about salvation through Jesus, the divine Son of God, can be powerful for a generic theist.

My father, who worked for four decades with Japanese high school students, often explained Christianity using three simple points: sin, savior, salvation. When fleshed out, Dad's brief outline explains the Christian message pretty well. But Yoshieda San, a wise Japanese colleague, told Dad one day that his outline is incomplete and, for a Japanese person, requires augmenting. The outline needs four points: God, sin, savior, salvation. In a broadly theistic culture, the first point—God—is often assumed by both parties in apologetic conversation. In Japan, however, a meaningful dialogue must begin with something apologists in America used to presuppose. Evidential apologetics works well for those who already assume God.

The two-phase strategy raises an important question: How rigidly must the two phases be distinguished? At times, classical apologists argue that these two phases must be separated very clearly and cleanly. An evidential argument will not work, they insist, until a theistic world view is in place to serve as a context for interpreting facts. One cannot move to phase two (evidence) until phase one (world views) is complete. Now this clarity on the difference between defending theism in general and Christianity in particular is an important strength of classical apologetics. C. S. Lewis's *Miracles* is superb on this point.

Although the distinction is correct, however, some are too rigid about it. Though my point of view affects my assessment of evidence, I can empathetically see the world through another's point of view. Without adopting another world view as my own, I can get inside it, understand it, and begin to consider its merits. A world view is not like eyes, but like glasses. No one can put in another person's eyes and see exactly what things look like to him. But people try on different pairs of glasses all the time. So apologists should keep the two phases of classical apologetics clear in their own minds. But conversants may legitimately wander back and forth between the two stages as they assess the total cumulative weight of the case for Christianity.

Classical apologists are prone to overconfidence in reason. They sometimes claim that a defense of Christianity must be airtight or useless. For instance, Sproul states, "if proofs do not prove, it is unreasonable to believe them as arguments. To do so is to say with the mind, that they do not prove and with the will, that they do prove. This is what we usually call fideism rather than rationality."[5] This feature of contemporary apologetics is a remnant of Enlightenment evidentialism and as such is baseless. But shorn of such overstatement, classical apologetics (with its helpful distinction between the two phases, its appeal to various kinds of evidence, and its recognition of the influence of points of view) resembles the epistemology I favor.

Audience-Sensitive Apologetics

This overview of the four current apologetic options suggests that each has both strengths and oversights. Thus it might seem that dialogical apologetics is an eclectic apologetic, a fifth position that borrows selectively from the other four. The epistemology I will flesh out does share certain features of these views. But dialogical apologetics involves more than this. It is not a *fifth view* in addition to the four current options, but a *second class or category of views*. The first group of options (the four positions) is, in theory, content-oriented. But

5. R. C. Sproul, John H. Gerstner, and Arthur Lindsley, *Classical Apologetics: A Rational Defense of the Christian Faith and a Critique of Presuppositional Apologetics* (Grand Rapids: Zondervan, Academie, 1984), 122–23.

dialogical apologetics is person-oriented both in practice and in theory. Much apologetic practice does follow varied strategies for different persons. But most apologists do this in spite of their theories. Dialogical apologetics makes a person-oriented stance central to the definition and theory of apologetics. The unique qualities of individuals, not an abstract theory about how all human beings know, guides apologetic practice.

The One Right Method

Despite their evident and profound differences, the defenders of the four contemporary options often share certain common qualities. First, each tends to assume that proof is either absolute or useless. Rationalists like Sproul say this explicitly. Sproul and friends presuppose that an apologetic must be definitive to be effective (and then claim that their arguments fulfill the requirement). Surprisingly, fideists join rationalists in assuming this questionable premise. They concur that rational methods must be definitive to be effective. Then they argue that reasoned approaches are not conclusive and conclude that rational apologetics is best abandoned. In this way, those at opposite ends of the rationalism/fideism spectrum share the same faulty premise.[6]

Second, as they are usually practiced, all four positions presuppose that there is only one appropriate way to know something. Though they do not agree on what that one correct epistemology is, they believe their chosen epistemology is right for all persons. Those who do not follow proper procedures, who fail to meet a single set of rational standards, or who miss the one correct strategy are not doing it right. Only those who follow rules that apply to all persons alike, many apologists assume, have a right to make knowledge claims.

This shared assumption runs afoul of the person-relativity of knowledge and proof. While truth is one (presumably it is one with God's perfect knowledge), human knowledge, the human *apprehension* of truth, is more varied. Despite important objective factors, knowledge is still relative to the individual who knows. Good epistemology therefore does not seek what some ideal human-in-the-abstract knows. It does not set standards that each person must fulfill in

---

6. By now it should be quite obvious that rational thought does not always lead to deductive certainty. Reformed epistemology clearly shows that a claim of deductive certainty depends on self-defeating and discredited classical foundationalism.

exactly the same way. It seeks to understand how particular, concrete, flesh-and-blood persons know what they know. Even Thomas Aquinas, the greatest natural theologian ever, recognized that different people can rightly know about God in different ways.

Third, since they surmise that all humans must find truth in the same way, many people assume that there is only one right way to practice apologetics.[7] The tendency is to presuppose without reflection that one correct apologetic method must apply to all apologetic situations. One size fits all! Given this assumption, apologists should develop and students should practice a system of apologetics that presumably matches everyone's needs. The only question is whether the right method is existential or presuppositional, evidential or classical.

So let the debate begin! Evidentialism is wrong, says the presuppositionalist, for unbelievers cannot grasp the facts as they are. One must posit Christian truth before any facts make sense. But the classical apologist thinks this approach entails fideism. One cannot merely presuppose a world view as true. Anyone—a Muslim, an atheist, a Buddhist, a New Ager—can do that. One must first use natural theology to show that we live in a theistic universe. But someone blinded by sin cannot grasp the theistic arguments, complains the presuppositionalist. And on and on the arguments go. This is exciting stuff for the apologetics junkie. But he should realize that some find it amusing or maybe irrelevant to the practice of apologetics.

In the final analysis, why is finding the one right apologetic method so important? The jury who will judge my case is deeply affected by a wide variety of presuppositions, attitudes, beliefs, and prejudices. Why must I be so concerned to ask what human-in-the-abstract can or cannot know? I have never spoken to a human-in-the-abstract. Why is it so critical to decide whether the noetic effects of sin prevent an unbeliever-in-the-abstract from accepting the theistic proofs? I have never talked with an unbeliever-in-the-abstract. When I am speaking with the man on the Bower Street bus, I try to find out what *he* knows and work from there. If knowledge is person-centered, then my apologetic should start with what *this man* believes.

7. To be clear, I repeat that *knowledge* can be warranted in different ways (e.g., one person can know that God exists because he experiences answer to prayer and another because he adopts the cosmological argument). I am not claiming here that *truth* is varied (e.g., God can be found equally well through Jesus or Buddha, through the Book of Mormon or the Koran). "Epistemological subjectivity does not itself necessitate metaphysical subjectivity." Arthur F. Holmes, *Contours of a World View*, Studies in a Christian World View (Grand Rapids: Eerdmans, 1983), 48.

Those who partake with gusto in debates about proper apologetic method forget that in addition to being a *rational* defense of the Christian world view, apologetics is also a rational *defense* of the Christian world view. As a *defense*, apologetics takes an advocacy point of view. It seeks to *persuade* particular persons of Christian truth, not just to *prove* the faith into thin air. Those who debate apologetic method often forget that *in practice*, apologetics must be audience-sensitive. Within the guidelines of proper epistemology, apologists help real people become convinced of the truth of the Christian world view.

Person-Centeredness

As a new approach to conceptualizing apologetics, dialogical apologetics does not formulate the arguments for Christian faith in some new way. It is not, most basically, a new apologetic method that rivals existential or presuppositional, evidential or classical apologetics. Dialogical apologetics calls into question basic presumptions about apologetics often shared by advocates of all current apologetic methods. I have already discussed several of these. The most basic one is this: apologetics is primarily conceptual and philosophical. Though advocates of different approaches debate each other on the fine points of epistemology, they often share the view that apologetics is an intellectual activity first and foremost.

As a distinct class or category of apologetic methods (not a fifth method of apologetics), dialogical apologetics encourages user-friendly, other-focused, and service-oriented apologetics. It uses the word *dialogical* because it stresses what happens in one-of-a-kind interactions between those who wish to share their Christian faith and those who need Christ. *Dialogical* here means, not just conversation with individuals, but audience sensitivity, a trait that can characterize writing and public speaking as well. It is *person-centered* because it stresses the critical personal dynamic of these encounters. Apologetics happens in dialogue, meetings of real people who approach each other with loads of baggage. This luggage—intellectual, attitudinal, cultural, and emotional—is complex and cannot be ignored. An apologist defends the Christian world view before a jury of real live persons who come to court carrying heavily laden bags.

Dialogical apologetics as I conceive it posits a soft rationalism and preserves the strengths of several traditional approaches.[8] It avoids the all-or-nothing impasse of absolute proof or skepticism, the dilemma of rationalism or fideism.

Dialogical apologetics balances two competing principles: it accepts with great seriousness both a common human rationality and the noetic effects of sin and finiteness. The first makes defending Christianity possible while the latter makes it very challenging.

Dialogical apologetics looks at things world viewishly. A person's view of fact and logic is affected by her point of view. But reality forces itself to be accepted at least to some degree; real facts have enough fiber, enough cartilage, to intrude on pet theories or ideologies. Thus world view choices are rationally decidable even if they are not simple.

Person-centered apologetics understands that these principles are incarnated in a unique way in each audience. The apologetic strategy, therefore, is to ask, Can I enter into dialogue with this audience, or this person, in all her particularity, and lay out the case for faith in terms that will make sense to her?

Since dialogical apologetics presents the Christian world view as the best way to interpret the whole of experience, dialogues must appeal to objective criteria and wide ranges of evidence. Now suppose someone is persuaded of the truth of Christianity by a personal vision of Jesus. In that case, an apologist is right to move directly to an invitation to exercise faith. As this new Christian matures, however, he may begin to wonder why Buddhist visions do not carry the same evidential weight as his own. The recourse here is to the cumulative case, the broader ranges of evidence by which anyone discriminates among conflicting experiences. The web of Christian belief can help a young Christian interpret and assess his vivid experience.

Dialogical apologetics, then, attempts to be both rational and personal. It is a rational enterprise in that it seeks to build a reasoned, probabilist, holistic, cumulative case for Christianity. But it is per-

---

8. "As I conceive it" is important. Theoretically, the person-centered, audience-sensitive character of dialogical apologetics could be wedded to another epistemology. I believe, however, that dialogical apologetics fits more naturally with an epistemology that recognizes the person-centered character of proof than it does with an epistemology based on classical foundationalism.

sonal in that it recognizes at the same time the roadblocks to faith thrown up by the audience's culture, psychology, attitudes, intellect, morality, *ad infinitum*. Dialogical apologetics encourages a strategy of dialogue with unique persons in which an apologist uses all the tools in the toolbox to move particular individuals toward an intellectual acknowledgment of the Christian world view and a heartfelt commitment of life and soul to the Savior that this world view declares.[9]

Dialogical apologetics is apologetics reconceived. It refocuses the attention of apologetic study, teaching, and practice on the relationship between the rational/philosophical dimensions of apologetic thinking and the dialogical context of that thinking. Traditionally, *apologetics* has been defined as the *art of the reasoned defense of the Christian faith*. This is the rational side of apologetics. To this rational dimension, dialogical apologetics adds the personal: apologetics is the art of the reasoned defense of the Christian faith *in the context of personal dialogue*.

Two Clarifications

This explication of dialogical apologetics may bring some objections to the surface. First, is dialogical apologetics just another name for what has been called *friendship evangelism*? Well, no. Dialogical apologetics is not any kind of evangelism, let alone friendship evangelism. Friendship evangelism advises the witnessing believer to build a long-term relationship with a friend as the basis for evangelistic interaction. Dialogical apologetics accepts this, but carries it much farther. In dialogical apologetics, a friend's personal qualities actually affect the *content and form* of the arguments.

Further, evangelism seeks to elicit a response of faith and trust while apologetics seeks to nurture agreement of the mind. These two activities must be distinguished in theory even though they are connected in practice. Thus while evangelism cannot serve those who have already trusted Jesus, apologetics does have a legitimate poste-

---

9. John Stott argues that dialogue must include concern both for the gospel and for the other person. If only the gospel is important, arrogance results. If only the person is, merely pleasant conversation results. Unless both ends are kept in view, dialogue becomes irrelevant. "The Biblical Basis for Evangelism," in *Let the Earth Hear His Voice*, ed. J. D. Douglas, International Congress on World Evangelization, Lausanne, Switzerland (Minneapolis: World Wide, 1975), 72.

vangelistic function. Most people do not follow a logically linear path to Christ. Some who believe as children or in times of crisis entrust themselves to God before they have clear conceptual reasons for doing so. Later, when Christians like these wander back to consider the rational bases of their spiritual commitments, apologetics provides a valuable resource.

Second, if dialogical apologetics focuses on apologetic conversation, is it then *practical* apologetics? This question will raise hackles. Apologetic purists, usually idea persons, disdain mere practicality. Ministry practitioners, often people persons, tend to value the practical and to dismiss the theoretical. Since they associate apologetics with philosophical theory, they tend to shun it. Dialogical apologetics reverses the basic assumption found too often among both apologists and nonapologists: both groups tend to abstract apologetics from real life. The difference? Purists think the abstractions are interesting and helpful; practitioners think not.

But dialogical apologetics seeks to connect the study and practice of apologetics to audience assessment. Apologetics is practiced in the context of personal dialogue with all the emotional and cultural baggage that involves. In this sense, dialogical apologetics is *about* a more practical apologetic. Master apologists understand that apologetic theory is supposed to pay off in real life, and they easily make this transition from theory to practice. But traditional definitions of apologetics and pedagogy have reinforced the impression that apologetics is abstractly philosophical. This hampers apologetic apprentices and journeymen alike. Dialogical apologetics is practical in the sense that it attends to the transition from theory to practice.

Purists may not want to shift the focus of apologetics. They may think I am advocating a watered-down approach to apologetics. "This is a good idea, but it's not what we mean by *apologetics*," some will say. I agree that no one needs diluted or infantile apologetics. But note that the basic thrust of dialogical apologetics complicates things. It is not enough to be historically and philosophically acute; one must be culturally, psychologically, morally, *ad infinitum*, attuned as well. By placing the study, teaching, and practice of apologetics in the dialogical context, dialogical apologetics does not deny the intellectual heritage of apologetics. It seeks to make the practice of apologetics more adequate and complex by placing that inheritance in its real life context.

People persons may wonder why dialogical apologetics is itself theoretical if it trumpets the call to relate theory with practice. The answer is simple: dialogical apologetics is a *talking about apologetic talking*. Dialogical apologetics is not a "how to" approach. This book is not entitled *How to Succeed at Apologetics in Three Quick Lessons*. (That title represents false advertising.) Dialogical apologetics is a theoretical discussion, a second-level theory about apologetic practice. In this sense, it is not just a practical apologetics. It is a theory that explores apologetics as it actually happens, whether at a kindergarten level or a postdoctoral level. Since dialogical apologetics focuses on practice of all kinds, this talking about apologetic talking must incorporate principles relevant to both. Thus dialogical apologetics is not milk-and-water apologetics.

The Nature of Dialogue

Given all this, we need to explore more specifically the meaning of apologetic dialogue. This is especially true since many religious pluralists today use *dialogue* for interfaith conversation that seeks only mutual understanding. I use *dialogue* for communicating in a way that takes account of the interests, abilities, perspectives, and commitments of the audience. This does not rule out defense. Dialogical apologetics seeks to build the case for Christianity, but to do so in the context of authentic relationship with another.

An Analysis of Dialogue

Those who defend the valley of apologetic dialogue will have guns trained on them from ridges on both sides. On the one ridge are those who promote proclamational apologetics as the only right form of interfaith conversation. They reject the word *dialogue*. They believe it is more blessed to give the truth than to receive it. On the other ridge are those who endorse pluralistic dialogue as the only appropriate form of religious interchange. They object to the word *apologetics*. It has connotations not unlike those of the word *sexist*. Pluralists believe dialogue must eschew persuasion or defense and seek only mutual understanding.

Dialogue is by definition bidirectional, other-centered communication. Dominance and control are abandoned; cooperation is sought. By contrast, *monologue* is a self-centered, asymmetrical stance of the speaker toward the hearer. The speaker controls the agenda; the hearer accepts that agenda tacitly at best, grudgingly at worst. The connection is not reciprocal. The attitudes of speaker and audience toward each other may be positive and open or hostile and aggressive. Many argue, however, that even when the relationship is positive, a superiority complex necessarily infects monological proclamation.

Today nearly everyone favors dialogue. Monologue is gauche; dialogue is chic. Beyond a general consensus in support of dialogue over monologue, however, conflicts arise. Deep differences lead each person to define *dialogue* in his own way. Lists are drawn up that reflect various understandings of the relationships between religions.[10] Then authors attach the word *dialogue* to the niche they wish to fill. Given this, the word *dialogue* is notoriously unclear.

Dialogue as I use it means something like this: apologists and dialogue partners, whether individuals or groups, come together as equals. They honestly admit their differences in world view and culture. But they display a serious desire to sharpen and broaden their understandings. They agree, at least tacitly, to listen carefully and sympathetically to each other, to explore the ground, structure, and rationale of various views, to sift what is culturally relative from what is universally applicable, and to look for what deserves the acceptance of all.

Given this, they can pursue a mutual search for understandings that best explain the totality of human experience and best interpret the human desire for ultimate meanings and values. Going in, the conversants may disagree on which of these understandings do best make sense of the world. Yet if each agrees to explore various views in the search for truth, the apologist's defense can be service-oriented, other-centered, and dialogical.

In this context, an apologist may rightly defend his viewpoint. Indeed, if communication is always persuasive, each person *must* do so. Given this, a clear demarcation between dialogue (which seeks only mutual understanding) and apologetics (which seeks persuasion and defense) is arbitrary and unrealistic. Contending for his views to the

10. Eric Sharpe, "The Goals of Inter-Religious Dialogue," in *Truth and Dialogue in World Religions*, ed. John Hick (Philadelphia: Westminster, 1974), 82–89; David J. Hesselgrave, "Interreligious Dialogue—Biblical and Contemporary Perspectives," in *Theology and Mission*, ed. David J. Hesselgrave (Grand Rapids: Baker, 1978), 235–37. Hesselgrave says that the question is not "Shall we engage in dialogue?" but "In what kinds of dialogue shall we engage?"

best of his ability is one way a person serves the other. Of course, an experienced apologist will not use his intellectual ability to crush an unskilled person. A good apologist will not take advantage of the partner. But when the other is willing and able, an apologist is not prevented from making his very best case by some rule of dialogue that floats down from on high. Clear defense and genuine dialogue are not incompatible.

What should dialogue partners agree to? Dialogue does not depend on a prior agreement of opinion. It does, however, require agreeing, at least tacitly, on method and purpose. Dialogue partners will agree together that truth is important and worth finding. They will feel out together a set of common meanings they will use to converse. They will want to move together toward concord on the nature of reasons and evidence. But consensus on where the dialogue will end up, on the specific truth they are seeking, is not necessary as a prelude to dialogue. Agreeing on which world view is epistemically best is not a prerequisite for dialogue.[11]

Dialogue and Mutuality

Those on the ridge of pluralistic dialogue will argue, however, that anything short of fully acknowledging the legitimacy of other religious traditions is monological. From this view, what I have offered so far is only sugar-coated monologue. For instance, Sri Lankan theologian S. Wesley Ariarajah defended storytelling but insisted that no one story can be the only true story.[12] To those of this general approach, *dialogue* entails a pluralism that rules out apologetics. This is the view of John Hick, Wilfred Cantwell Smith, John Cobb, and Paul Knitter, to say nothing of many important non-Western theologians.[13] Cobb argued,

> In faithfulness to Christ I must be open to others. . . . I cannot predetermine how radical the effects of [my] learning will be. . . . I cannot even know that, when I have learned what I have to learn here and been

11. Norman Geisler, "Some Philosophical Perspectives on Missionary Dialogue," in *Theology and Mission*, ed. David J. Hesselgrave (Grand Rapids: Baker, 1978), 249.

12. J. Wesley Ariarajah, "Toward a Theology of Dialogue," *The Ecumenical Review* 29 (1977): 3–11.

13. See, e.g., John Hick, *God Has Many Names* (Philadelphia: Westminster, 1982), 52–53; "Pluralism and the Reality of the Transcendent," *The Christian Century* (January 21, 1981), 48.

transformed by it, I will still see faithfulness to Christ as my calling. I cannot predetermine that I will be a Christian at all. That is what I mean by full openness. In faithfulness to Christ I must be prepared to give up even faithfulness to Christ.[14]

How should one respond to this suggestion? I agree that genuine relationship does mean I am open to the influence of the other. I cannot forever hold another at arm's length and then expect anything like authentic relationship. Apologists can recognize that learning something from the other is likely. They may even imagine circumstances under which their views might substantially change. So far, Cobb is right.

Yet Cobb's remarks elicit at least two responses. First, apologists rightly expect that dialogue will not easily reshape their own world view perspectives. Commitment to a world view is very deep, for a person's world view organizes her central beliefs and core values. For this reason, people cannot switch world views easily.[15] By contrast, I readily give up peripheral beliefs. Suppose I believe the sun will shine today. Then my friend shows me the weather report in the *St. Paul Pioneer Press* that says that rain is coming. I change my opinion in milliseconds. But core beliefs (like "Jesus rose from the dead on Easter") profoundly shape my sense of self. Reading an essay by a skeptical, German New Testament scholar will not quickly change that belief.

One writer put it this way:

> *Serious* dialogue indeed requires openness to change, but it also demands a sense of how significant changing one's faith would be. No doubt Christians have often lacked the first of these virtues, but many recent writers on these topics lack the second. . . . If we are honest, we will admit that we stand somewhere. If we are serious, we will feel serious commitments to the place we stand.[16]

As they defend the faith, apologists can remain open to learning, growth, and the possibility of revision in their views. But they also live with a sense of loyalty to the truth they have.

14. John Cobb, Jr., "The Meaning of Pluralism for Christian Self-Understanding," in *Religious Pluralism*, ed. Leroy S. Rouner (Notre Dame: University of Notre Dame Press, 1984), 174–75.

15. I am not implying that Cobb advocates this, of course.

16. William C. Placher, *Unapologetic Theology: A Christian Voice in a Pluralistic Conversation* (Louisville: Westminster/John Knox, 1989), 149.

Second, exclusivists, those who think one religion is true, can engage in dialogue. Conversely, pluralists, those who are open to the truth of all religions, can become monological. Those who insist that dialogue must assume pluralism are very open to nonexclusivist traditions. They must prejudge, however, that exclusivist traditions are ignorant of the superior insights of pluralism and consequently false at this point. In this way, those who require pluralism as a precondition for dialogue make a priori judgments that force other persons to adopt their agenda. In this way, they too can very easily revert to monologue.[17]

Dialogue and Objectivity

Those on the ridge of proclamational apologetics, on the other hand, may argue that I concede too much to subjectivity. A dialogical strategy for apologetics involves acknowledging the possibility that an apologist could learn from his dialogue partner. But faith should not waver like a little boat bouncing on ocean waves. To those of this general approach, *apologetics* precludes dialogue.

Is unwavering faith possible in light of epistemological uncertainty? How does the provisional character of human knowing (1 Cor. 13:12) square with the unconditional commitment faith requires (James 1:6)?[18] The difference between intellectual commitment to Christian teachings about God (i.e., knowledge) and personal commitment to God himself (i.e., faith) shows the way out of this dilemma.

Jumbling faith and knowledge together creates this question. Not keeping this distinction clearly in mind causes the problem because some people think they must somehow be consistent. Failing to distinguish faith and knowledge, they think consistency demands tentativeness in both areas or unshakable commitment in both. But the distinction solves the problem: if faith and knowledge are somewhat distinct, different stances are possible. Because faith is not knowledge, one can exercise total *commitment to God* while accepting the provisional nature of all human *knowledge about God*.

17. David Lochhead, *The Dialogical Imperative: A Christian Reflection on Interfaith Encounter*, Faith Meets Faith Series (Maryknoll, N.Y.: Orbis, 1988), 26; see Paul Griffiths, "An Apology for Apologetics," *Faith and Philosophy* 5 (1988): 415.

18. See Basil Mitchell, *The Justification of Religious Belief* (New York: Seabury/Crossroad, 1973), 117–34.

To illustrate, the objective knowledge a groom possesses of his bride must, in a technical sense, be provisional. His evidence that she will be true to him until death they do part does not reach deductive certainty. Yet he can rightly entrust himself to her as she does to him. When he does so, he commits himself to her by a final, all-or-nothing decision. If, instead, he waits for conclusive evidence that this woman will be unwaveringly true to the very end, he will never wed. And that has certain drawbacks.[19]

A common intuition, the concept of proportionality, magnifies this problem. Some assume that they ought to proportion their beliefs precisely to the available evidence. Thus if the probability of some idea is 80 percent, a proportionality principle says that commitment to the idea should be at the 80 percent level and not more. But this principle is unrealistic in personal relationships. Evidence of the bride's faithfulness is always less than complete. Had he followed his evidentialist rules, Clifford would have remained a bachelor. The groom is right to have a robust allegiance to his beloved even though he can never demonstrate, to the satisfaction of technical canons of deduction, that she will always be faithful to him.[20]

Even scientists must lay aside a rigid proportionality principle. Those who tried to spell out precise principles of probability for science failed in the attempt. Further, "the scientist as spectator is dead."[21] As Kuhn argued, scientists sometimes display tenacious commitment to paradigms that are, strictly speaking, unwarranted. Those who first adopt a new scientific paradigm must, in the early stages, accept it without evidence as they try to flesh it out. Thus demanding precise proportionality between evidence and belief is unrealistic.[22]

Of course, proportionality is true in a rough sense. Only the naive adopt utterly unfounded beliefs. Only the gullible trust proven scoundrels. But it is an error to calcify this rough rule of thumb into a strict principle requiring precise equivalence between probability

19. William James uses this illustration: an agnostic mountain climber comes to a dangerous crevice. In the arena of *belief*, he can remain uncommitted about whether he could clear the crevice. But in the realm of *action*, neutrality is impossible: he must either jump or turn back.

20. C. S. Lewis, "On Obstinacy in Belief," in *They Asked for a Paper* (London: G. Bles, 1962), 193.

21. Stephen Toulmin, *Return to Cosmology* (Chicago: University of Chicago Press, 1974), 252.

22. Lewis, "On Obstinacy in Belief," 184–85.

and degree of commitment. This has proved unrealistic and impossible. Since a strict proportionality principle is flawed, therefore, it does not preclude combining total commitment with tentative knowledge.

One's personal allegiance to God will always outdistance any evidence for intellectual commitments. This does not mean, however, that theistic beliefs are ungrounded or that believers are sinking in a swamp of subjectivity. Christian truth is in touch with universal laws of logic, spheres of action, and ranges of experience.[23] Genuine objectivity is possible even though absolute neutrality or indifferent detachment is not. *Objectivity in commitment* requires an interest in grounds of belief, a sensitivity to relevant evidence, a willingness to test convictions, and an openness to adjusting beliefs accordingly— all of which can happen in dialogue.[24] Though conclusive proof is elusive, objective intellectual grounds for faith are not.

In comparison to the alternatives, the case for Christianity is solid. As Lewis writes,

> We know, in fact, that believers are not cut off from unbelievers by any portentous inferiority of intelligence or any perverse refusal to think . . . . I will never believe that an error against which so many and various defensive weapons have been found necessary was, from the outset, wholly lacking in plausibility. All this "post haste and rummage in the land" obviously implies a respectable enemy.[25]

The Apologist's Goal

What then is my goal as an apologist in dialogue? It is this: to present the best case I can for the truth as I see it for the benefit of others. I should not evaluate the success of dialogue only by whether my partners agree in the end. From my viewpoint, success in dialogue is presenting the case for Christianity, by the Spirit's power, with rational force, cultural appropriateness, and personal sensitivity in the context of relationship. Of course, I hope the other is convinced of Christian truth. But if, in addition to making the case, I understand

23. Holmes, *Contours of a World View*, 52.
24. Holmes Rolston III, *Science and Religion* (New York: Random House, 1987), 22.
25. Lewis, "On Obstinacy in Belief," 186–87.

his views better, develop a relationship with him, or grow intellectually or personally, then I have succeeded.[26]

Moral values like love and justice will characterize dialogue of this kind. One who practices dialogue recognizes the other as an individual made in God's image. He expresses genuine openness to the other person, a willingness to hear as well as to speak, and a recognition of the dialogue partner as an individual with the right to think and act as an adult and an equal. Dialogue cannot force a person to accept a particular point of view. Force or undue pressure causes a reversion to monologue. This means fundamentally that a dialogue partner is given the freedom to say *no!* John Stott once put it this way:

> Dialogue becomes a token of Christian humility and love, because it indicates our resolve to rid our minds of the prejudices and caricatures we may entertain about the other man; to struggle to listen through his ears and see through his eyes so as to grasp what prevents him from hearing the Gospel and seeing Christ; to sympathize with him in all his doubts and fears.[27]

Genuine dialogue presupposes a fundamental integrity. Rather than hiding my belief that I stand in a certain place, integrity requires getting that fact out in the open. If I know something my friends may need, integrity requires that I not keep this a secret. If I am honestly what I am, I will share my concerns with others. I can will what is best for my partners (love), allow them the right to say *no!* (justice), and still believe that what I think is right. Indeed, is it possible to believe anything else? Who could enter a dialogue believing that what she thinks is wrong? Even the pluralist enters any dialogue believing pluralism is right and exclusivism is wrong.

From an apologist's perspective, then, dialogue should be other-centered, not self-centered. In entering dialogue, I do not see a partner as an instrument for reaching my selfish ends—achieving my success or my agenda. Entering dialogue means operating without

26. Paul J. Griffiths, *An Apology for Apologetics: A Study in the Logic of Interreligious Dialogue* (Maryknoll, N.Y.: Orbis, 1991), 81–82. William Lane Craig says, "Effectiveness in apologetics is presenting cogent and persuasive arguments for the gospel in the power of the Holy Spirit, and leaving the results to God." *Apologetics: An Introduction* (Chicago: Moody, 1984), 27.

27. Stott, "The Biblical Basis for Evangelism," in *Let the Earth Hear His Voice*, ed. Douglas, 72.

self-centered, ulterior motives. I seek to serve my partner by presenting the case for the truth as I see it as persuasively as I can. I should
expect the same from him. My purpose in so doing is to help him and
me find what is true. I need not enter with the assumption that my
view, as I now understand it, is the final, uncorrectable word on truth.
I believe that what I have to say is true in the main, but I can remain
open to the instruction of my dialogue partner.

This attitude can diffuse tension in discussions of religious belief.
Many a would-be apologist, like the sixteen-year-old on his first date,
enters conversation with fear and trembling. The apologist feels the
weight of the world on his shoulders. He bears all the responsibility
for convincing this person of God's eternal truth. But a more modest
goal can bring relaxation. An apologist will do the best he can to help
the other understand the Christian faith, its existential strength and
its intellectual fiber. He will remain open to learning and growing
through the process.

On the other side, the dialogue partner, like the sixteen-year-old's
date, is usually nervous, too. Many people fear the usual conversations about religion. (Yet everyone enjoyed those late-night, college
bull sessions, remember?) Why? Religious discussions often strike
people as pushy. Sometimes a person who speaks to an apologist feels
like an object—like yet another notch on the handle of a gunslinger's
six-shooter. An apologist's dialogue partners do not always sense genuine concern for them. This negative feeling can build tremendous resistance. People pull hardest when they are pushed hardest. Understanding and acceptance happen best when there is less pressure.[28]

Consider an old Chinese parable. If an owner wonders whether
his captive bird loves him, he sets it free. If it flies away, it never loved
him. If it returns on its own, it belongs to the owner forever. In the
same way, genuine dialogue sets a dialogue partner free. In fact, relaxation may even promote better results than obsession with results.
An apologist may be more persuasive precisely when she ignores the
results.[29] Entering dialogue means forgetting countable results in the

28. This does not mean that a good apologist will with cunning and calculation *appear* to be uninterested in the result. It means that a good apologist will genuinely value
the conversation and the opportunity to build relationship by sharing something deep and
profound: her reasons for faith.

29. This is like the hedonistic paradox, which says that pleasure is found in its rich-
est forms when a person is not directly seeking it. Pleasure is an unexpected byproduct of
virtue.

short run. They are God's business anyway. The apologist should simply present her case as clearly as possible and enjoy the discussion.

Summary

While existential apologetics cannot discriminate Christian experience from other sorts of experience, it is right to include experience of God as part of the case for Christianity.

When it overstates the noetic effect of sin and lack of common ground, presuppositional apologetics tends toward fideism. Yet it correctly highlights the effect of a point of view on evidence.

Evidential apologetics, in contrast, does not fully recognize the effect of world views on evidence, but it is right to insist on connecting the case for the Christian faith to objective evidence.

Although, like evidentialism, classical apologetics can be too rationalistic, it does helpfully balance the integrity of evidence with the effect of world views on evidence.

Unlike these four views (whose proponents tend to argue that apologetics must be done their way), dialogical apologetics stresses the uniqueness of each apologetic conversation and calls for a variety of strategies in response to the unique characteristics of each partner.

Dialogical apologetics is a second *class* of apologetic methods, however, not just a fifth apologetic method. It is a completely different *category* of apologetics from the traditional types, for it rejects a single method in favor of flexibility in apologetic practice.

Dialogue in this context means neither a pluralistic acceptance of all viewpoints as true nor monological declaration of truth, but apologetic discussion that involves real give-and-take.

Dialogical apologetics recognizes both the person-relativity and the objectivity of evidence. Commitment in faith and tentativeness in knowledge are mutually compatible.

The task of an apologist is not to determine ahead of time what some person can or cannot know. Rather her job is to find out in the relationship of dialogue what he does know and then, with that as context, to present the best case she can for the truth as she sees it for his benefit.

Since all communication is persuasive, an apologist is right to try to persuade the other. But an apologist succeeds when he clearly expresses his faith by the Spirit's power, not just when the other is converted.

Dialogical apologetics sees dialogue, which is the context for apologetics, as a complex and mutual human interaction at a variety of levels. Because it involves interchange between unique persons, dialogue has many dimensions. We turn now to ask, How do the conceptual, attitudinal, and cultural aspects of dialogue affect apologetics? What can help a Christian to present the best case he can for the truth of Christianity as he sees it for the benefit of the other?

PART TWO

Strategies for Dialogical Apologetics

6

The Word on Words

"When I say *God*, what do you think of?" asked Dad in Japanese. Following Yoshieda San's advice, Dad was explaining the Christian message to four Japanese high school girls by starting with the concept of God. But four confused faces revealed the wisdom of Yoshieda San's guidance. Dad gestured toward the first student.

"I think of a cloud floating along above the ground," said the first girl tentatively.

"Do you mean a ghost?"

"Yes, a ghost," she replied, her face brightening. Dismayed, Dad turned to the second girl.

"God is *pachi-pachi*," suggested her friend. She meant the sound heard at Shinto shrines when worshipers announce their presence to the local deities by giving two loud claps. Not much illumination here, but two others remained to answer.

"God is in the human heart, isn't it?" asked the third hesitantly. This is getting worse, thought Dad, but we have one more to go.

"I think of an old man with a beard who zaps bad people and puts them up in a tree. He takes money from the rich and gives it to the poor," said the fourth with more confidence than her friends. She combined the ideas of antiquity, the supernatural, and goodness—Merlin the magician, Robin Hood, and Santa Claus all rolled into one. Clearly, Dad had to backtrack before these girls could follow his train of thought. Radically different conceptions of the word *God*, rooted in very different cultures, virtually prevented effective communication. "Merlin the magician loves you and has a wonderful plan for your life." Talk about ships passing in the night!

Dimensions of Dialogue

What happened in this dialogue? Initially one might be tempted to analyze this by saying that the word *God* needed clearer focus. The problem, in other words, lay in different definitions of the same word. This is true as far as it goes. But the words people use reveal more complex factors. Words are like the proverbial iceberg tips, for they betray a variety of interlocking conceptual realities that lie below the surface of apologetic conversation. Indeed, a good apologist will recognize that dialogue is a complex tapestry of dimensions, each of which affects the quality of relationship and understanding.

Learning how to defend the Christian faith effectively in personal dialogue requires knowing the message (the Christian faith) as well as understanding the medium (personal dialogue). Assuming that a Christian understands his faith, this suggests we should turn to an analysis of dialogue. Speaking broadly, *to analyze* means to break something that is whole into parts for better understanding of its nature or function. (Putting the parts back together, called *synthesis*, is equally important, but not my focus here.)

Thinking about analyzing things requires caution, however, for not all things have parts as such. My fourteen-year-old nephew is a whiz with broken lawn mowers. He routinely reconditions mowers that have stumped mechanics at small-engine repair shops. When Jeremy fixes a mower, he first analyzes it. Is the fuel system in good shape? Are the electrical components working? He breaks the problem into parts and then into subparts, concentrating on one at a time until he finally finds the offending mower part. Then he either replaces or adjusts the part and chalks up yet another success story.

Unlike lawn mowers, certain other things in this world cannot be broken into parts. Theoretically, all the parts of a lawn mower could be separated physically and spread out on the driveway. (Of course, I would not trust a repairman who actually did this, but it could be done.) But consider a symphony. Its "parts" are sounds played by various instruments. In a sense, one could take the symphony apart, playing each note by itself. But playing a symphony well means playing the notes at an appropriate tempo, with expressive crescendos and decrescendos, with nuance and feeling. These cannot be spread out on a floor like the parts of a lawn mower. Pure loudness all by itself is impossible. Volume is a quality of the note, not a different thing from the note.

The aspects of a dimensionally structured reality only exist together. Tone of voice, for example, cannot be distilled out of a dialogue; tone of voice does not exist if there is no voice. For this reason, a dimensionally structured thing is highly interwoven. Since it is a dimensionally structured reality, dialogue has a special "all-at-onceness" about it. True, lawn mowers work only when the parts are properly attuned to each other. These parts exhibit a degree of interconnectedness. Leave out the spark plug, and the mower simply will not run.

But in dialogue, the degree of interweaving is even greater. It is not just that the aspects do not work; some do not even exist except together. A conversation, in other words, is more like a symphony than like a lawn mower. It does not consist of pieces that can be taken apart, but of a whole series of interpenetrating aspects. Dialogue is a very complex relating of persons. As such it is no simple matter to break a conversation into parts. A dialogue cannot be divided up cleanly, for it is made up of dimensions.

Because of the degree and quality of interconnectedness, each dialogue has its own unique character. The fact that conversations involve interaction between complex and somewhat unpredictable persons heightens their individuality. Dialogues will differ from each other much more than fifty Sears lawn mowers will. The apologist's task, therefore, is to reflect on the various dimensions conversations will display. But like the symphony's rate and volume, melody and harmony, these aspects all happen simultaneously to create a reality with its own unique qualities.

What dimensions do dialogues have? Plato had distinguished persuasion directed to teaching truth (and thus requiring knowledge in the persuader) from that aimed at making people merely believe something (and therefore not requiring knowledge). Plato feared the second of these, what he called *rhetoric*. Teaching ought to promote the good of the soul or person. But Plato believed rhetoricians fail to accept this responsibility, aiming instead at immediate success and personal gain. So Plato believed rhetoric to be a dangerous counterfeit.[1]

1. Plato *Gorgias* 454d; 501d–503a; 513c–514a; 517b–d.

Against this background, Aristotle wrote the classic systematic work *Rhetoric*. This work has exerted powerful influence on Western thinking about the art of human communication. In it Aristotle gave a broader meaning to *rhetoric* than did Plato, defining it as "the faculty of discovering the possible means of persuasion in reference to any subject whatever."[2] "Possible means of persuasion" led Aristotle to his famous distinction of three kinds of proof: *ethos*, *pathos*, and *logos*. *Ethos* denotes the influence on the listener of her assessment of the speaker's character. *Pathos* refers to the emotional aspect, the effect of the hearer's feelings on his receptivity to the message. *Logos* means giving evidence or reasons; it consists of facts, explanations, examples, statistics, testimony, and the like. *Ethos*, *pathos*, and *logos* are three sorts of proof that combine to move an audience toward a conclusion.[3] And they can be used to promote factual opinions, judgments, or actions.

Although Aristotle laid out these various elements, he emphasized the logical. Since humans are emotional beings and since a persuader must adjust to his audience, *ethos* and *pathos* are important. But Aristotle believed *logos* was the more legitimate mode of argument, and thus he focused on developing logical arguments for a persuasive purpose.[4] Interestingly, in the centuries after Aristotle, the discipline of rhetoric continued his categories, generally speaking, but not his emphasis; it tended to accent not logic, but language and style.

The discipline of apologetics among evangelicals today, however, is more Aristotelean. The emphasis in apologetics recently has been more on the logical than on the rhetorical. *Ethos* and *pathos* have been relatively neglected. To use Aristotle's terms, then, dialogical apologetics is all about restoring attention in apologetic practice to all three elements of proof. Dialogical apologetics encourages a recognition of all elements of dialogue in their "all-at-onceness." In developing the dimensions of dialogue, I will alter Aristotle's organizational pattern somewhat by identifying three aspects of persuasion, the conceptual (*logos*), the attitudinal (sometimes wrongly identified with *pathos*), and the cultural (no Aristotelean category here). I will conclude with some remarks about *ethos*.

2. Aristotle *Rhetoric* 1.2 (1355b26).
3. Ibid., 1356a1–20.
4. Two qualifications: First, ancient rhetoricians understood everyday reasoning. They valued the tradition of *informal logic*, especially informal fallacies (errors of thought not related to form, but instead to content). Second, the theoretical study of logic is valuable in its own right even if it is not as immediately usable as critical thinking.

The Structure of Arguments

Logic is the study of proper standards of inference. It is the search for appropriate guidelines for thinking. Logicians have traditionally considered their discipline a science, not an art. A set of strict rules guides logical thinking. It emphasizes syllogisms, symbolic notation, and truth tables. This view of logic as a geometrical science concerned with formal validity has its roots in Aristotle. This is what all logic students learned until a generation ago. Yet changes in how logic is taught today reveal increasingly positive attitudes toward practical logic, giving rise to a way of teaching logic that recognizes the artfulness in logic and has important consequences for dialogical apologetics.

Aristotle's Enthymemes

Logic in its traditional sense places a great deal of emphasis on formal validity. A *valid* argument is correct in *form* or *structure*. Assessing an argument as valid, however, says nothing about its *content* or *substance*. In this respect, logic is like math. If I say, "One million philharmonic orchestras plus one million philharmonic orchestras makes two million philharmonic orchestras," I am formally correct. In terms of form or structure, "1__ plus 1__ makes 2__" is always correct. Since there are fewer than one million philharmonic orchestras in the universe, however, that computation is defective as to its substance. But math cares about correctness of form, not of content.

An argument that is correct in both form (i.e., a valid argument) and content is said to be *sound*. According to traditional logic, a sound deductive argument (i.e., a valid argument with true premises) always produces a true conclusion. The classic example of a sound syllogism as everyone learns it in Logic 101 is:

All men are mortal.
Socrates is a man.
Therefore, Socrates is mortal.

This syllogism is clearly valid according to the rules Aristotle specified, and of course everyone will acknowledge its premises. Consequently, the argument is sound, and its conclusion is true.

The study of syllogisms along with other logical forms is challenging and invigorating. It is appropriate and valuable. But years of teaching logic have convinced me that instruction in formal logic must be fleshed out with a study of practical reasoning. The problem with traditional logic is that its connection to everyday thinking is not always immediately clear. Making it clear takes pen, paper, and lots of conceptual elbow grease. In apologetic dialogue, this attention to detail and exactness of form is rarely possible. The folks most apologists talk to simply do not have the patience for it.

Aristotle recognized this fact. He noticed that those who sought to persuade others often omitted key steps in the argument. They tended to say things like: "Since Socrates is a man, he is, of course, mortal." This way of putting it obviously makes no explicit mention of "All men are mortal," although the truth of this unspoken premise is presupposed. Aristotle called this kind of argument an *enthymeme*. An enthymeme is an argument that lacks a premise or depends on an unstated assumption the audience already accepts. In a sense, an enthymeme is an incomplete syllogism.

Aristotle argued that the enthymeme is the basic form of argument in rhetoric. To put it another way, the enthymeme is the rhetorical counterpart of the syllogism.[5] It generally involves the combination of an assertion plus a reason for that assertion. But the ancients preferred the syllogism to the enthymeme. They accepted the enthymeme because every enthymeme could be translated into its fuller, ideal (i.e., syllogistic) form.

Contemporary teachers of logic have also noticed the difficulties involved in relating traditional formal logic to everyday thinking. Consequently, many have become interested in what is sometimes called *critical thinking*. Critical thinking is an approach to logic geared to the analysis of everyday thinking and arguments. It is, in effect, practical logic. Numerous textbooks with *critical thinking* and *practical logic* in their titles attest to its popularity.

In sum, the traditional study of logic makes a sharp distinction between form and content. It stresses form or structure as the more important facet of logical reasoning. Indeed, some have tried to make assessing correct form the heart of all epistemology.[6] Those

---

5. Aristotle *Rhetoric* 1.2 (1356b5).

6. Confirmationist Rudolf Carnap wrote, "the problem whether and how much [hypothesis] *h* is confirmed by [evidence] *e* is to be answered merely by a logical analysis of *h* and *e* and their relations." *Logical Foundations of Probability* (Chicago: University of Chicago Press, 1950), 20.

who make the syllogism preferable to the enthymeme agree with this in spirit even if they are less extreme about it. For purposes of apologetics, however, an analysis that accounts for a greater variety of logical forms is preferable because it better reflects everyday reasoning.

Toulmin's Categories

Many textbooks on communication theory present a model for argument assessment that does just this. Historian of science Stephen Toulmin developed it in *The Uses of Argument*.[7] Rhetoric texts often pluck Toulmin's model out of a larger essay with a broader agenda. According to Toulmin, the traditional view of logic is wrong-headed. Because it exalts syllogistic deduction, the discipline of logic is too rigid and impractical. Instead, logic should follow the practical sort of reasoning everyone accepts in courts of law. The practice of law applies a probabilist style of assessment that yields positive results, is truer to everyday reasoning, and avoids skepticism.[8]

Toulmin's agenda shares the spirit of those in various disciplines who seek more flexibility in epistemology. In his words, the *working logic* of normal human reasoning differs from the *idealized logic* logicians study.[9] *Idealized logic* seeks a set of comprehensive rules, he argues, but the criteria of logical appropriateness cannot be legislated for all academic fields at once:

> "Can" and "possible" are . . . like "cannot" and "impossible" in having a field-invariant force and field-dependent standards. . . . all the *canons* for the criticism and assessment of arguments . . . are in practice field-dependent, while all our terms of assessment are field-invariant in their *force*.[10]

The meaning (i.e., force) of a criterion like *explanatory adequacy*, in other words, is constant in various fields (e.g., history, science, or theology). But the standards (i.e., canons) for deciding whether some

7. Stephen Edelston Toulmin, *The Uses of Argument* (Cambridge: Cambridge University Press, 1958).

8. Evangelical apologist John Warwick Montgomery studied law, hoping to apply its rules of evidence to apologetics. For various reasons, Montgomery has not fully developed in print the benefits that might have come through this suggestion.

9. Toulmin, *Uses of Argument*, 146ff.

10. Ibid., 38.

particular explanation is in fact adequate will differ somewhat from field to field.

In a similar spirit, Ludwig Wittgenstein and ordinary language philosophers reject the quest for an idealized logical language and plead instead for ordinary language as it is. Alvin Plantinga and his allies in Reformed epistemology argue against a rigid classical foundationalism that accepts only what is known certainly by deduction from undeniable premises. Thomas Kuhn and defenders of new forms of philosophy of science claim that even the sciences, the ideals of rationality, do not use rational principles in one predetermined way. I do not accept Wittgenstein, Plantinga, or Kuhn in every detail. In my view they grant too much independence to different fields. But they are right to resist the domination of all thought by a single set of rigid, universal principles applied in just one way.

The heart of Toulmin's model for argument assessment is the distinction between *datum* (D), *claim* (C), and *warrant* (W).[11] D is the evidence presented as the basis for the claim. C is the conclusion the argument seeks to establish. W is the link between the data and the claim. Using these definitions, arguments have this form: "D so C since W."

The difference between D and W is important. Speaking loosely, both support the conclusion. More precisely, D includes *specific evidence* while W is a *general rule* that justifies the move from D to C. It is like Swinburne's "primary inductive principles" (see chap. 3). W grants the license to use D in this case to support C. It tells whether D-ish facts actually support C-ish claims. W is the general statement, in other words, that certifies all arguments of a certain kind. To borrow Toulmin's legal model, D involves questions of fact, but W is a question of law. Given that the law allows certain kinds of evidence in cases such as are now being argued (i.e., assuming a proper W), a prosecutor enters appropriate evidence (D) in hopes of achieving a positive verdict (C).

Consider this example: "My Ford Mustang is smaller than your Chevrolet Caprice so it is cheaper to run." D is "My Mustang is smaller than your Caprice," an observable fact. C is "My Mustang is cheaper to run." Left unstated here is W, "Smaller cars are cheaper to run." In debating what kind of car is cheaper to run, most people will unconsciously assume W. As with all arguments, however, some W

11. This model is presented in the chapter entitled "The Layout of Arguments." Ibid., 97–107.

(which functions to give permission for moving from a D to a C) must be tacitly acknowledged before anyone will accept the conclusion. Without a W relevant to a particular field, no rational argument in that field is possible. Arguments all require that some W be assumed even if it is left unstated.

Note that this example can be expressed in syllogistic form:

Smaller cars are cheaper to run.
My Mustang is smaller than your Caprice.
My Mustang is cheaper to run than your Caprice.

This argument has the same structure as the "Socrates is mortal" argument. Both are valid and both have true premises, so the syllogistic format adequately shows both to be sound arguments. What then is the advantage of Toulmin's argument layout?

Suppose W is challenged. Of course, no one is likely to dispute either "All men are mortal" and only economists of a certain bent will question "Smaller cars are cheaper to run." But in other arguments, W does come into question. What then? For Aristotle's syllogism, the answer must be to move back to a prior inductive argument in defense of W. But for those who assume that deductive or syllogistic forms of logic are the preferred or ideal logical form, this raises a problem. It means that in actual arguments, a nondeductive argument becomes the background or foundation for the syllogism. The syllogism works only if this background argument works; the syllogistic house is only as solid as its inductive foundation.

Since it begins with observations about actual human reasoning, however, Toulmin's model puts in place a category that shows how an arguer could defend W if and when it is challenged. Toulmin calls this *backing* (B). Like D, the *nature* of B can be a series of factual statements. But unlike D (which supports C), the *function* of B is to support W. In this illustration, "Smaller cars are cheaper to run" could be supported, for example, by the masses of statistics gathered by car rental companies that correlate size and cost.

Now an obstinate person could question not only the use of W_1 in support of C_1, but also the use of B_1 in support of W_1. This challenge might require one to back up to develop an argument for W_1. Now this argument for W_1 based on B_1 obviously assumes a prior warrant, W_2. This hypothetical obstinate person could then dispute

W_2 backed by B_2. This might require one to form an argument for W_2 based on B_2 and assuming a prior warrant, W_3. Theoretically, this process could proceed until rigor mortis sets in. Unless dialogue partners agree to some W, no rational argument will ever work. This is consistent with my claim that the chain of reason giving must end somewhere. Unless we can know something without logical reasoning, we can know nothing with it.[12]

Two more terms complete Toulmin's model. First, sometimes D might support C subject to some *qualifier* (Q). Since arguments like these are probabilist, one may need a qualifier to indicate the degree of strength conferred by D on C. Q could be a word or phrase like "presumably" or "almost certainly." It signals that C might turn out to be false under certain conditions. Second, one may also want to spell out some of the reasons a conclusion might not follow. These are *conditions of rebuttal* or *rebutters* (R). For instance, the smaller car might cost more to run in cases where the smaller car is a souped-up sports car or if we factor in the medical costs associated with accidents in which small cars are involved. This fact is clearly relevant and might overturn C even though W ("Smaller cars are cheaper to run") is *generally* justified (by B).

In graphic form, Toulmin's layout of typical arguments looks like this:[13]

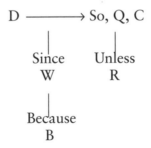

In prose form, the layout of typical arguments reads like this: Datum so, qualifier, claim since warrant (because backing) unless rebutter. "My Mustang is smaller than your Caprice, so it almost certainly is cheaper to operate; smaller cars are cheaper to run, according to rental-car-company statistics, unless the smaller car is a souped-up sports car."

12. See pp. 22–23.
13. Toulmin, *Uses of Argument*, 104.

A major criticism of Toulmin's model is that it gives help for *identifying* the parts of an argument, but not for *evaluating* those parts. Traditional instruction in logic emphasizes argument assessment. It stands to reason, however, that both skills are important, and that identifying precedes evaluating. Thus apologists can use this model as a starting point to help sort out the conceptual dimensions of dialogue. By asking these questions, assessment will become easier:

What is C? What exactly is the claim being advanced in this situation? What is the arguer claiming is the case?

Does D support C? First, what precisely are the facts, observations, or truths the arguer is advancing as evidence for C? Second, do these facts actually give reason to accept this claim?

Does W support the use of D for C? First, what exactly is W, the general rule the arguer claims gives permission to use this D for this C? Second, is this the right W, that is, does this W really grant license in this case?

Does B support W? First, what exactly is B, the facts or reasons advanced to support W? Second, does B actually give good reason to believe W?

What is Q? What degree of certainty is the arguer claiming for this argument?

Is there an R? Does some R show that the arguer misapplied W in this situation? In other words, what reasons might suggest W has not been used properly or is not relevant here?

Trouble Spots in Arguments

Toulmin's model, based on observations of working logic, provides workable categories for delineating the various elements of arguments. With this in place, we can turn to a discussion of some stumbling blocks commonly encountered in apologetic conversations. Seasoned debaters could list many such trouble spots, but mastering a short list of common conceptual difficulties will upgrade any apologist's dialectical skills.

What the Word Means

In apologetics, an argument is not a lovers' spat. It is not a dispute, a quarrel, or a war. Creating an argument means building a case for, or reasoning in defense of, a C. The basic building block of an argument is the statement. An argument is one statement, a C, supported by one or more other statements like D and W. The building block of a statement is the word. Words are linguistic units. They are symbols that evoke ideas or images in the mind. Words can represent concrete, physical objects one could point to in the world (e.g., a door) or very abstract notions that are impossible to point to (e.g., freedom).

Clear definition is a problem common in all communication, especially when it involves abstract ideas—as apologetics does. The same linguistic symbol can evoke different ideas in different people. For example, *capitalist* denotes someone who invests money in a business venture, hoping to make a profit. In a looser sense, the concept can identify anyone who advocates capitalism as the best economic system. For one steeped in socialist ideology, however, *capitalist* might connote a rich, selfish oppressor. The ideas evoked when two people hear *capitalist* may not be the same. A single verbal unit can have a double meaning.[14]

Puns depend on this double meaning. "Susan, I see your husband is suffering from depression. Would you like the name of a good economist?" This silly example clearly shows that punning is the lowest form of humor. When an *argument* turns on a double meaning, however, it commits the fallacy of *equivocation*. In cracking jokes, double meanings are fun. In discussing Christian beliefs, equivocation is deadly.

Equivocation is actually a single verbal symbol standing for two different words. Semanticists call this *polysemy*. Some might insist that a double meaning is actually one word with two meanings, not two words with one sound and spelling. But translating into another language shows why this is absurd. Take the word *hot*. The Japanese translate it *karai* (when it means *spicy*) and *atsui* (when it means *high temperature*). Any claim that *karai* and *atsui* are one word with two meanings befuddles a native Japanese speaker. To turn this around, the sound *hashi* can mean *bridge* or *chopstick* in Japanese. Is *hashi* one word with two meanings? English speakers think not. *Depression* (like *light, will, just, mine, still*) is not one word with two meanings, but two words that, in English, happen to have the same linguistic symbol assigned to them.

14. This example is suggested by David Chilton, *Productive Christians in an Age of Guilt-Manipulators: A Biblical Response to Ronald J. Sider,* 3d ed. (Tyler, Tex.: Institute for Christian Economics, 1985), 13–14.

People equivocate when they fail to recognize polysemy.[15] I once read a news item in a Christian magazine describing trends in American attitudes toward the family. The editors pointed out that Christians believe Americans should return to *traditional family values*. Then they quoted this statistic: only 10 percent of American households are *traditional families*. (*Traditional family* is defined as any family with a wage-earning husband, a work-at-home wife, and two or more dependent children.) The editors presented their readers with an enthymeme that had an unstated but implied conclusion: only 10 percent of Americans believe in the traditional family, and so Christians who do so are out of step with Americans generally.

This conclusion may be true, but this argument hardly proves it. Equivocation on the phrase *traditional family* bamboozled the editors. It means (1) a certain set of values (e.g., valuing maximal parental involvement in the lives of children over two incomes). It also denotes (2) a particular family structure (wage-earning husband, a work-at-home wife, and two or more dependent children). Deriving the 10 percent figure by counting Americans who fit sense 2, the editors fallaciously applied the 10 percent number to sense 1 (those who hold traditional values).

Notice that the concepts reflected in abstract words come in *matched sets*. A concept can be paired with other words to form a set of *categories*. A person's set of categories (i.e., one's total set of matched concepts) forms a grid for interpreting the world. Evaluations of the world reflect these grids. Thus the comment, "Christian conversion can be explained psychologically, so it is not a spiritual reality," implies a set of categories. It reflects pieces of the speaker's conceptual grid: in this case the speaker assumes, "Either an experience is psychologically explicable or it is spiritually induced." Surprisingly, humanists can share this piece of grid work with some fundamentalists. The humanists use it to discount spiritual reality; the fundamentalists, to reject psychology.

But both parties are victims of inadequate categories that are over-

15. J. P. Louw uses this biblical example: *flesh (sarx)* can denote the body (flesh as muscle tissue) or the sinful nature (the principle of sin). Because these two words coincidentally have the same verbal symbol, Christians may think that the body is more sinful than the soul. This is false. Jesus Christ was God in the flesh, that is, in a body (1 John 4:2). Our human bodies are the temple of the Holy Spirit (1 Cor. 6:19). The body-flesh is good even though the sinful nature-flesh is not. *The Semantics of New Testament Greek* (Philadelphia: Fortress, 1982), 39–40. See David K. Clark, "Interpreting the Biblical Words for the Self," *Journal of Psychology and Theology* 18 (1990): 309–17.

ly rigid and simplistic. The categories are inadequate because they rule out something that is clearly possible: an experience caused by spiritual power and at the same time describable by or interpretable through psychological categories. The two categories (*spiritually induced* and *psychologically explicable*) are not mutually exclusive. They overlap. Some phenomena might fit both categories; others might fit neither. More sophisticated and nuanced categories lead to clearer and more adequate understandings of the world.

How can one detect flawed categories? Finding a good counterexample will uncover defective categories. A counterexample is a case that clearly begs to be interpreted and yet does not neatly fit available categories. The inadequacy of the conceptual grid is revealed by its inability to incorporate the counterexample. A good counterexample forces one to reshape the categories so that all instances can be classed in what seems a natural and appropriate way.

Consider the *traditional family* example. The equivocation on this phrase led some to presuppose without careful thought something like this: Those who fit a narrow definition of the traditional family (working dad; nonworking mom; two kids) are those who hold traditional family values. But of course one could easily find counterexamples to that claim. Grandparents, empty-nesters, young marrieds, divorcees, singles, and widows do not fit the narrow definition, but many of them do hold traditional family values. In this case, an effective counterexample easily shows that two categories were wrongly united into one.

Or consider this illustration: a commonly accepted truism says, "You can't legislate morality." This sets up two mutually exclusive categories: (1) things that can be legislated and (2) things that have to do with morality. Accepting this truism as a W, one could easily argue for a prochoice law. (C is "You can't legislate against abortion.")

But are the categories adequate? Here is a counterexample: rape. Government rightly legislates against rape, but it is also clearly a moral issue. So in which category does rape fit? It fits both, of course, which shows that the categories implied in "You can't legislate morality" are too simplistic. This truism and its unsophisticated cubbyholes should be rejected in favor of a more nuanced approach. (These examples do not show that we should outlaw everything that is immoral, but they do reveal the importance of good categories.)

Equivocation and the muddled categories that often accompany it may not always be so obvious. But ferreting it out can often solve theological dilemmas. Resolving these puzzles often requires uncovering the conceptual flaws in the categories lying behind and implied by a particular discussion. Consider these examples:

Artificial insemination is immoral because it is adulterous.
Abortion is a moral issue and is therefore not the business of the state.
The idea of a positive self-concept is unbiblical because the Bible teaches Christians to crucify the self.
Since creation is a religious belief, it cannot be taught in public school.
I want to love God with all my heart, so I have no need for theology.

All of these as well as many other theological puzzles may imply faulty grids. They are like the proverbial "Have you stopped beating your wife?" Answering the question requires accepting one of two implied and equally unacceptable options. So questions built on faulty categories cannot be answered; they must be rejected and rephrased.

If someone understands and uses words clearly, it is because his categories are sharp. They neither overlap nor leave out important possibilities. Carefully using words and listening to others' words is important. The more abstract the subject of discussion, the more this is important. Concrete questions are easier to work with (e.g., Which lawn mower does the best job on this lawn?). Abstract ones are tough (e.g., Does the human right to life imply that capital punishment is morally wrong?). Clear definitions reflect better categories, and the result is higher skill in thought, communication, and argument.

What the Data Imply

Using words clearly to form statements is critical for good conversation. Combining statements properly in building and evaluating arguments is equally important. A category of common trouble spots in apologetics is the misuse of evidence. A complete list of informal fallacies would be very long. I have space only for a few. But any study of critical thinking will pay an apologist rich dividends.[16]

One common error in thinking is the fallacy of hasty generalization. This occurs when someone asserts, after examining too few in-

---

16. See, as two examples among many, Vincent Ryan Ruggiero, *Beyond Feelings: A Guide to Critical Thinking*, 2d ed. (Palo Alto, Calif.: Mayfield, 1984); A. J. Hoover, *Don't You Believe It!* (Chicago: Moody, 1982).

stances, that a claim is always true. In everyday thinking, in fact, people are often tempted to draw general conclusions after observing only a single case of some phenomenon. In terms of Toulmin's model, hasty generalization can occur either when justifying C with D or when certifying W with B. In both cases, argument builders will use individual facts to ground a broader generalization. If an arguer examines only one or a few facts, hasty generalization is likely.

Suppose someone argues, for example, that the moral fiber of American culture is weakening and American society is sliding downhill. In support of this he points to increased drug use and tells a story about a fourteen-year-old pushing crack in his local junior high school. This piece of evidence vividly supports his view that America is in moral decline. But does all the evidence confirm his view? What about heightened awareness of racial discrimination or sexual harassment? Are social attitudes improving in these areas? If so, such evidence is surely relevant to a broad generalization like "Society is going downhill." Despite the vivid story of the crack pusher, this claim needs more evidence.

The fallacy of special pleading I described is much like hasty generalization. Both fallacies occur when someone bases a conclusion in too little evidence. But special pleading adds this feature: some regulating principle filters out contradictory evidence, allowing only the facts that fit the conclusion to get through the sieve. The North Sea fisherman committed this fallacy because the size of his net holes systematically filtered the evidence. A hasty generalization leads to a firm conviction that in turn becomes a filter that permits a person to see only part of the evidence (viz., only what supports his preconceived view).

Anecdotal evidence, which supports a conclusion by touching the imagination, can commit either or both of these fallacies. Anecdotes do have several proper functions, however. First, importantly, anecdotes can exert unusual persuasive force. Because they are vivid, stories help a person experience a point concretely, and this makes them very persuasive.[17] Second, they do give valid instances as data for the generalizing process. A single story (e.g., the junior high school crack pusher story) does offer one case in support of the generalization. But since generalizations need other supporting cases, an arguer should assess other facts in a fair-minded, comprehensive way before affirming a conclusion.

17. See the evidence on this point in chapter 7, pp. 163–64.

Apologists should use anecdotes, but they should employ them carefully. Because telling stories raises the risk of committing a fallacy, it is best to augment them with argumentation. Then it is appropriate and effective to help a friend confront the point in a visceral and experiential way by using narrative that stirs the imagination. Part of C. S. Lewis's great appeal is his use of very concrete, imaginative illustrations even—or especially—when he is discussing very abstract matters. But using a story as the only evidence can be special pleading. Professors of preaching regularly preach this sermon: illustrations only illustrate.

Another form of fallacious reasoning is begging the question, or circular reasoning. This occurs when the parts of an argument are tied to each other rather than to something outside the argument. It is using the conclusion as a premise or assuming the truth of the claim in developing the argument. I argued that appealing to an experience without supporting it with other tests can lead to circularity. Suppose someone says, "I know Allah is the one true God because I experienced him." "But how do you know it was an authentic experience?" "Because it was an experience of the true God." The circularity here is obvious.[18]

Even well-known scholars can beg the question. I shall never forget discovering, as a student, in the pages of Julius Wellhausen, defender of the Documentary Hypothesis of the Pentateuch, this circularity: the Jewish tabernacle came from a period later than the writing of Deuteronomy. Any reference to the tabernacle in the Pentateuch, therefore, is later, Priestly material. Once these later sections are laid aside, what is left, the original Deuteronomic material, never refers to the tabernacle. Since there is no textual evidence for an early date for the tabernacle, it must be dated late. Maybe Wellhausen had other reasons for the date he assigned to the tabernacle, but circularity fatally flaws this argument.[19]

The problem of circularity raises the distinction between demonstrative and circumstantial evidence. Everyone knows that circumstantial evidence is unacceptable in court. But why? A piece of cir-

18. This problem came up in chapter 5, pp. 103–4. See also the discussion of coherentism and circularity in chapter 2, pp. 46–48.

19. Julius Wellhausen, *Prolegomena to the History of Ancient Israel* (New York: Meridian, 1957), 34–38. According to the Documentary Hypothesis, the Pentateuch is a composite of four major writings (two of which are Deuteronomy and the Priestly Code) written by different authors and collated at a later date.

cumstantial evidence is equivocal because it fits equally well with several interpretations of an event. Since it fits several theories, a circumstantial fact cannot narrow the options to just one hypothesis. By itself, therefore, circumstantial evidence cannot make a case.

For instance, imagine that a murderer attacks and kills his victim on the steps outside my office window. Later a lab test finds that my shirt is covered with the victim's blood. Does this prove I am the murderer? No. The evidence is circumstantial; it fits with several hypotheses. Perhaps I murdered the victim, but then again maybe I gave the victim CPR in his last moments of life. Either theory is compatible with the observed fact of the bloody shirt. With sufficient other evidence, the bloody shirt could help to convict me. Say the police found the murder weapon with my fingerprints in my office trash can. But even then a frame job is a possible explanation. A clear eyewitness account, however, is demonstrative and would very likely convict me.

How does the circumstantial nature of the bloody shirt relate to circular reasoning? One who presupposes his theory is tempted to overestimate the weight of circumstantial evidence. If Sergeant Ertsgaard of the St. Paul Police is convinced, for whatever reason, that I am guilty, the facts that fit with his hypothesis will jump out at him. He will wrongly see them as actually *confirming* his theory. This is a kind of circularity. One could also see it as a kind of special pleading. The conviction Ertsgaard starts with (viz., I am guilty) becomes the grid that filters the facts. When all the facts that make it through Ertsgaard's sieve unanimously support one theory, he pronounces the case solved.

Take a real case. The empty tomb is circumstantial evidence (D) that is easily misused. Consider how it relates to several hypotheses:

C^1: "Jesus bodily arose from the dead."
C^2: "The disciples stole the body."
C^3: "The women went to the wrong tomb."
C^4: "Jesus's body never left the tomb; decades later legends about a risen savior grew up in the church."

In isolation, D fits equally well with C^1, C^2, and C^3. Therefore, C^2 and C^3 must be ruled implausible *on other grounds*, not merely on the ground that the tomb was empty, before we can validly conclude

C^1. In a comprehensive cumulative case, however, D is helpful for it negates one theory, C^4.

Now someone who holds C^4 could argue that the D, the alleged fact of the empty tomb, is not really a fact. She could question the authenticity of the New Testament documents, for example. But this is a different tack altogether. Given that this D, the empty tomb, is a historical reality, it decisively discredits C^4. No one could credibly argue, "I acknowledge D, but C^4 is the best interpretation for D." A circumstantial fact can contribute to a good case if, *in concert with many other circumstantial facts*, it falsifies all possible theories of explanation *but one*.[20]

This is exactly the strategy commonly employed in arguing for the resurrection of Jesus. Apologists falsify alternative hypotheses one by one, using the combined effect of circumstantial evidence. This procedure leaves one hypothesis, C^1, as the best and the (probably) true explanation of the available facts. This strategy represents a cumulative case, probabilist argument. And it follows, as Toulmin points out, the model of jurisprudence.

What the Argument Presupposes

Properly using words and correctly combining statements to form good arguments is difficult enough. But another factor lurks in the background. This category of trouble spots in apologetics is the unwarranted assumption. As I have argued, all arguments presuppose something. Unless something is known without argument, nothing is known with argument. Every argument needs raw materials. But this fact does not warrant just any presupposition. Thus identifying and evaluating assumptions is imperative.

The sources for presuppositions are many. Some, like Swinburne's primary inductive principles, are rational guidelines posited in all thinking whatever. Some are part of the fabric of specific points of view. Some are very personal and individual, growing out of some vivid, life-changing experience.[21] Some derive from culture.[22] The first

---

20. See chapter 4. Facts must be interpreted in the context of several comprehensive theoretical systems. But facts are not entirely at the mercy of conceptual schemes. They have enough resilience to force certain theorists to abandon or modify some schemes.

21. See chapter 7.

22. See chapter 8.

thing to assess about assumptions, however, is not their *source* but their *role*. What is the function of this presupposition for this world view or this argument?

Some presuppositions are rational, that is, they reflect general rationality. Their role is to guide all thinking no matter what the point of view or world view. Consequently, assumptions of this kind do not depend on particular points of view. A test for truth like coherence, for instance, is assumed by all thought or any point of view whatsoever, and so it is proper to accept it. To take another example, a principle like the uniformity of nature is necessary to science in general even though science cannot prove it. Since the knowledge science produces when it assumes uniformity is acceptable, the assumption too is acceptable. In this way, if a general rational principle really is assumed in large ranges of human thought, I can appropriately accept it as properly basic.[23]

Other assumptions are philosophical, that is, they arise out of a point of view, perhaps a particular philosophical world view or a scientific paradigm. Every complex conceptual system or point of view needs central explanatory principles. These central beliefs direct traffic, showing how that conceptual grid organizes into a coherent whole the phenomena humans observe. These presuppositions can be acceptable. They are justified if they are critical to a world view that is coherent, accurate, and liveable.

In effect, both conceptual relativism and presuppositional apologetics entail that *all* assumptions are philosophical. Both these views claim that no rational principles exist independently of a point of view. In contrast, a soft rationalism distinguishes the rational principles all world view thinking assumes (like coherence, accuracy, and livability) from the philosophical principles or central beliefs that particular world views posit for their own internal work.[24]

For instance, since the Newtonian point of view assumes that objects move in a straight line when no external force disrupts normal motion, the movement of an object that follows a straight line needs no explanation. Newtonian physics accepts this idea as fundamental: Straight line motion is normal. A planet moving in a curved path,

23. This is a transcendental argument. In general, such an argument works like this: some principle is the unprovable but necessary precondition that makes a second act or claim possible. Since the second act or claim is appropriate, right, or true, its necessary precondition is, too.

24. See chapter 4, pp. 83–87.

however, demands explanation. Thus scientists begin to look for an object large enough to exert gravitational force to move the planet out of straight line motion. Certain forms of Greek physics, however, took circular motion as basic or normal. In such systems, it is linear motion that demands an explanation.

An assumption like "Straight line motion is normal," since it is necessary to thinking within a certain point of view (rather than necessary to all thinking whatever), must be used a bit more cautiously. A principle like this is justified if the system built around it meets other tests like explanatory adequacy (as Newtonian physics does). But positing a principle like this can lead to circularity unless caution is exercised. If the assumption runs roughshod over the evidence (rather than explaining it naturally and smoothly), fallacious reasoning can result. Of course, the judgment as to when evidence is being explained and when it is being explained away is not simple.

Still other assumptions are attitudinal. They are reflected in connotations of words, images, or ideas. Prejudices or stereotypes are attitudinal assumptions learned usually from culture. These factors profoundly influence language and thought. For this reason they are critical for apologetics.

In sum, there is no thinking without assumptions. But this does not imply that all presuppositions are created equal. Unwarranted assumptions do plague human thought. How can good apologists identify guides for the proper use of presuppositions? Once assumptions are identified, these three questions are worth asking:

Is this presupposition warranted by facts or observations (in cases where this is possible)?

Is it being applied consistently in various areas or on different topics?

Is it consistent with itself or does it involve self-defeat?

The first of these questions is fairly straightforward. If a person assumes that he will never trust someone of a certain racial group, has he succumbed to an unwarranted stereotype or is his prejudice really warranted by the facts?

The second is also obvious. Suppose that, during a debate on abortion, a person claims, "There are no moral absolutes," and then uses this assumption to reach her prochoice conclusion. A critic would be right to ask whether she applies this same point consistently to all moral issues. Does she, for example, apply her assumption in the arena of sexual harassment? Or does she think, as I do, that sexual harassment is absolutely wrong? If she posits different assumptions in different contexts, then she bears the burden of proof to explain this apparent inconsistency. She needs some new criterion to determine when absolutes apply and when they do not. Naturally, subjecting this new criterion to critical review is perfectly in order.

The third, the principle of self-defeat, is a little trickier. Successfully showing that a position is self-defeating is a powerful critique. Sometimes, however, apologists can be too quick to label a particular position self-defeating. I argued that "There are no moral absolutes" is not self-defeating.[25] Since this statement is not itself a moral absolute, it is in order. It could be criticized as in the previous paragraph (i.e., by checking to see if its defender applies it uniformly). But if a position really does self-defeat, as in the case of classical foundationalism, then uncovering this point constitutes a very powerful critique.

A Sample Conversation[26]

Adam the Apologist 1 (a young Christian): Since you are a Mormon, I assume that we both believe in God. But we obviously have different understandings of him. Could you explain to me how you judge the truth of religious understanding?

Fred the Friend 1 (a Mormon elder): The answer is as varied as the number of people who believe. Basically, I know what is true for I experience it. I simply know.

[Adam recognizes the possibility of equivocation on the word *God*, but passes over that to talk about W. Fred's C is not explicit, but it is probably something very broad, say, "The Mormon world view is true." Fred says his W is something like: "Those who experience what is true can know for certain that they have the truth."]

Adam 2: But if you know only intuitively, then how can we ex-

25. See chapter 2, pp. 38–40.
26. All sample dialogues are adapted from real apologetic conversations. But, as they say, the names have been changed to protect the innocent. In none of these samples do I claim that either Fred or Adam makes the best possible case or follows the best possible strategy. I offer these samples as extended models of the interplay between different elements of typical dialogues.

plain the fact that different people have significantly different understandings about God? There must be something more than just feeling it is right.

Fred 2: Okay, I'll tell you how I test for truth. There are several
things. The first is the personal experience. I would describe this like
what you see in the comics when a person has an idea and you see a
light come on above him. It's a revelation. People have new revela-
tions from God all the time. The Holy Spirit tells us new things about
truth and God. I know this experience is true because if it is right, I
have peace in my heart.

[Adam questions W on the grounds that different people have
used that W and yet not agreed with Fred's C. Adam implies that at
the very least Fred needs some Q like "probably" or "possibly." Fred
essentially repeats himself, although he narrows the sort of experience
he refers to in W by saying it is marked by a sense of peace.]

Adam 3: How can you know what you feel is right? Many people have a similar sense of peace and draw different conclusions.

Fred 3: In addition to personal knowing, a second test for truth is
consistency with the scriptures as we have them. We go to the Book
of Mormon and the Bible to see if an idea is true. We look to Moroni
10:4–7, which is very similar to James 1:5. It tells us to ask God if we
need clarification about anything. We have the right to ask God for
wisdom. A third test we use is the concurrence of the body of believers in the church. If my revelation is out of line, they have the right
and responsibility to correct me.

[Adam repeats his point. So Fred augments his W by adding something like "Whatever the scripture says is true" and "Whatever the
body of believers agree to is true."]

Adam 4: As I listen to your tests for truth, I realize they are not
that different from some used in our tradition. We believe the Holy
Spirit instructs us in evaluating our experiences. We agree that the
Scriptures are authoritative, and concurrence of the body of Christ is
important. How is it, then, that we have such differences? This is important, and we can't both be right. We need an adequate test for
truth.

Fred 4: All you can do is read the Book of Mormon. Then you
will know I am correct.

[Adam points out that the threefold W Fred has suggested still
does not guarantee arriving at what is true. The problem is that
"Whatever the scripture says is true" and "Whatever the body of be-

lievers agree to is true" do not answer the question Adam and Fred are discussing. For two believers operating within a biblical world view, for example, "Whatever the scripture says is true" is a good W. But since they are discussing whether the biblical world view is better than the Mormon world view, this W does not help. Fred senses the problem and changes his tack. He suggests that arguing will not prove his C, whereas Adam actually experiencing Mormon truth for himself might.]

Adam 5: But it seems there are contradictions between the Book of Mormon and the teachings I find in the Bible. How can I reconcile this?

Fred 5: The Book of Mormon is a fuller revelation of God and Jesus. After Jesus' resurrection, he came to the new world—to the ten lost tribes—and preached. We know this because Joseph Smith had this revealed to him as he earnestly sought the true religion. God told him that all religions had strayed and that he was to have nothing to do with them. He was to start a new, "reconstructed" church of God. He was given a miraculous ability to translate the plates of Moroni from the original language. The Bible has been translated at least three times, and it contains errors. These men were earnest men, but they translated in their own power. But Joseph Smith translated with the help of God.

[Adam too moves to a different line of discussion. He questions one of the basic presuppositions Fred implied in **Fred 3** (viz., the Bible and the Book of Mormon are consistent). Fred's response is not unusual: though Mormons like to say the two books are consistent, when pressed they give the Book of Mormon priority over the Bible. This new C is supported by these D: "Joseph Smith, who translated the Book of Mormon, was helped by God; those who translated the Bible were earnest, but they were not helped by God." This argument presumes a different W: "Books written with God's help (or inspired, etc.) deserve priority."]

Adam 6: What makes Joseph Smith unique? Can't I do the same thing?

Fred 6: He was in the line of Ezekiel and Isaiah and Jesus. You are not.

[Adam accepts the new implied W for now. So he questions Fred's D. Adam asks whether Smith really was helped by God. Without really supporting his D, Fred simply restates it: Smith *was indeed* helped by God as were Ezekiel and the others.]

Adam 7: Why not?

Fred 7: Because you have not had the revelation.

[Adam repeats his request for verification of D. Fred begins to argue in a circle. "God helped Smith translate the Book of Mormon. Anything God helps someone translate is true. So the Book of Mormon is true." How do you know God helped Smith? "He is in a line of prophets. Anyone in a line of prophets is helped by God." How do you know he is in that line? Could I be in a line of prophets? "No, you are not a prophet because you have not received the revelation."]

Adam 8: Can you tell me how you know this really is a revelation of God rather than a heresy?

Fred 8: Ezra Taft Benson would tell us if it was wrong. Prophet Benson is the prophet in the line of Joseph Smith. Peter came to the new world and appeared to Joseph Smith and ordained him. Peter was ordained by Christ. Prophet Benson was selected by a body of twelve Apostles to whom God had revealed this choice.

[Adam restates his request. Fred adds more links to his circular claim. It is becoming clear that the C implicit in **Fred 1** ("The Mormon world view is true") is acting as the filter that guides Fred's argument toward his C. This philosophical assumption dominates his thinking.]

Adam 9: But Prophet Benson is a man like we are. Is he infallible? Maybe he is deluded.

Fred 9: We have experienced the truth, so we simply know. Do you have a copy of the Book of Mormon?

[Adam points out that the W, "Whoever experiences God has the truth," could be subject to this R, "Unless he is deluded." Fred reverts to his original argument (from **Fred 1**) and strategy (from **Fred 4**)].

Adam 10: No, I don't.

Fred 10: Let me get you a copy. (He left and returned shortly with a copy.) Read this every night for two weeks and turn to the last page, Moroni 10: 4–7, and if you ask the Holy Spirit to guide you, you will be convinced I am right.

Summary

A dialogue is a complex tapestry of dimensions. These aspects all affect the quality of interpersonal relationship and of communication.

Aristotle gets at these dimensions when he introduces the classical categories: *pathos*, *ethos*, and *logos*. Additionally, apologists must consider attitudinal and cultural components.

Aristotle emphasized *logos*, the rational dimension. Any apologetic will have a strong *logos* element. But dialogical apologetics seeks to incorporate insights about other dimensions of dialogue as well.

Toulmin's model gives categories for separating the tightly woven strands of dialogue: "Datum so, qualifier, claim since warrant (because backing) unless rebutter."

Apologetic arguments can get derailed over word meanings. Clear definitions are very important, not only in their own right, but because words point to concepts that reveal the shape of a person's world view.

Arguments are also susceptible to poor reasoning. Among many others, hasty generalization and circular reasoning cause problems, as do the misuse of anecdotes and circumstantial evidence.

Presuppositions are necessary to all thinking, but not all assumptions are created equal. Good presuppositions are either necessary to all thought or clearly justified within a point of view. They are applied consistently and without self-defeat.

We have now examined the first dimension of any dialogue. In apologetics, the conceptual aspect is particularly important. But it is not the only significant facet of apologetic interaction. Other aspects remain; these include the attitudinal, cultural, and emotional. So we turn now to assess the attitudinal dimension: How do attitudes form and how do they change? What effects do a person's attitudes have on his decisions and perspectives, and how is this influence important in apologetic dialogue?

7

The Man's Got an Attitude

Fifty-five scholars gathered to hear the lecture. An enthusiastic professor delivered a big build-up, formally reading Dr. Myron L. Fox's impressive credentials. Dr. Fox, distinguished professor at the Albert Einstein University, arose to speak on "Mathematical Game Theory as Applied to Physical Education."

After the lecture, the organizers polled the audience for its responses. Most believed they had learned something of value. Some judged the lecture outstanding. One responded, "Excellent presentation, enjoyed listening. Has warm manner . . . lively examples . . . extremely articulate."

Not one of the fifty-five members of the audience figured out the truth: the lecture was a hoax. Dr. Fox was an imposter, armed with fake credentials. Three professors of medicine had hired an actor to deliver the lecture. He deliberately gave an incoherent presentation full of meaningless and conflicting statements. He sprinkled his speech with academic double-talk and scholarly jargon. During the Q and A, he purposely talked in circles. Yet Dr. Fox successfully bamboozled every member of his professorial audience![1]

Understanding Attitudes

How could these professors be duped? What factors lead people to accept falsehoods?

People react to truth claims in complex ways. They often form judgments, not by evaluating evidence directly, but by looking to established opinions or assessing contextual clues. Several social science disciplines study these factors by using a major concept, the idea of

---

1. "An Exercise in Education Flimflam," *Parade* (May 12, 1974), 17; quoted in Vincent Ryan Ruggiero, *Beyond Feelings: A Guide to Critical Thinking*, 2d ed. (Palo Alto, Calif.: Mayfield, 1984), 107–8.

attitude. A richer understanding of attitude and its relation to persuasion can enhance one's skills of apologetic conversation.

Defining Attitude

"The concept of attitude is probably the most distinctive and indispensable concept in contemporary American social psychology."[2] But *attitude* is notoriously difficult to define. One theorist says his colleagues have suggested five hundred different definitions.[3] Nevertheless these definitions do have some common features. Gordon Allport defined attitude as *"a mental and neural state of readiness . . . exerting a directive or dynamic influence upon the individual's response to all objects and situations with which it is related."*[4]

This definition highlights a fundamental assumption about an attitude: it is an inclination, a *"state of readiness,"* as Allport put it, to believe, feel, or do something about something in a certain way. It is a propensity to respond to a specific *attitude object* (which is anything—a person, an institution, or an idea—that elicits an attitudinal response). A commonly cited definition reflects this notion: attitude is a "predisposition of the individual to evaluate some symbol or object or aspect of his world in a favorable or unfavorable manner."[5]

Psychologists consider attitudes to be a readiness for action or response. Since theorists never directly observe attitudes, however, they must posit or assume that attitudes influence emotions, behaviors, or stated opinions. They confirm the presence and character of attitudes by checking for tendencies in observed behaviors and verbal reports. When grouped together, patterns emerge from these inclinations to respond in certain ways. These patterns congeal into values and value systems. Attitudes, therefore, are tendencies, rooted in a person's value system, to react to or evaluate things in the environment in certain ways.

Since attitudes express fundamental values, they relate to beliefs. But scholars debate the exact connection between attitudes and beliefs. Some analyze attitudes into three aspects: cognitive, affective (i.e., emotional), and behavioral. In this view, beliefs are one compo-

---

2. Gordon Allport, "Attitudes," in *A Handbook of Social Psychology*, ed. Carl Murchison (Worcester: Clark University Press, 1935), 798.

3. James F. Engel, *Contemporary Christian Communications: Its Theory and Practice* (Nashville: Nelson, 1979), 180.

4. Allport, "Attitudes," 810.

5. Daniel Katz, "The Functional Approach to the Study of Attitudes," *Public Opinion Quarterly* 24 (1960): 168.

nent of attitudes. Researchers study the relationship between these variables and attitude.[6] For example, how do behaviors relate to attitude? Are the actions of a person who says he is not prejudiced against a particular racial group consistent with his claims? Many theorists, including some Christians, have adopted this definition of *attitude*.[7]

This analysis builds on the so-called faculty psychology, which divides human persons into mind, will, and emotion. Given this, cognition relates to mind, and behavior connects with will (the intention to act). By a process of elimination, attitude gets associated with emotion. In this way, *attitude* includes an evaluative dimension that is defined as affect or emotion.[8] This approach to attitude, however, is defective. For one thing, the psychology it depends on is flawed. Faculty psychology has fallen on hard times because it bifurcates the human psyche too sharply.

Further, critics say, although attitude is *related to* emotion, it is wrong to say an attitude *is* an emotion.[9] The alternative to subdividing attitude into belief, feeling, and intention is reconceiving an attitude as a special kind of belief. In this view, attitudes are not the *result of* beliefs, they *are* beliefs. This shift appears in this helpful definition: "An attitude is a relatively enduring organization of beliefs around an object or situation predisposing one to respond in some preferential manner."[10]

Although all attitudes are beliefs, however, some beliefs are not attitudes. So what is the difference? Consider this statement: "Unions

6. See Milton Rosenberg and Carl Hovland, "Cognitive, Affective, and Behavioral Components of Attitudes," in *Attitude Organization and Change: An Analysis of Consistency among Attitude Components,* ed. Milton J. Rosenberg et al. (New Haven: Yale University Press, 1960), 1–14; Martin Fishbein and Icek Ajzen, *Belief, Attitude, Intention, and Behavior: An Introduction to Theory and Research* (Reading, Mass.: Addison-Wesley, 1975), 12.

7. Engel, *Contemporary Christian Communications,* 179; David J. Hesselgrave, *Counseling Cross-Culturally: An Introduction to Theory and Practice for Christians* (Grand Rapids: Baker, 1984), 278; Em Griffin, *The Mind Changers: The Art of Christian Persuasion* (Wheaton: Tyndale House, 1976), 15–18.

8. Fishbein and Ajzen, *Belief, Attitude, Intention, and Behavior,* 12.

9. Carolyn Wood Sherif, "Social Values, Attitudes, and the Involvement of the Self," in *Beliefs, Attitudes, and Values,* ed. Monte Page, Nebraska Symposium on Motivation, 1979 (Lincoln: University of Nebraska, 1980), 11–13. Later, Fishbein correctly described attitudes as having cognitive and *evaluative* components.

10. Milton Rokeach, *Beliefs, Attitudes and Values: A Theory of Organization and Change* (San Francisco: Jossey-Bass, 1968), 112; cf. Robert Bostrom, *Persuasion* (Englewood Cliffs, N.J.: Prentice-Hall, 1983), 47; Mary John Smith, *Persuasion and Human Action* (Belmont, Calif.: Wadsworth, 1982), 39.

are losing power." I believe this is true. Union membership is declining among American workers. Supreme Court decisions are limiting what unions may do to organize workers and pressure employers. But if I say without expression, "Unions are losing power," my hearer would never know how I evaluate the situation. Am I glad unions are losing power, or not?

Attitudes differ from other beliefs in having a *valence*, a positive or negative value. Attitudes involve an evaluation, pro or con, about an attitude object. A friend and I may share the belief, "Unions are losing power," but have opposite attitudes. I might be glad for the fact; my friend might not. A Russian and I might agree that *Soviet Union* is now an oxymoron yet have opposite attitudes about the fact. Thus at the center of the concept of attitude is the notion of a tendency to evaluate something pro or con. And this should help explain why cognitive argument alone is not enough for apologetics. I may prove to someone that Jesus claimed to be God's Son without convincing her to be glad about the matter.

Attitudes may differ not only in valence, but also in *intensity*. People hold some of their beliefs lightly and others deeply. A Bosnian freedom fighter and a first grader at Ketler Elementary School may both believe that freedom and democracy are good. That is, they will both have a positive attitude toward these ideals. But the level of intensity is likely to be very different. The first grader's intensity will run far higher when his mother decides to ground him from playing his Nintendo game than when his teacher leads his class in a discussion of current events in Bosnia. And note: valence and intensity are in no way directly connected. Positive and negative attitudes can either be intense or not.

Attitude Formation and Change

Attitudes are rooted in nurture, not in nature. Since attitudes are beliefs with an evaluative component, children do not arrive on this planet with a suitcase full of attitudes. Attitudes are caught, not taught. Children develop attitudes when they observe significant people in their lives in order to learn how to interpret and survive in their world. They adopt attitudes from their parents and later from peers and other adults. Individuals, groups of various kinds, and whole cultures can model and transmit attitudes. Attitudes result from an "individual's efforts to process information about an object in a particular motivational context."[11]

A classic study of attitude formation followed shifts in the political perspectives of women from conservative homes who attended exclusive Bennington College as freshmen in 1936. The young, liberal faculty at Bennington shaped student attitudes so powerfully that researchers discerned significant differences between freshmen, sophomores, juniors, and seniors. A follow-up study twenty years later showed that Bennington's influence lived on, especially among those alumnae who married liberal men.[12] Attitudes can still form in the adult years.

Because each person catches attitudes from his immediate surroundings, a boy may develop attitudes about things with which he has no direct contact. He may learn from his father to cheer the Minnesota Gophers and boo the Iowa Hawkeyes, for example, even if he gets no closer to them than a television screen. On the other hand, direct and personal experience with an attitude object can be more potent. Traumatic experiences like being attacked by a gang member can very forcefully shape attitudes.[13] According to one study, attitudes formed through direct experience are more stable, clear, and powerful than those formed in other ways, and thus they lead to a greater consistency between attitude and behavior.[14]

Practically speaking, theorists hope this work can contribute to the practice of persuasion. Persuaders try to nurture attitude formation. They also look for two kinds of attitude change: sometimes they hope to *prevent change* by intensifying current attitudes, and other times they hope to *induce change*. So writers commonly identify three types of persuasion: attitude *formation*, *reinforcement*, and *change*. The question therefore becomes, How do attitudes grow and change?

11. Herbert Kelman, "The Role of Action in Attitude Change," in *Beliefs, Attitudes, and Values*, ed. Monte Page, Nebraska Symposium on Motivation, 1979 (Lincoln: University of Nebraska, 1980), 127.

12. Theodore Newcomb, "The Persistence and Regression of Changed Attitudes: Long Range Studies," *Journal of Social Issues* 19 (1963): 3–14.

13. Harry Triandis, *Attitude and Attitude Change*, Wiley Foundations of Social Psychology (New York: John Wiley and Sons, 1971), 104–5.

14. Dennis Regan and Russell Fazio, "On the Consistency Between Attitudes and Behavior: Look to the Method of Attitude Formation," *Journal of Experimental Social Psychology* 13 (1977): 28–45.

What understandings can form a solid foundation for effective practice of persuasion?

Theories of Attitude Change

Theoretical explanations of attitude change abound. They focus either on the desire for intellectual consistency, the effect of group influence, the impact of perceived needs, or the human activity of information processing. Since those who investigate attitudes are usually social scientists, researchers test these theories experimentally. In general, the results are trending toward theories that are quite promising for apologetics. Many currently accepted theories stress that human persons form attitudes by actively processing information about their world in light of their perceived needs.

Cognitive Consistency Approaches

I spoke once with a Christian leader who had divorced his wife to marry another man's wife. He claimed his actions were blessed by God because he and his new wife were enjoying spiritually rich devotions! Doing or saying something that goes against basic beliefs stimulates attitude change. When a person acts in a new way for the first time, he may feel that such actions are not appropriate. This stimulates him to produce original messages to convince himself the actions are not too bad after all. Since these new thoughts clash with the internal network of beliefs that functions to justify behavior, he will tend to reformulate his former attitudes to fit the new behaviors.

This well-documented phenomenon is called *counter-attitudinal advocacy*. This phrase describes the tendency of humans to change attitudes to line up with their public pronouncements. A person will come to believe things he *says* even when they differ with prior beliefs. Theorists have advanced several explanations for this phenomenon. Some of these emphasize *cognitive consistency*. Cognitive consistency theories have in common the view that human persons actively process information, sorting through arguments and modifying disharmonious beliefs in order to achieve intellectual coherence. A highly influential example of the cognitive consistency approach is the *cognitive dissonance theory* proposed by Leon Festinger.[15]

According to Festinger, my thoughts or cognitions include beliefs about myself and my relations to my surroundings. My belief that I do not smoke is such a cognition. So is my belief that God has made me a steward of my body. These two cognitions relate well to my total life view. But two of my beliefs could be *dissonant*, that is, in logical conflict. I could simply ignore this dissonance. But assuming I want my beliefs to be consistent (because inconsistency or dissonance causes discomfort), I hunt for dissonance-reducing strategies. Often I reshuffle my cognitions, eliminating dissonance by altering certain attitudes.

Festinger's work stimulated a large volume of research on attitudinal change. But it has not avoided criticism. An oft-cited problem is its simplicity; it assumes that cognitive dissonance accounts for all attitude and behavior change. In fact, it appears that many factors affect attitude change. Critics therefore argue that the theory works only in narrowly prescribed areas. It is not, in other words, a general theory that explains everything. It suffers "empirical shrinkage"; research has restricted its application to increasingly limited situations.[16] Yet Festinger's theory shows that *arguments a person generates from within are most persuasive*. People purposefully integrate their knowledge into a consistent world view. This is critical for apologetics.

Another theory interprets counter-attitudinal advocacy differently. James Tedeschi developed an *impression management theory*, suggesting that attitude changes reflect the human desire to project a positive public image. All people want others to see them as consistent, stable, and credible. So they shift their attitudes to make them consistent with behaviors. In popular language, this is face-saving. Its force is the reason behind a well-documented human tendency: when responding anonymously, people tend to display their true opinions. But when forced to take a public stand, many people conform to those around them. Public commitment tends to prevent attitude change because a well-publicized change of opinion will tarnish a public image.

Tedeschi modifies earlier cognitive balance theories in several ways. According to Tedeschi, attitude changes tend to happen in small

15. Leon Festinger, *A Theory of Cognitive Dissonance* (Stanford: Stanford University Press, 1957).

16. Smith, *Persuasion and Human Action*, 128–29.

increments rather than in large leaps (although very dogmatic persons sometimes take one large jump from strongly pro to strongly con or vice versa). Further, changes of attitude after counter-attitudinal advocacy may be short-lived. Without reinforcement, people tend to drift back to their previous positions.[17]

Tedeschi's theory is right to caution against assuming without evidence that attitude change is permanent or complete. But some criticize impression management theory because it seems to exaggerate its claim that changes following counter-attitudinal advocacy are temporary. Presenting a positive picture of the self is not a superficial concern. It is deeply ingrained in the human desire for the approval and acceptance of others. Thus attitude change designed to save face can be forceful and permanent. If anything, impression management theory does not give its central insight enough weight! Self-presentation goals motivate people powerfully.[18]

Group Influence Approaches

Impression management theory highlights the human concern for others' views. Many theories place this social context at the center of their understanding of attitudes. These hypotheses stress this assumption: attitudes form against the backdrop of others' attitudes. Theorists developed these views to account for conformity and polarization. People define their attitudes by either moving toward others (conformity) or away from them (polarization). In both cases, others strongly influence attitudes. Of course, Americans scoff at conformity, valuing the individual who goes his own way. They forget this: not only *endorsing* a position because the majority does, but *rejecting* it for that reason means that others' views have largely shaped one's own opinions.[19]

Solomon Asch produced a very famous experiment on conformity. Asch showed groups of people a set of lines of various lengths. Then he showed them another line and asked them which line among the first set was the same length as this new line. But there was a catch: all but one of the group members collaborated with the experimenter.

17. James Tedeschi, Barry Schlenker, and Thomas Bonoma, "Cognitive Dissonance: Private Ratiocination or Public Spectacle?" *American Psychologist* 26 (1971): 685–95.

18. Smith, *Persuasion and Human Action*, 138; see Prov. 16:2.

19. Ruggiero, *Beyond Feelings*, 59.

Only one was a naive subject unaware that the researcher had instructed his confederates to answer wrongly. Under various conditions, Asch observed whether a subject gave the clearly right answer or followed group pressure. Surprisingly, a large majority of the naive subjects ignored the obvious truth and caved in to group pressure at least once![20]

Experiments like these confirm common sense: under the right circumstances, social conformity is a powerful force. But the theoretical interpretations of the effects of conformity are still underdeveloped. Thus researchers have proposed several forms of *social learning theories*. Some such theories, like B. F. Skinner's, view human action mechanistically. In this view, reinforcement happens unconsciously. But others are less mechanistic. Albert Bandura argues that humans purposefully search for if-then relationships: If I do X, what results will arise? When outcomes positively reinforce certain behaviors, people repeat them. These results help people learn to live in their environment as it is now and to anticipate how it will be in the future.[21]

Out of social learning theories come several significant strategies for persuasion. One is *modeling*. Modeling occurs when someone observes another's behavior producing positive results. Not surprisingly, people look to models who are like themselves, are competent, have high status, and behave consistently. They follow these persons because they believe their behaviors will bring good results for themselves as well. Another strategy is *role play*. When a person places himself in a specific situation to experience its consequences first hand, significant attitude and behavior change can occur. According to research, direct and emotional involvement with new situations powerfully affects attitudes.

A significant reason for the effects of these methods is that personal experience tends to shape attitudes very powerfully. For example, in a classic study, Irving Janis and Leon Mann investigated attempts to persuade people to kick the cigarette habit. A ten-year anti-smoking campaign failed dismally. But when medical personnel and family members watched a lung cancer patient suffer and die, they successfully quit smoking. The researchers hypothesized that an

20. Solomon Asch, "Effects of Group Pressure upon Modification and Distortion of Judgments," in *Readings in Social Psychology*, 3d ed., ed. Eleanor E. Maccoby et al. (New York: Henry Holt, 1958), 174–83.

21. Albert Bandura, *Social Learning Theory* (Englewood Cliffs, N.J.: Prentice-Hall, 1977), 16–31.

emotional empathy with the patients helped the medical staffs and families realize deeply that the same thing could happen to them. So they created an experiment to test whether actively engaging in role play could change attitudes and behaviors more significantly than passively watching public service messages on television.

They found twenty-six women with similar attitudes who were moderate to heavy smokers. Fourteen role-played cancer victims. The role-players entered a room set up like a doctor's office and furnished with X-rays of cancerous lungs. The "doctor" told them bad news, and then they expressed their feelings about health, smoking, and "their" cancer. To ensure that they heard the same information, the other twelve listened to the role-play sessions on audio tape. Two weeks later, follow-up showed far greater attitudinal and behavior change among the role-players. While the control group members reduced their smoking 4.8 cigarettes a day, the role-players cut down by 10.5 cigarettes per day! Involvement in emotional role-play brought significant change.[22]

Vivid experiences form strong attitudes. Thus an apologist can inadvertently touch a sore spot and elicit strong reactions. She need not conclude, however, that *she* is the offending cause. Nor should she presume that these intense attitudes constitute opposition to the gospel. She could assume that the other was wounded by some previous experience. Based on this, she could cautiously probe, looking for the background for the strong feelings. Properly done, this strategy can give the apologist insight, help the other blow off some emotional steam, and establish rapport.

Another kind of theory that emphasizes the social environment is *attribution theory*. According to views of this type, a person will scan his environment, looking for attitudinal cues to help make sense of unexplained behavior. This can include observing oneself, for people sometimes create their own attitudes by observing their own behaviors. Attribution theory has its critics. But even a defender of attribution theory admits that a person does not *shape* his own attitudes by observing his own behaviors when existing attitudes are clear and strong. Thus self-attribution helps *form* attitudes, but it does not *change* existing attitudes.[23]

22. Irving Janis and Leon Mann, "Effectiveness of Emotional Role-Playing in Modifying Smoking Habits and Attitudes," *Journal of Experimental Research in Personality* 1 (1965): 84–90.

23. Daryl Bem, "Self-Perception Theory," in *Advances in Experimental Social Psychology*, ed. Leonard Berkowitz (New York: Academic, 1972), 2–30.

But attribution theories do reveal that humans pursue their goals within the boundaries of their socially perceived world. Many years ago, I hired a man to do some carpentry work. In talking over a fair wage, he said, "I'm a fifteen-dollar-per-hour-man." I asked him what made him a fifteen-dollar-per-hour-man. "If you think you're a fifteen-dollar-per-hour-man," he said, "then you're a fifteen-dollar-per-hour-man." Social reality is what persons think reality is. *Social* reality is as important in conversation as *real* reality. Attitudes form within the lines of the world *as it is socially perceived.*

Growing out of attribution theory is a strategy for persuasion that has generated a good bit of study. It is called the *foot-in-the-door* phenomenon. Persuaders first try to get a person to comply with a small request in hopes he will later respond positively to a larger one. Fund raisers use this technique when they ask for a small donation, hoping they can come back later and successfully solicit a larger gift. According to attribution theory, when a person sees himself freely responding to the small request, he assumes the behavior reflects his true attitudes. He then begins to see himself as active and supportive on this issue, and these new beliefs in turn affect his future behavior.

A well-known experiment established the foot-in-the-door strategy. Researchers claiming to represent two fictitious groups, the "Keep California Beautiful Committee" and the "Community Committee for Traffic Safety," contacted 112 home owners. They asked home owners to promote one of these causes either by putting a small sign in a window of their home or by signing a petition. They made no requests of a control group.

Two weeks later, the researchers returned to make an outrageous request. Now claiming to represent "Citizens for Safe Driving," they asked all the residents whether they could place large, crudely lettered signs reading "Be a Safe Driver" in their front yards. The researchers made it clear that the sign would hide part of the house, would have to remain for over one week, and would leave behind a large hole in the yard. Of the control group, 16.7 percent agreed. Of those who had been asked for any one of the smaller favors, however, 55.7 percent agreed![24] This suggests that small initial requests induced the Palo Alto residents to see themselves in a new light, and this new self-perception dramatically changed later behavior.

24. Jonathan Freedman and Scott Fraser, "Compliance Without Pressure: The Foot-in-the-Door Technique," *Journal of Personality and Social Psychology* 4 (1966): 195–202.

The foot-in-the-door technique does not always work, however. Several important factors affect its success. The initial request must be large enough to engage a person's attitude structure yet not so large as to cause rejection. People accept trivial requests and reject outlandish proposals without a second thought. Further, the initial request must be accepted freely. A demand that is forced from without does not engage the attitude system and so causes little change. This suggests that when it involves undue pressure, persuasion may accomplish only short-term conformity, not long-term attitude change.

In the early 1960s, students at Yale caused a disturbance. The New Haven police restored order. Students widely accused the police of brutality. So researchers asked the students to write essays defending the police. They paid students either fifty cents, one dollar, five dollars, or ten dollars. Attitude change correlated with the amount of money paid. The first two groups believed they had defended the police freely. Not motivated by the pocket change, they came to think they supported the thesis because they really believed it. The second two groups experienced much less attitude change. Since they assumed their arguments to be motivated by money, they never came to think they really believed what they wrote.[25]

Need-Oriented Approaches

Phenomena like conformity and polarization emphasize the roles attitudes play in meeting human needs. The *functional theory* of persuasion focuses on this factor. In this view, attitudes form and evolve because of the needs they serve. *Instrumental* attitudes help a person adjust to the world. They develop positive attitudes toward things that meet his needs and negative ones toward those that thwart them. *Value-expressive* attitudes, as the name implies, embody one's central values and self-concept. *Ego-defensive* attitudes protect one from rude, unpleasant truths either about himself or about the world. Finally, *knowledge* attitudes constitute a point of view, the cognitive scheme by which a person organizes the chaotic world.[26]

A focus on the roles played by attitudes highlights this fact: humans act to resolve their felt needs. This theme, consistent with theories like Abraham Maslow's hierarchy of needs, has been called an

25. Jack Brehm and Arthur Cohen, *Explorations in Cognitive Dissonance* (New York: John Wiley and Sons, 1962), 73–78.

26. Katz, "Functional Approach," 170–76.

emerging trend in studies on attitude.[27] The desire to meet felt needs is like the energy that propels a car. Attitudes change when they fail to do their job: if a person feels hemmed in or stymied, then change will occur. "Some degree of dissatisfaction with one's self-concept or its associated values is the opening wedge for fundamental change."[28] For this reason, *"people will not change unless they feel a need to change.* Need activation is always the first step in any type of decision."[29]

The very concept of *felt needs*, however, agitates some Christians. The notion of felt needs fits North American culture. According to Daniel Yankelovich, 80 percent of Americans have accepted the claim that need fulfillment is the stuff of life.[30] But Christ came to meet *real* needs, some Christians argue, not just *felt* needs. Many years ago, a Christian observed that responding to felt needs is like ringing a bell— it attracts a crowd. But the bellman must have something of value to say. A bell, after a time, irritates those it initially attracts.[31] This is one way to resolve this problem: responding to felt needs is a *starting point* for communication. Eventually, however, a person must get past felt needs to substantive matters.[32]

Clearly, the Christian apologist cannot merely pander to felt needs. At the same time, functional approaches to attitude change teach that people do assess messages in terms of their own desires. "What's in it for me?" may not be a noble motivator, but it is a powerful one. Thus what people are willing to believe is not simply a matter of the credibility or legitimacy of the ideas, rules, and persons offered them. It is also a matter of their own need to believe. What they want from an authority is as important as what the authority has to offer.[33]

The concept of need grounds another important theory. *Commodity theory* treats information (e.g., a hot stock tip for a broker)

---

27. Abraham Maslow, *Motivation and Personality* (New York: Harper, 1954); Shelly Chaiken and Charles Stangor, "Attitudes and Attitude Change," in *Annual Review of Psychology*, vol. 38, ed. Mark Rosenzweig and Lyman Porter (Palo Alto, Calif.: Annual Reviews, 1987), 615.

28. Katz, "Functional Approach," 188.

29. Engel, *Contemporary Christian Communications*, 110.

30. Daniel Yankelovich, *New Rules* (New York: Random House, 1981), 3.

31. George Jackson, *The Fact of Conversion* (New York: Eaton and Mains, 1908), 225.

32. Engel, *Contemporary Christian Communications*, 117–20.

33. Richard Sennett, *Authority* (New York: Knopf, 1980), 25.

as though it were a commodity, something that can be exchanged from one person to another. Response to persuasion involves two steps: someone judges that information is valuable and then moves toward accepting the information. Information has a cost. Greater cost often means greater value. Value increases if the information is scarce, requires effort to attain, or is delayed. Having valuable knowledge (like gossip) gives one status. People tend to judge more valuable knowledge more decisively. This generates greater force leading to positive attitude change. Thus the more valuable the information, the more people will do to get it.[34]

Commodity theory does not specify the force that motivates people to seek valuable information. So one theorist suggests that psychological *reactance theory* fits this role. When freedom to do or have something is threatened or reduced, a person feels a discomfort called reactance. This motivates one to maintain or regain freedom by clutching the threatened thing. For example, the child whose toy is desired by another child suddenly wants to play with *that toy!* Once, as I considered the purchase of a fireplace, I suddenly valued the fireplace more when the seller let me know he had only one left and someone else wanted it!

According to reactance theory, the motivation for seeking what is scarce is the desire to think and act freely. Thus information I seek becomes even more desirable if it is scarce, requires effort, or is delayed. I can enhance my ability to have that information if I want it (i.e., I can enhance my freedom) if I accept its truth by moving toward adopting the position. Just as I must move decisively if I want that fireplace, so I must act aggressively to accept information that is in limited supply. If I cannot get the information at all (e.g., if it is censored), I can still restore a perception of freedom by valuing the information more highly. Lost alternatives are oh so attractive!

Learning Approaches

Like the commodity view, a final category of views places special stress on how receivers process information. An influential school of thought is the *Yale theory* developed by Carl Hovland and associates and modified by others like William McGuire. Hovland argues that

34. Timothy Brock, "Implications of Commodity Theory for Value Change," in *Psychological Foundations of Attitudes*, ed. Anthony Greenwald and others (New York: Academic, 1968), 243–75.

attitude change occurs as new information is learned and internalized (a perspective that offers encouragement for apologists). Hovland's approach considers the adoption of a new message to be a learning experience that is directed by proper rewards.[35] According to McGuire, persuasion involves the steps of reception and yielding. The Yale theorists tried to find which aspects of *source, message, channel,* and *receptor* affect yielding.

A more focused version of a learning approach is Martin Fishbein's currently popular *information integration theory.* Fishbein relates learning and change more loosely than does the Yale theory. But he still sees attitude alteration as a function of how individuals combine and integrate the relevant information about some object, using their attitudes to select important facts and to fill in where the data are spotty. This assumes that the individual plays an active and significant information processing role. It focuses on what people *do with* messages, not on what messages *do to* people.

Research by persuasion theorists into factors related to source, message, channel, and receptor provides evidence for claims like these:

Credibility of the source, what Aristotle called *ethos,* affects the impact of a message. I will raise this issue in the conclusion.

Information presented first is usually (not always) more persuasive. This is called the *primacy effect* (cf. Prov. 18:17).

Novel evidence is more likely to elicit attitude change. Evidence someone has heard before has already been processed, and a conceptual defense is likely to be in place.

Negative messages tend to be more powerful and persuasive than positive messages.

Emotionally intense messages are typically more persuasive than emotionally bland ones.

A clearer message is usually more persuasive. An incomprehensible message is ignored if it is incoherent or too complex.

Messages that present both sides of an issue are more persuasive to those who initially disagree with the message and to more intelligent people. They also have a longer range effect.

35. Carl Hovland, Irving Janis, and Harold Kelley, *Communication and Persuasion: Psychological Studies of Opinion Change* (New Haven: Yale University Press, 1953), 10–11.

Messages that present one side of an issue have a greater impact on those who already agree and on those who are less intelligent. They tend to have a shorter range impact.

Intelligent, high self-esteem people will more easily comprehend a message, but they are also more resistant to persuasion. The same conceptual tools they use to understand a message will help them find reasons for rejecting it.

Making an overall agenda clear from the beginning will aid comprehension and thus help persuasion. This should be done unless the audience is hostile to the message.

Messages delivered on videotape are more persuasive when they are simple. Complex messages are more powerful when written. One-on-one apologetic discussions have more in common with videotape than print, which suggests that simplicity is a virtue.

Changes in a person's life (like new roles or relationships, or times of passage) provide opportunities for attitude change. But they may not by themselves actually bring change.

Reasons a receiver constructs in support of a message are more memorable and persuasive than those a source provides.

But this recognition is most important: individuals will process information according to their own predispositions. Most messages are far too complex for receivers to handle exhaustively at a conscious level. Thus they use different strategies to reduce the density of information to manageable proportions. This means a receiver will use her cognitive framework to reformulate any message.[36] What counts, therefore, is not what the message *does to* the receiver, but what she *does with* the message.

Information processing theories, where the receiver is seen as an active participant in persuasion, are very popular in the literature. They generate less criticism than other views. This is not to say, however, that the other theoretical perspectives have nothing to say. Trends in the literature suggest that the wide-ranging general theories earlier researchers proposed cannot be sustained. Instead theories

36. Joseph Cappella and Richard Street, Jr., "Message Effects: Theory and Research on Mental Models of Messages," in *Message Effects in Communication Science*, ed. James Bradac (Newbury Park, Calif.: Sage, 1989), 27.

now cover smaller ranges of phenomena.[37] Thus a full-orbed understanding of persuasion must make room for the effects of social environment, the influence of psychological need, and the role of cognitive scheme, point of view, or value system in an individual's processing of persuasive messages.

A Sample Dialogue

Adam the Apologist 1 (a young Christian): Hi, Fred. I sure do appreciate your willingness to meet with me.

    Fred the Friend 1 (a middle-aged New Ager): No problem.

    Adam 2: I'm glad we can discuss spiritual things.

    Fred 2: Oh, you're going to be telling me what you believe?

    Adam 3: Yes.

    Fred 3: Oh. I don't know if I like that. I thought you'd be asking me questions about my spiritual views.

    [Adam should already be picking up an attitudinal reaction here. Fred is tense about this conversation. He is happy to give his views, but he does not want to hear Adam's.]

    Adam 4: Well, this is sort of like a survey, but it would be better to call it a conversational interchange or a discussion since both of us will be interacting with one another. I will be sharing my thoughts with you too. Will that be okay?

    [Adam tries to resolve Fred's misgivings. His approach implies sincere dialogue. Both will be sharing their views. But Fred is not convinced.]

    Fred 4: Well, I thought it would be a survey of my views and not a discussion. Are you going to be tape recording this?

    [Fred is still very skittish. Who knows why Fred thinks Adam will use a tape recorder? But that is irrelevant. The question indicates his anxiety.]

    Adam 5: Oh no! I want to strengthen my listening skills. I will not use a recorder. I'll be putting a great deal of effort into listening attentively.

    Fred 5: Oh, good. That's good. You know, some people just aren't as comfortable talking when they know they're being recorded. They're a lot more careful about what they say. Tape recorders are inhibiting for people.

37. Smith, *Persuasion and Human Action*, 310–12.

[Adam's promise to listen carefully is as important as his promise not to use a tape recorder. Listening carefully pays a dialogue partner a large compliment. Fred warms up a bit.]

Adam 6: I'm glad you feel okay.

Fred 6: Look, I consider myself a spiritual person, but I know we probably have great differences in views. I don't believe like I used to believe, but I do have my own religion—sort of a conglomeration of all the different spiritual trips I have taken throughout my life. I'm sure that on any subject we discuss we will find we have very different views.

[Adam may think he has convinced Fred of his sincerity. But Fred is still wary: "Look, don't expect me to agree with you or be convinced by you." Fred's signals are still defensive.]

Adam 7: Well, do you believe in God?

Fred 7: Well, I don't believe like I was raised, and I know I don't believe like you. I believe God exists out there somewhere surrounding the earth. God is a great power or energy that surrounds the world, and we can experience him. God doesn't control anything; he just is. We all have a little bit of Godness in us. I don't believe in the trinity—you know, Father, Son, and Holy Ghost. There is just a force that exists, and some call it God. I don't know if it is God, but I know it's there.

[Fred repeats that he does not want to be proselytized. "We believe differently. There's no way you'll change my mind."]

Adam 8: Have you always believed this way?

[Adam is taken aback by this sudden, wide-ranging statement. His question is good. He is probing for Fred's current beliefs and the reasons for his coming to these views. He needs a little history in order to understand Fred, so he stalls for time and information.]

Fred 8: No. This isn't how I was raised to believe. I was raised Christian. I was very active in church when I was young. My mother made sure we went to church every time it was possible. She was a very good Christian. I attended Sunday school and church services and even went to church during the week. I was baptized, confirmed, and a church member. In fact, I wanted to be a missionary at one time. I thought it would be very noble to help people in other parts of the world with their physical and spiritual needs. I think it is very nice that you are interested in helping people with their needs. I was very religious—or I should probably say Christian-like since I still view myself as a very religious person. Although I don't believe in attending church, I have a lot of spiritual trips. I had a very strong faith when I was young and wanted to serve God, but something happened that changed all that. Now I no longer believe in that. (Fred digresses to explain why he doesn't pray.)

[Fred is a talker. He gives Adam a lot of information. But Adam is still trying to figure out why Fred believes this way. So he asks another information-seeking question.]

Adam 9: What made you change your views?

Fred 9: The reason I rejected the way I was raised is due to a talk that I had with my pastor when I was young. See, a very close friend of mine died when I was young. He was a very special person to me, and it was hard for me to understand why he died. When he died, he was only twenty-three years old. I went to my pastor to find out why God would take such a young life. My friend was very vibrant and full of life, he had a lot going for him, and then at such a young age he no longer had a chance to live life as he once did. I no longer could share my life with him. It didn't make sense to me. It seemed so unfair. It just didn't seem right. So I asked my pastor why this would happen, and he couldn't answer my question. He said something about my friend having had a very good life, a valuable existence, but my pastor never could give me a reason why my friend had died.

[Fred's revelation is significant. A traumatic experience fostered a change in attitude. The experience of losing the friend *by itself* did not cause the shift. That experience *combined with the pastor's apologetic ineptitude* brought the change. Experiences of upheaval only create the possibility of attitude change. Unfortunately, that pastor had a much better chance of preserving Fred's perspective years ago than Adam does now of changing it. Clearly, since Fred's views have developed through significant and emotional experiences, the ideas he shares here will be deeply integrated into his cognitive schema.]

Adam 10: That must have been hard to understand.

[Adam expresses genuine empathy.]

Fred 10: Now I understand, though, why my friend died. Now that I'm older—I'm not ashamed of my age, I'm fifty-nine—now I understand that life is only a small period of time in our existence. It doesn't matter if someone lives to be ninety or only to nine years old, it's only a small portion of our total existence. Since I never got a good answer from my pastor I started to expand my faith and take some spiritual trips.

Adam 11: Spiritual trips? (Adam's eyes open wide.)

Fred 11: I went out to Berkeley in the sixties and tried everything. I went on a bunch of spiritual trips. I tried speed, LSD, mushrooms—everything. Everything I tried brought me through a spiritual trip and gave me greater understanding. I only did mushrooms once, but I remember going back home after that and running into the pastor I was telling you about. I told him I did mushrooms and finally understood everything he was trying to say when I was young about love and life. He looked at me like I was really strange. That was just one of many spiritual trips I have been on that have made me the kind of spiritual person I am now.

[Fred has totally restructured his world view. He developed the new set of interpretations to help him make sense of his friend's untimely death. Now vivid spiritual trips have confirmed this new restructuring.]

Adam 12: Does this make you bitter about your upbringing?

[Fred used a belief in life after death to solve his problem (viz., how could a short life have meaning?). Tragically, he came to believe in life after death in a reincarnational form. What if the pastor had included heaven as a part of his original response? Fred would not have been pushed off to consider reincarnation. In spite of all this, Adam has the presence of mind to focus on attitudinal and emotional issues. Factually, Fred has revealed that an important person in his life—his former pastor—thinks he is crazy. But what is Fred's attitude toward that? Favorable or not? And what emotional issues does this raise? Adam's question expresses empathy again.]

Fred 12: Oh, no. I believe it was one aspect—maybe a seed—in my spiritual journey. It was part of my spiritual pilgrimage. The teaching I got in the church was just one of my spiritual trips. It was very basic, simple; maybe I could call it primitive. Not that it's primitive for others. They're just at a different place in their spiritual journey, just on a different trip. I think we all have a spiritual journey we must encounter. You know the sayings, "seek first the kingdom of God" and "the truth shall set you free." We need to seek for truth, the energy that surrounds the earth, that we have within us, that force we will be released into.

That's why I have problems with my neighbor and her gentleman friend who call themselves atheists. They don't realize the importance of the spiritual. They make me so mad. I can get along better with fundamentalists than with those who deny a spiritual side of life. My spirituality often clicks with a fundamentalist's. But these atheists say things like, "Why do you live so far up here on a hill, so you'll get closer to God?" They don't need to say that.

[Note that Fred starts by brushing off the opinion of others who disagree with him. He gives a typical New Age answer: everyone is on the journey; some are farther along than others; everything is cool. But he changes his tune when he admits his atheist neighbors make him angry when they tease him. Which statement is the more accurate?]

Adam 13: Then why does it bother you that your atheist friends don't recognize the spiritual? To me, if God isn't personal, it won't matter whether someone considers it important.

[Adam ignores the New Age rhetoric about everyone being on a journey and spots Fred's point of pain. So he begins to explore the intellectual basis for Fred's attitude toward the atheists. Fred does not give an intellectual answer.]

Fred 13: I was with my mother when she died—in fact, I used to be interested in working with dying people—and there was some sort of glow right after she died. My dad wasn't very religious. But when my dad died I was with him too. I truly sensed his energy being released when he stopped breathing. It floated up into the outer atmosphere. This is what I believe God is. All the energy of people gathers together to form God. It's a oneness of sorts. I think it's cool. I can still feel that energy. It's a part of spirituality.

[Adam finds out that the reasons for Fred's attitudes are rooted in his interpretation of vivid experiences. Fred's Jungian, New Age theories about spirituality represent the way he made sense out of two difficult experiences. Mom and Dad did not face the judgment. They are now part of God.]

Adam 14: Do you feel your atheist friends are missing out on an aspect of life?

Fred 14: Yes, I think that's true. Our spiritual side is there even if we try to deny it. That's why I believe in reincarnation. (Fred goes on a long discussion of reincarnation.) I have a certain oneness with Jesus as well as other spiritual teachers. That's why I can get along with fundamentalists, because they have an understanding of spiritual things. But I really do not think anyone has a right to tell someone else what to believe. I have a closeness with spiritual people, but it is a very wide area of our existence. So, even though I get along with fundamentalists, they need to remember not to force their views on others. I can't stand it when people come over and give me booklets and talk to me on the bus about Jesus.

[Fred likes being religious. He feels good about other religious people, too. He comes back to a sensitive spot, however, because some spiritual people push their beliefs on him. Remember his anxiety that Adam would share his views (**Fred 2–4**)? His experiences with fundamentalists have probably been negative. If Fred classes Adam as a fundamentalist (someone who gives out booklets and talks about Jesus), Adam might encounter huge new barriers.]

Adam 15: Well, Jesus has made a great impact on the entire world and many have found him to make an impact on their personal lives. Just like you said, you were handing out pamphlets one time in order to stand up for a cause, these people have taken a stand on an issue they believe is essential to life.

Fred 15: Yeah, I guess I'm being a little inconsistent there. (Pause) I may hand out information sheets, but I never try to force my view on someone.

[Adam points out Fred's inconsistency. Fred tries to convince others of his view, but he gets mad when others do it to him. Fred's brain whirls. He creates an ad hoc distinction to resolve this bit of cognitive dissonance: handing out information is one thing; forcing a particular view on others is a different thing. Adam next asks a good question that leads Fred to admit that sometimes giving out information is good. Adam is hoping to hand out some information, too.]

Adam 16: Wouldn't it be ethically right to tell someone who was dying how to save his life?

Fred 16: Yes.

Adam 17: That's why people tell you about Christ, because it's a matter of life or death. I wish it wouldn't bother you that people give you booklets about spiritual matters, because I really wanted to give you this book by C. S. Lewis called *Mere Christianity*. Would you be interested in it? It's a book about Christianity by a British philosopher.

[Adam does not say, "You are wrong to be insulted when people give you books." He suggests his own feelings, saying in essence, "I'm very sorry you feel insulted when people give you books. I had hoped to give you a book, but I don't want to offend you." Adam then asks permission to give him a book. Fred has an out. Since he does not feel pressured, he willingly accepts the book.]

Fred 17: Oh, I like philosophy. I'd be interested in looking at the book. Sure, I'll take it.

Adam 18: Good. I hope you'll enjoy it. Maybe we can talk again.

[Adam has successfully overcome Fred's intense anxiety. What he will think when he reads Lewis is anyone's guess. Given the depth of the experiences out of which Fred's views formed, Adam has made real progress in establishing a positive relationship and defusing some of Fred's strong attitudes.]

Summary

Attitudes are beliefs with an evaluative valence. They are a tendency to judge some symbol, idea, or object in a favorable or unfavorable manner.

Attitudes are caught, not taught. They are caught both by observing others and by interpreting one's own experiences. Attitudes fostered by vivid personal experiences tend to be very tenacious.

Cognitive balance perspectives for understanding persuasion stress the human desire for coherence among their thoughts. In some areas, especially those related to face saving and self-image, this desire may affect attitude formation and change.

Group influence theories highlight the effect other people have on one's attitudes and beliefs. People want to be respected by others and so do not want to commit themselves to attitudes they think the larger group will find implausible.

Need oriented approaches emphasize the role attitudes play in meeting inner psychological needs. It is dangerous to cater only to felt needs. Yet any persuader must realize that humans generally change only when they see a need to do so.

Learning oriented views accentuate what a receiver will do with the information presented to her. Receivers are active participants in any successful persuasion.

Emotionally explosive attitudes often have experiential roots. Apologists should recognize that they may not themselves be the cause of strong reactions. Other root causes can be located.

We have discussed the cognitive and attitudinal aspects of dialogue. Armed with these broad perspectives, we will now turn to a force that powerfully shapes these aspects of dialogue, the influence called culture. What is it about group identity that shapes human thinking processes and attitudes? What are the cultural factors that alter every apologetic dialogue?

8

Conversation at the Cultural Crossroad

Strolling down the lane, two French poodles named Mimi and Fifi spotted the neighborhood hound coming the other way. The three dogs stopped at appropriate dog distance. Mimi and Fifi introduced themselves.

"I'm Mimi," said Mimi. Then, with an air of sophisticated nobility, she spelled it out: "M-I-M-I."

"I'm Fifi," said Fifi. She spelled it, too: "F-I-F-I."

The neighborhood hound was impressed, but not intimidated. "I'm Fido," he said. "P-H-Y-D-E-A-U-X."

Understanding Culture

Like the dogs in this silly story, all humans create images of themselves and others by using labels. Labels are cultural tags that identify a person by connecting him to a group or ranking him within a group. By using these tags, cultures affect people powerfully. The effect is sometimes powerfully positive, sometimes powerfully negative.

In some ways, each person is like all other humans. In other ways, each is unique. In yet other ways, however, each takes on the characteristic perspectives and attitudes of the social group with which he identifies.[1] The word *culture* includes the group dynamics and influences that shape all human self-awareness. Discerning a person's cul-

---

1. Clyde Kluckhohn and Henry Murray, "Personality Formation: the Determinants," in *Personality in Nature, Society, and Culture*, ed. Clyde Kluckhohn and Henry Murray, 2d ed. (New York: Knopf, 1953), 53–67.

tural identify and self-image, especially as it relates to the apologist's, is critical to dialogical apologetics.

Definitions of Culture

First defined in 1871, *culture* is the key concept for anthropology. As with the word *attitude*, however, scholars do not agree on one meaning. In *The Silent Language*, Edward T. Hall says culture is "the way of life of a people, . . . the sum of [a group's] learned behavior patterns, attitudes, and material things."[2] All cultures fulfill comparable roles; they are different answers to the same human needs. They are patterned ways that enable people to live together, systems of ideas, values, attitudes, and behaviors by which groups live.

Clyde Kluckhohn says culture is the knowledge a group stores up to use in the future.[3] It is shared by a society and passed to its children. It enables a group to interpret its world, and thus it provides the shared code by which a community views its environment, the rules of the game of life by which it adapts to its surroundings. People revert to the cues of their native culture to help them make sense of the unknown. They use these cues to relate the unknown to the known. For instance, when a Japanese woman sees an American man laugh, she may assume he is embarrassed, for this is what laughter often means in Japan. Humans assess the appropriateness and meaning of ideas, attitudes, and behaviors by their own cultural standards.

People do not usually sense the informal aspects of their own culture (although they are acutely aware of formal cultural dimensions like law). Culture is so *natural* that most people, especially those with no cross-cultural experience, feel only its absence. Because water is its natural habitat, the fish does not feel wet. Take the fish out of the water, however, and it is suddenly and desperately aware of its surroundings. To describe the guidelines provided by culture, Hall uses the phrase *hidden pathways*. Cultural pathways are out-of-awareness, and for that reason they are all the more powerful in shaping attitudes and behaviors.[4]

Becoming aware of my own culture usually happens only when I

2. Edward T. Hall, *The Silent Language* (New York: Doubleday, Anchor Books, 1981 [1959]), 18, 20.
3. Clyde Kluckhohn, *Mirror for Man: The Relation of Anthropology to Modern Life* (New York: Whittlesey, 1949), 23.
4. Hall, *Silent Language*, 29, 62–66, 120.

run up against the hidden ways of another milieu and find them strangely foreign and uncomfortable. Yet even then, if I am unreflective, I may still see only the foreign culture. I may simply dismiss the other as *foreign* in the sense of *unnatural* or *abnormal*. For instance, men in some eastern European countries kiss each other. That is weird! Or so I am tempted to think. When I step into another's shoes and turn to look at myself as he sees me, however, then I may suddenly notice that I too am a cultural being. Some of my ways look unnatural to him. A good way to become conscious of my own culture is to note especially the points where other cultures differ from my own.[5]

Cultures and Subcultures

People commonly think of cultures as divided along political or geographical boundaries. This is correct to a degree. One can speak properly about American culture, meaning the culture of the United States. Certain behavioral and attitudinal tendencies do tie Americans together. Other countries may have several distinct cultures. Canada, with its French-based culture in Quebec and its British culture in most of the rest of the country, is a nation of two major cultures. African nations, with their many tribal groups, may have hundreds of different languages and cultures. Yet certain generalizations about the cultural distinctives of Africa are possible. Africans, for example, place far higher value on kinship relationships than do North Americans.

Yet despite some similarities in American culture, subcultures of various sorts abound in the United States. Subcultures may divide along regional lines. The Deep South, the Big Sky Country, the Tex-Mex border, and Manhattan differ significantly. Subdivisions may form on ethnic lines. A Native American, Asian American, or Hispanic community will bond to itself, preserving its distinctives and language. Economic divisions are also important—lower class, middle class, upper class plus various shades in between. Other subcategories may break out along gender, age, professional, educational, or clan boundaries.

Every person possesses an identity based on culture group connections. I am a white Midwesterner; a middle-aged, middle-class male; a highly educated professional; a seminary professor by occupation. Some of these things are obvious by looking at me (light skin). Others will be clear by listening to my speech (no *ain'ts*). But the in-

5. Ibid., 32.

formation Americans consider most important is not immediately obvious. So most people ask, "What do you do?" Americans need to know the most important thing they cannot infer from obvious cues: occupation. Occupation is so important to Americans, in fact, that they are likely to ask an airline pilot wearing his uniform, "So, you work for the airlines?"

With these cues in hand, Americans know what to do with me. They can relate to me according to unwritten codes of cultural appropriateness. A high school sophomore from Brooklyn will use the information to assess me one way. He will act on that judgment unless he learns from personal experience with me that his image needs correction. A math teacher in the Baptist church in Mora, Minnesota, will evaluate the same cues differently. He too will act on his assessment until he learns from experience that it needs adjusting. He may assume initially that I know a lot about the Bible. But when I goof up some story (if I say Moses saved the animals in the ark from the flood that knocked down the walls of Jericho), he corrects his appraisal.

Within groups, individuals have rank—higher status or lower status. Rank may be assigned or earned. If it is ascribed, like royal status acquired by birth, it can be relatively rigid, as in a caste system. If status is achieved (e.g., based on performance in sports or business), it can change dramatically. This is called upward (or downward) mobility. Insiders, those who are on their home turf culturally, usually have more status than outsiders. An outsider breaking into a new group usually starts near the bottom. As the outsider learns to function smoothly in the new culture, she may in some contexts become an insider and gain status.

High rank or prestige in one cultural setting does not necessarily translate into high status in another setting. The high school chess champion is accorded high esteem in the honor society, but he will incite gales of laughter if the ball bounces off his head in gym class. People in different cultures use different information in making their assessments of rank. The criteria of status, in other words, differ according to cultural or subcultural context.[6]

The Japanese have a very formal and systematic way of arranging themselves. Part of this system involves ranking according to age. Unlike Americans, the Japanese give older persons greater respect.

6. Stephen A. Grunlan and Marvin Mayers, *Cultural Anthropology: A Christian Perspective*, 2d ed. (Grand Rapids: Zondervan, Academie, 1988), 129–33.

This leads them to ask Americans bluntly, "How old are you?" A middle-aged American, valuing youth over age, wants to keep his birth date a military secret. Not understanding the importance of this information in the Japanese ranking system, the American thinks the question rude. The Japanese, of course, feels uncomfortable when the American withholds information that is vital to proper social relationships in Japan. Clearly, whether it is appropriate to ask a person's age is culturally relative.

In all cultures, people form groups. A mob of college freshmen thrown together in what is affectionately called Welcome Week will immediately begin to divide themselves into smaller units. They will then signal their group affiliations by distinctive dress, speech, and behavior patterns. Indeed, humans send signals to each other by adopting these mannerisms and noting how others use them. I have a friend who works as a carpenter. He had built our home and later hired me to work on his crew, so we became good friends. When I invited him to church, however, he said, "I've never seen a pick-up truck in the First Baptist Church parking lot." In America, a person's vehicle sends a message that is easily decoded by anyone who has cracked the cultural code.

In the broader American culture, organically structured groups form along ethnic, economic, or professional fault lines. Intergroup contact is often limited. When it does happen, it typically follows clear, formal guidelines. A matronly woman will generally not speak to a lower-class male. If she needs to find the pickles at the grocery store, however, she may engage a stock boy in conversation. In accordance with the rules, the woman will be brief. The stock boy will mumble exactly as stock boys are supposed to:

"Where can I find the dill pickles?"

"Aisle 4, next to the mustard and catsup."

"Thank you, young man."

"Humph."

Most interpersonal relationships happen within groups. (Interpersonal relationships between people of different groups are often governed by the strict, formal, out-of-awareness rules employed in everyday commerce). Occasionally, intergroup relations lead to antagonism. For example, conflict between an ethnic group and a city police force may erupt over a case of police brutality. When this happens, loyalties and attitudes are forged largely by group identity. The lines between groups are fault lines. Major earthquakes happen only rarely. When they do, the earth usually slides along those predetermined cracks.

Effects of Culture

Culture provides a thought system by which a group's members adapt to each other and to their environment. To denote this, anthropologists use the phrase *world view*. Philosophers use *world view* differently. In philosophy, it means an all-inclusive system of thought. A world view is metaphysical; it addresses subjects like the nature and existence of God and the world, the purpose and destiny of human life, and the nature of values and the good. In anthropology, all this counts as part of a culture's world view (so the two uses overlap somewhat). But *world view* also includes a culture's preferred modes of thinking, artistic expression, and personal relating, including its views of space and time.

A sharp apologist will keep this double meaning in mind when reading missiological literature. Sometimes missiologists argue that evangelists must communicate a Christian world view.[7] They refer here to the philosophical sense of the phrase. Those who come to faith in Jesus Christ must think Christianly: God exists; he creates human life; humans are alienated from him; Jesus is God's Son; and so on. More commonly, missiologists speak of expressing the gospel in terms of a receptor's world view.[8] They mean here that cultural *idiom* should be retained when it is not germane to the gospel *message*. These two bits of advice may sound contradictory, but they are not, for the phrase *world view* does double duty.

A culture's world view is its "central control box," says Charles Kraft. A world view organizes the conceptual system of those enculturated in its use. One's view of time, for example, is world view based. Event-oriented peoples could care less about how much time an activity takes or about when it begins. Time-oriented peoples consider these matters very important and break out in hives whenever someone breaks the time code. Other polarities—group/individual, stability/change, freedom/security, oral/visual/written, conformity/creativity—are all world view matters. North American white culture

7. David J. Hesselgrave and Edward Rommen, *Contextualization: Meanings, Methods, and Models* (Grand Rapids: Baker, 1989), 212.

8. Friedrich Dierks, "Communication and World-View," *Missionalia* 11 (1983): 56.

values individuality, change, freedom, writing, and creativity. Not all other cultures do.[9]

Preferred styles of public discourse and thinking are world view based. This much is obvious. Every culture also prefers its own rhetorical style. (Think of the unique and powerful preaching patterns in the African American church.) Theorists sometimes carry this point farther by claiming that each culture has its own logic. They imply a kind of conceptual relativism in which different languages reflect entirely incommensurable logics. For instance, one writes that for some Africans, the question "whether God was personal or impersonal originated in a typically Western world-view." The Sotho-Tswana people of South Africa interpret the personhood of God "in nondualistic African thought-forms where a personal God and an impersonal divine power are not mutually exclusive concepts."

A careless person might assume that this shows the radical incommensurability of culture-based logics. Western logic is either/or; African logic is both/and. This is misleading. In the Sotho-Tswana language, it is claimed, *God* "does not belong to the noun class in which we find other personal beings but in a class which is predominantly used for impersonal objects."[10] But this example does not show that the Sotho-Tswana fail to distinguish personal from impersonal. It shows precisely the opposite! The allegedly Western distinction is *embedded in their language!* The difference in this case is not of incommensurable logics, whatever that could mean, but of classification.

All languages, including the speech of the Sotho-Tswana, use distinctions. It is not that some languages contain conceptual contrasts while others do not. The very nature of language requires conceptual distinctions. Languages differ, however, in the shape of their verbal categories and, therefore, in how they classify objects in the world. Different peoples assess what is good or bad, male or female, spiritual or natural in ways that do not fit universal sets or patterns. As my dad found when exploring the word *God* with the Japanese girls, concepts in one language do not match one-to-one the categories embedded in another language.

Consider this: English translations of Leviticus 11:19 and

9. The Sotho-Tswana people object to being asked, "How are you?" To these group-oriented people, the second person singular is offensive. The welfare of the individual is irrelevant. Only the well-being of the group matters. Ibid., 54.

10. Ibid., 49. See the discussion of conceptual relativism in chapter 4, pp. 76–82.

Deuteronomy 14:18 classify bats as birds. Modern biological categories, however, classify bats as mammals because they have fur instead of feathers. Assuming the distinction between furry mammals and feathery birds, modern critics wrongly claim that the Bible is in error. But the linguistic symbol translated by the English word *bird* does not precisely mean what a modern biologist means by *bird*. The Hebrew word badly translated *bird* denotes *flying creature*. The Hebrew root means *to fly*. Assuming Hebrew categories, the Old Testament classes a bat as a flying creature. Nothing startling here! Critics naively criticize the Bible on this point when they fail to grasp cultural differences.

Languages are pregnant with classifications. Every language provides its users with ways to sort out the rich variety of sensuous experience. As our examples show, these ways of organizing the world (i.e., the concepts a culture and its language use) differ from culture to culture. Learning a language opens up the classification system embedded in that language. As children learn their language, they pick up its concepts. Similarly, a nonnative speaker not only learns a language, he learns *from* a language. He discovers how a people group sees the world as he discerns the conceptual system embedded in its language.[11]

One very important dimension of a classification system involves attaching positive or negative evaluations to things. Beliefs with a positive or negative valence, of course, are attitudes. Attitudes congeal into values, those principles or ideas that people (either individually or in groups) consider most important.[12] As language relays the forms of a cultural world view to a new generation, it perpetuates attitudes and values. Thus a person's attitudes and values are strongly influenced by his cultural identity. One way to understand important parts of a person's conceptual network is to get inside his cultural heritage. This means grasping not just the kind of food he likes to eat, but the deeply ingrained thinking and evaluating patterns he prefers.

Along with everything else, cultures transmit attitudes toward religion. Religious life is never found except in a cultural milieu. People

11. Again, these differences are not radical. Although languages do not correlate in a simple one-to-one fashion, they do exhibit deep structural similarities. Significantly, almost anyone can learn another person's language. See Oswald Werner and G. Mark Schoepfle, *Foundations of Ethnography and Interviewing*, Systematic Fieldwork, vol. 1 (Newbury Park, Calif.: Sage, 1987), 104–19; Hesselgrave and Rommen, *Contextualization*, 206–7.

12. See chapter 6, pp. 155–58.

usually learn their faith, live it out, and pass it to their children in their own cultural context. Just like any other faith, the Christian gospel is influenced by cultural forms. This raises the thorny question missiologists study: Which aspects of the Christian faith are part of the essential core meaning and which are the cultural form? The problem arises because cultural elements tend to grow and eventually obscure the gospel core.

One writer uses the image of wainscoting. Normally, wainscoting (cultural elements) covers the lower part of the wall (the gospel). But too often the wainscoting grows toward the ceiling, gradually obscuring the wall.[13] Then one culture's wainscoting is transferred to another context as though it were the wall itself. The wainscoting that adorns the gospel in one culture is inappropriate to others. If the apologist in dialogue is to defend the faith effectively, she will strip away her own wainscoting, expose the wall, and form a new wainscoting that reflects the colors and patterns found in the new culture. The dialogue partner must hear the gospel in a form harmonious with his socioculture.

In sum, every apologist works with at least three cultures: biblical culture, his partner's, and his own.[14] Mature Christians approach the Bible with a clear understanding that its message comes in cultural forms. They seek to ferret out the biblical principles that are expressed in the ancient Near Eastern idiom. They are also well aware of other contemporary cultures. Often it is the third culture, one's own, that causes the biggest surprise. Apologists and evangelists expect the other person's culture to interfere with understanding the gospel but are sometimes shocked to find that their own culture disrupts comprehension as well.[15]

Prejudices and Stereotypes

Not only do language and culture pass on a world view, including attitudes, values, and preferred styles of expression and thought, they also transmit a group's ideas about other groups. Attitudes about

13. D. Jay Losher, "A Wainscoted Gospel: Christian Mission and Enculturation," *Asia Journal of Theology* 3 (1989): 485–86.

14. Taking off on Anthony Thistelton's *Two Horizons*, Hesselgrave speaks of "The Three Horizons: Culture, Integration, and Communication," *Journal of the Evangelical Theological Society* 28 (1985): 443–54.

15. Dierks, "Communication and World-View," 45.

groups of people are often stereotypes, especially when they are negative. Stereotypes play a critical role in everyday life as well as in apologetic dialogue. Not only does an apologist bring to a conversation prejudices about the other, but any dialogue partner will have a set of preconceptions ready to go as well. A good apologist must monitor both sets of prejudices.

The Meaning of Stereotypes

Walter Lippmann first discussed the idea of a stereotype in 1922.[16] He observed, for example, that a man will assess a woman from another group, not by making the effort to know her individually, but by plugging her into a preformed classification system. The real woman triggers what Lippmann called "a picture in our heads." The man sees her as a faceless representative of a *class* of persons. (Note the revealing comment, "They all look the same to me.") He assumes without evidence that his predefined concept and its attitudinal components aptly describe the individual. Thus a stereotype is *"an exaggerated belief associated with a category."*[17] He does not see *that woman*. The woman stimulates him to see *his concept*.

In theory, any feature a person possesses could activate a stereotype. But generally, either physical traits (age, sex, appearance, or race) or social/behavioral factors (religion, ethnicity, or a troubled past) form the basis for categorizing stereotypes. Perhaps the strongest and most prominent form of stereotyping is racism. In fact, racism, especially against African Americans in the United States and against Jews in Nazi Germany, has motivated much of the research on stereotyping. As with racism, stereotypes in general have a tendency to grow out of all proportion to real evidence.

A stereotype involves two qualities. First, it is agreed on by social consensus. This does not mean an image must be accepted by everyone *as true* in order to be a stereotype. Rather, people must agree on the *substance* of that image in order for it to be called a stereotype. For example, I may have an individual mental picture of motorcycle riders. If no one else shares this image, however, it is not a stereotype. Since an individual acquires it from a culture, a stereotype is some-

16. Walter Lippmann, *Public Opinion* (New York: Harcourt Brace, 1922).
17. Gordon Allport, *The Nature of Prejudice* (Cambridge: Addison-Wesley, 1954), 191.

thing most people in a society will recognize. An image is a stereotype only if a society as a whole identifies it as such.

Second, stereotypes are usually negative. Some images people use to classify others are positive. For instance, the phrase *movie star* immediately brings many positive images to mind—good looking, trendy, popular. When one thinks of a *stereotypical* movie star, however, the concept usually includes negative attributes like sensual, greedy, and egotistical. Common connotations of the word *stereotype* suggest that it is usually not positive.[18]

A stereotype is not the same as a prejudice, although the two ideas are closely connected. A stereotype is a concrete image with many associated qualities. If Jay Leno just utters the phrase *TV evangelist*, his audience erupts with laughter. They think of a cluster of traits: hypocritical, bombastic, greedy, tasteless, and libidinal. While a stereotype is a fuller image of some class of persons, a prejudice lacks the full set of associated concepts. It is an attitude, a negative or positive preconception about someone, based on group association. Stereotypes and prejudices are related of course. If I accept the usual stereotype of television evangelists as true, I will have a negative attitude, a prejudice, toward them.

Significant studies show that stereotyped attitudes build expectations that powerfully influence behavior. People behave in line with prior expectations. Original attitudes about other groups thus become self-fulfilling prophecies that reinforce themselves. For instance, researchers brought together two groups of people, Group A and Group B. They manufactured prejudices by telling Group A that some *arbitrarily chosen* Group B people were hostile. They told Group B people nothing. The psychologists then analyzed the groups' interactions. The results? Group B members whom Group A prejudged would be hostile actually acted with more hostility. The others acted less hostilely. Group B reflected Group A's prejudices *even though they knew nothing* about them!

In phase 2, Group B (which still knew nothing) encountered Group C. The experimenters also kept Group C in the dark, so they had no prejudices about Group B. When the so-called "hostile" Group B members from phase 1 interacted with Group C, some continued to act hostilely! Similarly, phase 1 "nonhostile" Group B mem-

18. Arthur G. Miller, "Historical and Contemporary Perspectives on Stereotyping," in *In the Eye of the Beholder: Contemporary Issues in Stereotyping*, ed. Arthur Miller (New York: Praeger, 1982), 28–31.

bers acted nonhostilely with Group C. Thus in their interaction with Group C, some Group B members continued to exhibit behaviors generated by Group A's prejudiced expectations. Group A's prejudices affected relationships even after Group A was gone![19] Forces like these profoundly affect interactions between people. The relevance of these findings for dialogical apologetics should be obvious.

Functions of Stereotypes

Researchers have adopted several (not incompatible) approaches to understanding stereotypes. From a sociological orientation, some emphasize the origins of stereotypes in a given culture or subculture. From a psychological point of view, others see stereotypes as important because they meet certain needs, an ego defense or a scapegoating need. Taking a cognitive approach, still others assume that stereotypes serve humans by reducing cognitive complexity. Since gaining exhaustive information about every person is impossible, all persons must generalize in order to keep information processing at manageable levels.

This third approach emphasizes a major theme in current research: stereotypes simplify life. They serve as "substitutes for observation."[20] They offer the advantage of economy of effort, even though they lack the virtue of accuracy. They are like the formal codes a society uses to automate life's experiences and thereby reduce stress. The codes simplify life. Notice how uncomfortable people become when they do not know the rules of behavior. For example, everyone gets nervous at weddings, partly because they are formal occasions with different rules that are too hard to remember. People relax when they know the rules.

Offhand comments can reveal an ignorance that is bred of the need for simplicity. Take the concepts Americans use to categorize Asians. Since I grew up in Japan, I use a more complex set of categories for Asians. I know how Japanese, Chinese, and Koreans differ; I even know what distinguishes Tokyoites and Osakaites. The need for simplicity in thought processing, however, causes many Americans

---

19. Mark Snyder and William Swann, Jr., "Behavioral Confirmation in Social Interaction: From Social Perception to Social Reality," *Journal of Experimental Social Psychology* 14 (1978): 148–62; cf. Carl Word, Mark Zanna, and Joel Cooper, "The Nonverbal Mediation of Self-Fulfilling Prophecies in Interracial Interaction," *Journal of Experimental Social Psychology* 10 (1974): 109–20.

20. S. I. Hayakawa; quoted in Miller, "Perspectives on Stereotyping," 20.

to clump all Asians together. A surprising number have asked me, "So, you were born in Japan! How interesting! Do you speak Chinese?" People who ask this inane question obviously have little experience with Asians. The concept *Asian* has for them no clear subcategories. "We stereotype more and more those we know less and less."[21]

Obviously, people tend to know more about people who are part of their own in-group. Whites know more about whites than they do about African Americans, and vice versa. Research shows that, *in general*, when humans gain information about other individuals, they modify judgments based on stereotypes.[22] Often, however, this does not happen. People begin with negative views of out-group members. Even when out-group members are admired, group rivalry can generate negative attitudes. These negative attitudes filter out positive evidence so powerfully that the facts cannot overcome the bias. Thus while lack of contact with other groups maintains stereotypes, contact between groups does not guarantee that people will generate more positive attitudes.

Prejudice and bias due to group loyalty cause systematic misinterpretation of other peoples' words or behaviors. How does this work? Consider the difference between *dispositional* (individual and personal) and *situational* (group or cultural) influences. When some act is influenced by dispositional factors (e.g., a personal choice), others hold the actor responsible. When an act is influenced by situational factors (e.g., cultural conditioning), however, others tend not to hold him responsible. For instance, those who think teens *choose* to have sex blame them for their pregnancies. But those who think social pressures *cause* teens to engage in sex see pregnant teens as victims.

When an out-group member fails, people typically point to *dispositional* factors; success they ascribe to *situational* ones. In this way, they blame him for failure, but give little credit for success. When an in-group member fails, however, people point to *situational* influences; but success they attribute to *dispositional* ones. In this way, they give him credit for success, but not blame for failure.[23] These

21. Harry Triandis, *Attitude and Attitude Change*, Wiley Foundations of Social Psychology (New York: John Wiley and Sons, 1971), 104.

22. Lee Jussim, Lerita Coleman, and Lauren Lerch, "The Nature of Stereotypes: A Comparison and Integration of Three Theories," *Journal of Personality and Social Psychology* 52 (1987): 536–46.

23. People tend to apply this interpretive pattern for their own benefit. Its effects are enormous. See David G. Myers, *The Inflated Self: Human Illusions and the Biblical Call to Hope* (New York: Seabury, 1980).

identifiable patterns in the interpretation of others' successes and failures are often unconscious. But they reveal deep biases.[24] Their effects are real: some in this society feel them every single day. When this attribution mechanism operates on the basis of racial identity, it unleashes a devastating force called racial prejudice.

Ethnocentrism and Cultural Relativism

The tendency to give the benefit of any doubt to one's own group, its values, standards, and ways of living, is rooted in *ethnocentrism*. In his classic work *Folkways*, William Graham Sumner defines *ethnocentrism* as the "view of things in which one's own group is the center of everything, and all others are scaled and rated with reference to it."[25] An ethnocentric person will see his own group as superior or virtuous, as embodying what is natural, normal, or universal. He will see other groups as defective and inferior in the ways and to the degree they differ from his own. Americans, for example, tend to think of foreigners as "underdeveloped Americans."[26]

The antidote to ethnocentrism is *cultural relativism*. According to Sumner, cultural relativism implies that "everything in the mores of a time and place must be regarded as justified with regard to that time and place."[27] Thus to look at a culture without the jaundice of ethnocentrism, I must lay aside my own cultural biases and get inside the other culture. The standards for assessing a culture's norms and values must be gained from within that culture, not superimposed from without. A cultural pattern in any society is good, not because it is similar to mine, but because it fits and functions well in its setting.

Both ethnocentrism and cultural relativism have taken some heat. American Christians who come to understand ethnocentrism can see that much of American culture is not acceptable biblically. Missiologists make this point repeatedly and correctly. While ethnocentrism is a deadly disease, however, Christians are not sure they want the cure. Cultural relativism seems to require that no practice, attitude, or aspect of another culture can be criticized. This entails ethical relativism, or so it seems.

24. William Gudykunst, *Bridging Differences: Effective Intergroup Communication* (Newbury Park, Calif.: Sage, 1991), 85–87.
25. William Graham Sumner, *Folkways* (New York: Mentor, 1960 [1906]), 27–28.
26. Hall, *Silent Language*, 24.
27. Sumner, *Folkways*, 65.

Despite appearances, cultural relativism does not imply ethical relativism.[28] (Ethical relativism is the denial of universal ethical norms. It says all ethical norms are relative to situational, cultural, or personal decisions or factors.) Now if cultural relativism does entail ethical relativism, and a Christian criticizes ethical norms in another culture on the ground of universal (even biblical) norms (i.e., he denies ethical relativism), then he is unavoidably ethnocentric. Can one argue against a practice like cannibalism on moral grounds and still avoid ethnocentrism?

One way to view this matter places ethnocentrism and cultural relativism at the two poles of a single continuum.[29] This is a mistake. Given this model, in order to avoid ethnocentrism, I must slide toward cultural relativism. If I wish to stop short of relativism, then I *ought* to, it is good to, remain partly ethnocentric. This analysis is simplistic. Even if every person *is* ethnocentric, it does not follow that everyone *ought* to be ethnocentric or that being ethnocentric is good.

A better solution involves the use of the common missiological distinction between form and meaning and the philosophical contrast between descriptive (observational) and normative (evaluative) judgments. First, the forms. (This includes cultural preferences along the group/individual, oral/visual/written, freedom/security, stability/change, conformity/creativity polarities as well as preferred modes of artistic expression, personal relating, and thinking—including views of space and time.) *Descriptively*, as a matter of fact, cultures value different forms. The phrase *cultural variety* clearly denotes the fact of differences in these values.

Normatively, however, the *fact* of cultural variety entails nothing about how to evaluate cultural norms. Cultural variety shows neither that one set of cultural preferences is superior in some way nor, alternatively, that all sets are equal on some scale. That they are different shows merely that they are different. The Japanese eat on, sit on, and sleep on the floor. Americans like platforms; they eat on tables, sit on chairs, and sleep on beds. Following their cultural patterns, they consider floors dirty. As a matter of fact, then, these cultures differ. Not much can be inferred from that fact alone.

Cultural relativism requires that we judge these customs from within each culture. What is right about cultural relativism is that it

28. Marvin Mayers, *Christianity Confronts Culture: A Strategy for Crosscultural Evangelism,* rev. ed. (Grand Rapids: Zondervan, Academie, 1987), 245–47.
29. See Grunlan and Mayers, *Cultural Anthropology,* 254.

is a commitment to understanding *a culture's forms* on its own terms. I should not judge any one set of cultural ways as better than any other simply on the grounds of my group identity or loyalty. Of course, I feel more comfortable with white ways because I am white. That I am white, however, does not show that white forms are *better* in some absolute way. In relation to cultural forms, Christians should affirm as full a commitment to cultural relativism as possible. Accepting cultural relativism may even require that I recognize and compensate for my own natural biases toward the familiar.

Second, as for meaning, Christians are committed to Christian truth content. Christian truth (as God understands it) is absolute. (The same truth *as I comprehend it* is less than absolute; my knowledge is surely flawed.) I am committed to the Christian truth I have, but *not because it is Western or white*. I accept it because it reflects the transculturally relevant Word of God. Thus *speaking generally*, no mode of expression particular to one culture has priority. The church in a particular place builds its theology as it allows the Word to interact with its culture. Christian truth relevant to that culture emerges from the dialogue between Scripture and culture.[30]

Given this, cultural relativism does *not* eliminate the ground for judging immoral practices like *suttee* (burning widows) or cannibalism.[31] It does mean, however, that one must "*take such customs seriously within the cultural context in which they occur* and attempt to appreciate the importance of their function within that context."[32] On the one hand, for instance, understanding the reasons for polygamy may unearth important insights into fundamental thought processes and values of a particular group. Such values (e.g., caring for unattached kinsfolk) may be laudable. If I restrain the urge to judge such patterns too quickly, I may recognize the validity of the *values* that those forms express even if the *forms* offend my cultural sensibilities.

On the other hand, recognizing the truth of cultural relativism implies two things. First, in criticizing cannibalism, I assess it as immoral on the ground of biblical principle, *not because it is un-American*. Sec-

---

30. See William Dyrness, *Learning about Theology from the Third World* (Grand Rapids: Zondervan, Academie, 1990), 24–34.

31. *Ethical* relativism may imply that the *content* of cultural practices like these must be accepted as morally right in their context.

32. Charles H. Kraft, *Christianity in Culture: A Study in Dynamic Biblical Theologizing in Cross-Cultural Perspective* (Maryknoll, N.Y.: Orbis, 1979), 50.

ond, I must offer biblical critique of my own culture just as I would any other. Some American cultural values (e.g., rampant materialism and individualism) desperately need biblical response. If an African says my faith is too white for him, I will agree. This is not a criticism, but a fact. I must defend the gospel, not my white culture. I can and should admit the limited relevance of my own preferred ways and disconnect them from the good news about Jesus. An African needs Jesus, but not my white, American, middle-class ways.

Communicating in Cultures

The pervasive influence of culture and the magnitude of cultural differences imply that communication across any cultural lines is difficult. That the dialogue partners' cultural commitments operate out-of-awareness only complicates the matter. Every telling of the Christian story to a non-Christian will cross cultural boundaries. As with ethnicity, gender, national identity, class status, and profession, cultural fault lines separate people of different religious affiliations. *No apologist can have an entirely same-culture dialogue with a non-Christian person.*

Communication Difficulties

Three areas of difficulty plague cross-cultural communication. First, all communication encounters problems even in the best of circumstances. Every textbook on communication spells out the cycle of communication: sender, message, receiver, feedback. The sender codes his message in symbols and sends it to the receiver. The receiver decodes the symbols and then reconstructs a message that may or may not be identical to what the sender intended.

Communication scholars often cite Herbert Spencer, who said that good writers adapt words to express new meanings.[33] Spencer's dictum has become a truism: words do not mean; only people mean. Because people actively encode and decode, all communication suffers meaning leakage. Pessimists justify their gloomy perspective by pointing to factors like these: communicators

33. Herbert Spencer, *The Philosophy of Style* (Boston: Allyn and Bacon, 1892), 42–43.

know another person's thoughts only imperfectly;

depend on ambiguous signals;

use defective coding systems;

allow biases to affect the use of these coding systems;

misjudge the accuracy of their own beliefs.[34]

Naive views, by contrast, see communication as a transfer of information bricks from one mind to another. The teacher drives up the forklift and offloads tons of bricks into students' skulls. Sophisticated skeptics realize this model is false. But the opposite extreme is wrong, too. Information a communicator sends is not like bricks, but like clay. Receivers will shape the clay, but only within limits. Meaning is recreated by the receiver within a latitude of correctness established by general use.[35] Communication is neither perfect nor impossible. Some estimate communication reaches at best an 80 percent accuracy level.[36]

Second, effective communication is even more difficult across cultural fault lines. A major problem is negative expectations. Serious communication with those who are different is typically viewed in terms of *cost* rather than *benefit*. After the gawking tourist stage, people assume that communication with those of different cultures will be frustrating and unproductive. So they avoid it when possible and dread it when unavoidable.[37] Of course, these expectations powerfully influence the experience. (Recall the experiments that labeled certain people as *hostile* and *nonhostile*.) Communication anxiety, an interpersonal cousin to stage fright, becomes a self-fulfilling prophecy. This dynamic hampers many apologetic dialogues.

Third, nonverbal aspects of communication cause special problems in cross-cultural experiences. According to one estimate, only 35 percent of the social meaning of a message comes through verbal

34. Aaron Beck, *Love Is Never Enough: How Couples Can Overcome Misunderstandings, Resolve Conflicts, and Solve Relationship Problems Through Cognitive Therapy* (New York: Harper and Row, 1988), 18–26.

35. Kathleen Reardon, *Interpersonal Communication* (Belmont, Calif.: Wadsworth, 1987), 4; G. B. Caird, *The Language and Imagery of the Bible* (Philadelphia: Westminster, 1980), 49.

36. David J. Hesselgrave, *Communicating Christ Cross-Culturally*, 2d ed. (Grand Rapids: Zondervan, 1991), 91.

37. Gudykunst, *Bridging Differences*, 64.

channels.[38] If so, nonverbal codes and signals are obviously important aspects of the meanings humans share. Nonverbal communication is "an elaborate and secret code that is written nowhere, known by none, and understood by all."[39] If the verbal and nonverbal do not cohere, most people will take the nonverbal, which is more difficult to control, as the more reliable indicator. If I swear I feel just fine, but I am sweating profusely, I will not likely be convincing.

Theorists organize nonverbal aspects in a variety of ways. One is *proxemics*, the use of space and distance. All persons have a culturally determined comfort zone. Moving into an intimate zone when the relationship is not intimate causes high stress. Unfortunately, what is normal speaking distance and what counts as intimate distance differ with culture. Many Africans maintain a very close distance. An American who accepts that tight comfort zone will communicate more effectively. In Japan, however, one must keep at a safe distance or risk causing anxiety.

Kinesics, a variety of motions and actions, includes body movement, orientation, and lean, as well as hand and eye movements. Looking directly at a person's eyes or touching others is always powerful. They can be powerfully *painful*, of course, as in cases of sexual harassment. Here cultural and gender issues significantly affect the rules. In general, one's own kinesics should be monitored so they express openness, relaxation, and warmth. Irritating behaviors like finger drumming should obviously be avoided. Kinesics of the dialogue partner need to be watched as well. Backing up or looking at the watch signal one thing; leaning forward or an earnest look signal something else.

A third general category is *paralanguage*, the use of any vocal behavior other than word choice or sequence. Obvious examples are volume, pitch, or inflection. The meanings of these areas of nonverbal communication are heavily influenced by culture, although not entirely so. A complete discussion of dos and don'ts is obviously impossible here, but here are three reminders. First, apologists should force themselves to admit the power of the nonverbal and pay close

38. Randall Harrison, "Nonverbal Communication: Explorations into Time, Space, Action, and Object," in *Dimensions in Communication*, 2d ed., ed. James Campbell and Hal Hepler (Belmont, Calif.: Wadsworth, 1970), 258.

39. Edward Sapir, "The Unconscious Patterning of Behavior in Society," in *Selected Writings of Edward Sapir in Language, Culture and Personality*, ed. David Mandelbaum (Berkeley: University of California Press, 1949), 556.

attention to it. Second, when in Rome do as the Romans. Apologists should follow the rules the other person reveals. Third, they can send up trial balloons. Lean forward when making an important point. Then monitor the result, and adjust accordingly.

Cross-Cultural Strategies

Good apologists understand several important cross-cultural lessons. First, all communication of the gospel is cross-cultural. Some are tempted to think cultural issues are relevant only in defending the faith in foreign lands. Obviously, Christians do defend the faith in Asia, Africa, Europe, and Latin America. But apologists also work in North American cultural contexts—African American and Hispanic; rural and metropolitan; northern and southern. Dialogical apologetics recognizes distinctives in the chemist's culture, in the businessman's, the feminist's, the collegian's, and the welder's. *All apologetic dialogue with non-Christians (and most of it with Christians) is cross-cultural!*

Second, cultural sensitivity and stereotyping are similar in some ways, but they must be separated. If I look to culture to understand a person's world view, attitudes, values, nonverbal codes, or verbal and mental concepts, I place him in a category. If I look to a stereotype, however, I also interpret a person by placing him in a category. In both cases, I initially assess a person by his group identity. In this way, cultural sensitivity and stereotyping are remarkably similar. Yet apologists must distinguish them. The first is helpful; the second is disaster. How can I gain the values of cultural understanding without stereotyping?

Stereotyping misuses culture-sensitive modes of thinking (i.e., the habit of seeing a person's attitudes and behaviors as rooted in group patterns). It uses cultural explanations to blame, belittle, or avoid individuals from other groups, often to shore up a weak self-image by tearing others down. Cultural sensitivity, on the other hand, illuminates the world view preferences, the attitudes, values, and verbal or nonverbal codes of other people. It uses classification to promote genuine understanding, not avoidance. The major difference between stereotyping and cultural sensitivity is the purpose to which the cultural generalization is put: the former builds fences, the latter builds bridges.

Cultural sensitivity, therefore, does *not* rule out classification. Indeed, the whole point of cultural study is to learn about an individual by understanding the patterns typical of his group. While a sensitive apologist will use the cultural information, however, he must augment it with the personal. While he must categorize people in groups, he must also search out the features that distinguish individuals from the category. The rule is: first classify, then particularize or "decategorize." Knowing someone well means understanding how he differs from others in his group.[40]

Several strategies help overcome stereotypes. I can intentionally give dispositional or personal factors priority over situational or cultural factors in interpreting a person's behaviors. Personal information allows me to make my perceptions of the other person more complex and accurate. My knowledge of the other need not depend solely on group-based generalizations. I gain knowledge by asking honest questions, signaling openness and safety (verbally and nonverbally), and listening carefully. I must also assume that any question the other asks is a request for information, not an implicit criticism. An apologist should make asking questions acceptable, not taboo.[41]

Third, all apologists are stereotyped. When people discover that someone is a pastor or a Christian, that tidbit of information accesses a whole network of ideas and attitudes. These may be negative or positive. Most are probably a conglomeration. I should be aware that, in conversations with real people, *I am not myself*, at least at first. I am whatever the dialogue partner *thinks* I am. I am the image that words like *pastor* or *Christian* or maybe even *fundamentalist* pull up off her hard disk onto her screen.

Apologists must accept responsibility for disarming stereotypes. It is just part of the job. I cannot expect the other to meet me halfway. In my case, my job (professor of theology) combines two negative stereotypes: *professor* and *theologian*. I have two strikes against me whenever someone discovers the title before she has a chance to form opinions based on the real me. So I defuse. "I have a friend from Texas," I say, "whose spiritual gift is keeping me humble. He always asks me, 'How is a Texas longhorn like a philosopher?' The answer? 'A point here, a point there, and a lot of bull in between.'" This is pitiful humor, but it contains a powerful coded message: "I'm normal; you can relax." Self-depreciating humor can defuse stereotypes.

Fourth, cultural adjustment is something I should expect to do in

40. Gudykunst, *Bridging Differences*, 82, 145.
41. Ibid., 109.

all cases. Again, I cannot expect the other to meet me halfway, and I certainly can't become incensed when he does not. Several years back, my wife and I enjoyed the company of a young Christian couple. Though they were our age, they had only recently come to faith (and marriage) out of a swinging singles lifestyle. But every meeting caused a problem: they were huggers; I was not. When they came to our house for dinner, both of them would hug both of us. Hugging Alice was one thing—that I could handle. But hug Ted? You must be kidding! I tensed up, rigid as a tree. Obviously, I did not make the cultural adjustment.

What is worse, I came to realize that I was blaming Ted for his failure to adjust. That is, I was indicting him for not doing what I was not doing. I found myself thinking, "Why can't Ted see I'm not comfortable with this? He should relate to me on my wavelength!" I expected him to accommodate me without ever considering that I should do so for him. Months later I realized that I bore responsibility to accommodate him. Indeed, I now think I have *more* responsibility than the other to make the adjustment. So I have taken hugging lessons; I can now hug when appropriate. I am all things to all huggers, so that I might win some (1 Cor. 9:22).

The intercultural barriers to communication caused by stereotyping and other problems may seem overwhelming. It may seem more reasonable to deal only with one's own cultural kind. Three realizations should prevent this. First, all apologetic conversation with nonChristians is cross-cultural. If I wanted to avoid cross-cultural encounters, I would have to abandon most apologetic dialogues. Second, cultural differences are more intrusive early in a conversation, but become less so as relationship and dialogue move forward.[42] Third, the common humanity of dialogue partners, the potential for cultural adjustment, and the Holy Spirit's power should give hope.[43] Successful cross-cultural apologetic dialogue is possible.

A Sample Conversation

Adam the Apologist 1 (an African Christian): Are you saying that all religions are totally wrong or that they are all partly wrong?

42. Ibid., 140.
43. Hesselgrave, *Communicating Christ Cross-Culturally*, 189.

Fred the Friend 1 (an African American pluralist): All these religions—Baptist, Lutheran, Jehovah's Witness, Catholic—are partly right.

Adam 2: Do you include Islam and Hinduism and others?

Fred 2: Of course.

Adam 3: Do you think they all contain truth?

Fred 3: Yes. But the problem is that people use the religion they think is right to do what is wrong. Why is it that black people, for example, are always the ones to suffer? Everywhere blacks are oppressed. In America they are oppressed. In Africa they are oppressed, oppressed, oppressed! This is because of religion, you see? The Bible says Adam was the first person to sin, and Adam was a black man. God punished everyone because the black man sinned.

[Adam is seeing red lights flashing here. Obviously, part of Fred's cultural world view is that the black peoples on both sides of the ocean are oppressed. Further, he blames this oppression on religion in general and biblical teaching in particular. This is critically important. The worst thing any apologist—especially a white person in this context—can do is try to convince someone who feels the sting of racism that he should not feel the pain. White apologists may interpret Fred as meaning, "I am oppressed and you are the cause." Some will take offense. But an apologist's task is to present Jesus, not justify white racism. So he must not assume that he is being attacked personally. This requires a high tolerance for ambiguity.]

Adam 4: That's interesting, but I don't think the Bible says Adam was black. Even if he was, where have the other people come from? They also came from Adam, so you cannot lay Adam's sin only on black people.

Fred 4: I didn't know that.

[Adam does not agree that God created a black man. Empathy ("I feel badly that you have experienced oppression") might have been more helpful. As he does later, Adam should have tried to find out why Fred believes as he does. But Adam does salvage the situation with a good argument: if Adam and his descendants are blamed for sin, then whites deserve blame, too, because everyone descended from Adam. An effective point!]

Adam 5: You know, I don't think we're as oppressed as you think. We have a bright future even if we have been oppressed. We are no longer being oppressed. If you don't believe me, look at where you and I are [studying at a major university]. How many blacks were able to study this much in the old days? Brother, we need to develop a healthy view of ourselves.

Fred 5: Yes, I think you're right. The Bible also says Jesus was an African, and I think to some extent God is black.

Adam 6: Why do you say God is black?

[Adam will shortly respond fairly bluntly to Fred's claims about God being black. But note that this time he first asks Fred why he makes these claims. This is a better strategy, for understanding should precede criticism. Lying behind the interchange is the fact that Fred cannot identify with a white Jesus and the white God dominant culture presents. Fred is clearly hurting, and the white God is not helping.]

Fred 6: I mean, look at the way the black man is discriminated against, yet he can still smile. If it's not God within him, how can he manage? He is struggling all the time.

Adam 7: Well, brother, I think God is neither black nor white. In fact, God is colorless. I know God loves all people, but really God helps those who fear him. It seems to me we need to clarify some biblical teachings. I think we need to know, first, who God is, and second, who we are. God is perfect and the judge of all truth. We are sinful and in need of salvation. But before I go on, what do you think about what I have said?

Fred 7: The problem is we can't see God, even though he is obviously the creator. Where did he come from? And he isn't all that perfect. Remember Noah's ark? By the way, Mount Ararat is in Africa, right?

[Adam sees that Fred has some objections to the biblical view of God. Fred also continues to connect everything in the Bible to Africa. Some whites will jump on this and dispute the Africa connection instead of talking about God. But the location of Mount Ararat is irrelevant. Adam does something better. He senses that there are cultural reasons why Fred keeps doing this. So before he criticizes, he again probes why Fred thinks this way.]

Adam 8: I don't think so, but why is it important?

Fred 8: Well, God made a mistake and was trying to correct it by using the flood, you see? God made people who were behaving badly so he decided to wipe them out to correct the situation.

Adam 9: Are you saying God is evil, or what?

Fred 9: I guess I'm saying God is both good and evil.

Adam 10: If God is both good and evil at the same time, then how can we know what is right or wrong? On what basis can we fight for justice? It seems as though *rightness* and *wrongness* no longer exist.

Fred 10: Hmm. Tell me what you think is right.

[Adam has shown Fred a difficulty in his view of God without alienating him by contradicting every single claim. Fred now asks for Adam's view. This shows that Adam has done well. Fred has used up his ammunition, and explanatory problems still exist. This is a window of opportunity. Fred is open. Adam is ready with a punch line.]

Adam 11: Tell me, brother, do you believe truth depends on the situation?

Fred 11: Yes, of course. Truth is relative to the situation.

[Fred had claimed that all religions have some truth (**Fred 1–3**). Adam recalls some threads from Fred's initial statements and beautifully weaves them into the discussion.]

Adam 12: Given that truth is relative, why do we still talk about the oppression of the blacks? It seems to me you have just been saying that oppression is absolutely bad. Are you trying to say that some oppression is good and some is bad?

Fred 12: Oh, no! Oppression of blacks is always wrong.

Adam 13: I agree with you. All oppression is wrong. But if truth is relative, I don't see how oppression could *always* be wrong. Let me suggest this idea: God is perfect and has told us about himself through Jesus. If we can get ahold of Jesus, we will know God.

Fred 13: Hmm. Good point.

[As a foundation for his argument, Adam skillfully uses something that runs deeply in Fred's culture, his experience of oppression. Some white apologists, interpreting Fred's claim that he is oppressed as an accusation, might try to convince Fred that he is not oppressed. Others will spend persuasive capital debating side issues. Unlike Adam, apologists who take these paths will alienate Fred and miss this opportunity. Adam has established rapport and learned some important things about Fred. Fred is now ready to hear about a biblical view of God.]

Summary

Culture is the patterned ways a group of people lives together and adapts to its environment. These ways are powerfully influential, but usually out-of-awareness.

Cultural issues affect all relationships. Within groups, relative status or rank is important; between groups, group differences are significant.

Cultures are guided by a world view, a system of thoughts, attitudes, and values including preferred ways of thinking, interpreting, and communicating. A world view guides a group's thinking about itself and its environment.

Stereotypes are images people use to assess members of other groups. General images simplify their thinking about others, but such classifications often distort perceptions.

Cultural sensitivity, like stereotyping, classes people in groups. But unlike stereotyping, it uses these classifications not to demean or destroy, but to understand.

Ethnocentrism is evaluating other societies by my cultural standards. Cultural relativism is accepting cultural forms on their own terms. Commitment to cultural relativism with regard to most cultural forms (not the same as ethical relativism) is appropriate for Christians.

All communication is strewn with cultural land mines. Cross-cultural communication is even more difficult. All dialogical apologetics is cross-cultural.

Appropriate cross-cultural communication requires proper use of cultural knowledge. Apologists must overcome their own stereotypes as well as those of others.

We have now journeyed through three dimensions of apologetic dialogue: the conceptual, the attitudinal, and the cultural. Every dialogue involves complex interpenetration of these forces. In the final chapter, we turn to a discussion of strategy. Given that we can defend the faith with rational appropriateness (as argued in part 1), and assuming that we understand some of the complexities of dialogue (as discussed so far in part 2), we now need to know: What strategies will allow an apologist to defend the faith most appropriately and effectively?

9

Tipping the Scale

"But why is my father suffering so? The doctors have said he can't survive this cancer. So why doesn't God just take him?"

I was on a retreat with an adult Sunday school class fifteen years ago. They knew each other well. As the new teacher, I had gone along to get acquainted. Most members were in their thirties or early forties; most practiced a profession or worked in business.

During chat time, Rose Williams kept pressing her seemingly unresolvable question. No one was able to offer more than a superficial response. Each would-be comforter failed to speak meaningfully to her need. Eyes gradually turned toward me, the newly installed class guru. What would the novice teacher say?

I had wrestled with the theoretical problem of evil as a graduate student. In those dark days of doubt, I had wondered whether the concept of God made sense in light of human suffering. Gradually, I had resolved my uncertainties and accepted the classic *free will defense*. This response to evil says that God gives all humans freedom so that they will love him without coercion. But that freedom, being real, can be and sometimes is misused. Evil arises from the abuse of creaturely freedom.

Armed with a conceptual response that had once rescued me, I tried to speak to Rose's pain. I told her that God was right to make free creatures who could choose either to love him or to go their own way. Because he values freedom for his creatures, God permits some persons to do evil despite the pain and suffering it causes. More broadly, God often allows events in this fallen world to follow a natural course even though this means allowing pain. God does not always prevent the pain of cancer, but he does give grace and courage.

I felt I had clearly expressed the free will defense. But my ideas—helpful in my dark hour—bounced off Rose like ping-pong balls off granite. The conversation ended in frustration for all. Like the others, I utterly failed to connect with Rose in a meaningful way.

I raise Rose's case to illustrate this fact: not all apologetic-sounding questions are purely intellectual. Rose's question reflected primarily emotional undercurrents. My attempted answer engaged the conceptual, however, and thus failed to connect with her need. I heard her words, but I utterly misconstrued her question. The intellectual side I emphasized in my answer is only one aspect of real life. Rose's problems needed pastoral care, at least initially. Later the more intellectual side of apologetics became more pressing. But on that particular day, the emotional dimensions needed attention.

Setting the Stage

I have come to realize that some apologetic discussions suffer from a similar defect. I resolved to rethink apologetics to account for the other relational and emotional aspects of conversation. This book is one result. It sees apologetics as a process of defending the faith in the context of personal relationship and dialogue. The last question, therefore, is, What strategy enables an apologist to do this?

Developing the Right Attitude

"Dad, can I have a glass of water? I'm really thirsty."

"Son, how can you be thirsty? You've already had three cups." Like the seven-year-old avoiding bedtime, would-be apologists can think of many reasons not to defend the faith. Specifically, two objections often arise. Developing proper attitudes on these issues can alleviate anxiety. First, perhaps persuasion is inappropriate. Some writers claim that any act of persuasion is an act of violence. Is an attempt to persuade others ever right in a pluralistic society?

Definitions of persuasion differ. Some say a communication must *successfully* create, reinforce, or change another person's attitude before it can be called persuasion. This seems wrong, however. The *intention* to affect another's beliefs and attitudes is the main criterion. A television ad featuring a pickup truck-driving hound dog to sell a new strain of corn seeds is a case of persuasion even though I utterly ignore it.

All intentional communication, including normal, everyday comments, is persuasion.[1] If I say that my kids go to Pike Lake School, I intend my statement to affect others' thinking, and I expect them to accept my statement as true. As in this case, the vast majority of communication acts are successful acts of persuasion. Most people accept most of what they hear without question. Thus apologists need not be tense about persuading. People do it all the time. Apologists just need to expand their skills to deal with more challenging cases. One should not limit the concept of *persuasion* only to the difficult cases where clear differences of opinion or perspective raise doubts about the success of attempted persuasion.

Second, perhaps the dialogue partner will be antagonistic. Will he be rude and aggressive, a fire-breathing, dragon-like monster? Apologists can create stereotypes of the other that are all out of proportion to the facts. Like stage fright, stereotypes create anxiety. They are deadly, for preconceptions like these can become self-fulfilling prophecies.[2] Anticipating a tense conversation with someone with whom I disagree, I tense up. Then I convey this tenseness nonverbally to the other. He reflects the tenseness back, and this confirms my expectations and dulls my resolve.

Apologetic conversation is not as relaxing as soaking in a hot tub. Indeed, a certain amount of tension is unavoidable. It reflects biological changes, such as the release of adrenalin, that occur when people enter unfamiliar surroundings. God made the human body that way. However, certain adjustments in attitude can help create a healthier frame of mind:

Success in dialogue is presenting the case for faith clearly and persuasively; drawing people to faith is important, but not the only criterion of success.

Changing a person's heart is God's business, not mine. Since God is sovereign and gracious, it does not all depend on me.

Major changes in a person's point of view require a process. One-shot dialogue rarely brings radical change. Progress can be success.

I need not achieve perfection. I can admit my need for personal growth and accept the other's help in that area without spoiling the dialogue. Genuine willingness to learn can be a positive force.

1. David J. Hesselgrave, *Communicating Christ Cross-Culturally*, 2d ed. (Grand Rapids: Zondervan, 1991), 88.
2. See chapter 8, pp. 187–90.

My arguments need not be watertight before I begin. I can recognize that I am still developing the case and be thankful for any help the other might give me. Even if he does not accept my argument, his sharp critique aids the kingdom.

Willingness to be open to mutual learning means I can establish a partnership. Dialogue partners need not be sparing partners; they can be fellow travellers on the road to truth.

Dialogical apologetics is service. I offer my help to the other person (although I too have a lot to gain). Unlike a car salesman, I am not just trying to win a trip to Hawaii by selling the customer a car he does not need.

A dialogue partner is a person, not a *pagan* or *vile sinner* or *unbeliever blinded by the devil*. Seeing others as real human beings with real needs can reduce my negative stereotypes.

The other person will often feel nervous about discussing "religion." I can have the satisfaction of helping her relax.

Lots of strategies can help reduce the tension and open the way for an enjoyable, profitable sharing and assessing of ideas. I have the ability to learn and employ these skills.

One important objection might be lodged against this set of attitudes: they are unbiblical. I argued that change is a process. But the Bible says, "Now is the day of salvation" (2 Cor. 6:2). I counseled learning from the other. But "do not love the world" (1 John 2:15). I advised partnering with a non-Christian. But "do not be yoked together with unbelievers" (2 Cor. 6:14). I claimed that a dialogue partner is on the path to truth. But humans "suppress the truth by their wickedness" (Rom. 1:18). I suggested that one should not visualize a dialogue partner as blinded by the devil. But the "god of this age has blinded the minds of unbelievers" (2 Cor. 4:4). What to say?

My general response is this: I accept these texts as half of the biblical message. But allowing my image of the other to be dominated by these biblical ideas (i.e., not balancing them with other biblical themes) *encourages destructive stereotypes*. These foster negative stance and attitudes, which in turn create mental blocks both in the apologist and in the other. If the Christian communicates this negativity nonverbally, he will build resistance in the other. In this way, a theology intended to help people see their need for Christ actually has the opposite effect. Focusing on how godless, wicked, worldly, and blind his partner encourages the apologist to push the other away subconsciously.

To tell someone he is a sinner is speaking truth, but it can antagonize him. Driving him away by telling the truth in the wrong way and at the wrong time is hardly good communication. Effective communication must not only be true, but loving as well. It is not loving to tell a person the truth before he is ready to hear and in such a way that it produces the reverse effect.[3]

Someone once criticized D. L. Moody's evangelistic techniques. He responded, "You don't think much of my methods? I don't either. But I like my way of doing it better than your way of not doing it." Moody was a great evangelist. But not all attempts at evangelism have been better than nothing. Surprisingly, some evangelism is actually counterproductive.[4] Due to psychological reactance,[5] insensitive methods can technically enunciate the gospel while actually hurting the cause. That is a very poor trade-off. The point of the attitudes I defended is to help ensure that if a person rejects the gospel, she actually rejects the *message*, not the *messenger* or the *method*.

Hearing the Other

Armed with these attitudes, an apologist can turn to understanding his dialogue partner. The most important skill here may be the forgotten art of listening. Listening is arduous. For one thing, my thoughts are like my babies—I love my own the best. Listening insists that I go against the grain: it forces me to look at someone else's baby pictures. Further, some people are just plain hard to listen to. Some never stop talking. Others never finish a complete thought. I listened to a man who talked nonstop for ten minutes at a party one night without ever completing a sentence. I understood not one thing! Knowing what I was thinking, my patient wife smiled at me and nodded her encouragement.

Problems like these make effective listening difficult: defensive-

---

3. Note that Jesus used forceful language against self-righteous religious leaders, and his words drove them away. But he dealt with those who were at all open to his words both directly and kindly. I interpret his strong words to the Pharisees as a strategy of last resort with those who lacked the ears to hear.

4. Em Griffin, *The Mind Changers* (Wheaton: Tyndale House, 1976), 178. Remember Joseph Bayly, *The Gospel Blimp* (Havertown, Penn.: Windward, 1960)?

5. See chapter 7, pp. 167–68.

ness, the urge to talk, spouting too much information, stress, fatigue, and negative attitudes.[6] But a serious commitment to active listening is as critical in apologetic discussion as it is difficult. Listening time is not down time, like time spent waiting for a red light to turn. It is like the time Kirby Puckett spends in the on-deck circle watching a pitcher work on the previous batter. Unlike hearing, listening requires conscious, focused attention. It is not an "internal monologue" in which a person thinks ahead to his turn.[7]

To get at *what* is said and *why* it is said, good listening examines *how* something is said. By attending carefully, an apologist tries to get inside the other person's perspective. This includes listening for and noting intellectual commitments, attitudes, and feelings. A careful listener discerns the other's cultural identity and self-concept as well. She hears both the conceptual content of words and their emotional feel.

Careful listening helps one identify another's felt needs.[8] This is important, since usually a person changes his world view only when his previous point of view fails to do its job. "Some degree of dissatisfaction with one's self-concept or its associated values is the opening wedge for fundamental change."[9] Change can come when a person feels blocked or frustrated and feels a crack in his central value system. Without this cracking, world views tend to reinforce and perpetuate themselves like a self-fulfilling prophecy. This means good apologists look for conceptual cracks. The key is for the apologist to connect the truth he knows to the psychic motives and cognitive needs already present in the other. According to a clearly emerging trend in current studies, people do things for their own reasons, not someone else's.[10]

Listening can be dialogical. In ordinary conversation, people often fail to make their ideas clear on the first try. The listener can prompt the speaker to expand on incomplete or unclear ideas. If a person talks about her faith and then gets off the subject, an apologist can redirect: "I'm interested in what you said about. . . ." If someone

6. Norman Wakefield, *Listening: A Christian's Guide to Loving Relationships* (Waco: Word, 1981), 23–29.

7. William Howell, *The Empathic Communicator* (Belmont, Calif.: Wadsworth, 1982), 80–82.

8. See chapter 7, pp. 166–67.

9. Daniel Katz, "The Functional Approach to the Study of Attitudes," *Public Opinion Quarterly* 24 (1960): 176, 188.

10. Shelly Chaiken and Charles Stangor, "Attitudes and Attitude Change," in *Annual Review of Psychology*, vol. 38, ed. Mark Rosenzweig and Lyman Porter (Palo Alto, Calif.: Annual Reviews, 1987), 615.

makes a cryptic comment, a defender can probe: "Help me understand what you meant by. . . ." If someone is unclear, a listener can use reflection (repeating back a person's ideas) to clarify: "Tell me if this is what you're saying. . . ." Thus a good dialogical listener will help sharpen the other's speech.

What qualities do speakers value in a listener? A dialogue partner will appreciate the listener who remembers her name, understands her problem, is willing to help, shows patience, and is friendly no matter what happens. On the other hand, a dialogue partner will not like the listener who responds by talking down to him, refuses to hear him out, insists on introducing other topics, is friendly only when there is agreement, or pretends to know more than he really does.[11] It is not hard to see which qualities others appreciate. What is difficult is actually developing those traits. The commitment to do so is a promise to love the other selflessly.

By listening in this way, an apologist sends a critical message: real listening signals openness. I use the word *signal* because this message often comes across nonverbally and out-of-awareness (and for that reason powerfully). In fact, a careful apologist will use nonverbal cues to provide positive attitudinal feedback (i.e., acceptance and affirmation) while the other is speaking. This must include following culturally appropriate time and distance rules as well as using open body language (e.g., eye contact) and friendly mannerisms (e.g., nodding the head).

Defusing Emotions

The positive feedback that attentive listening offers goes a long way toward defusing intense emotions. Experiencing an emotion means feeling arousal. It is sensing one's surroundings or responding to them with a sensation of a particular kind. Emotional states often have a physiological aspect, including variations in heart rate or blood pressure, changes in glandular secretions, or erection of body hair. Emotions "are immediate, intense, and bodily ways of being moved by a situation."[12]

An emotional life has both conscious and unconscious facets. On

11. Ernest Bormann et al., *Interpersonal Communication in the Modern Organization* (Englewood Cliffs, N.J.: Prentice-Hall, 1969), 186–87.
12. James Olthuis, "Straddling the Boundaries Between Theology and Psychology," *Journal of Psychology and Christianity* 4 (1985): 10.

one view, the more unconscious tendencies to experience emotion are concerns or *passions*. Concerns and passions are cherished ideals or values. *Concerns* function as stable bases for emotions and so are called emotion-dispositions (i.e., they predispose someone to have emotions of a certain kind). *Passions* are particularly central concerns that integrate a person's life. A set of circumstances that touches a concern or passion evokes a negative or positive emotion. For instance, suppose Walt has a concern for his stock market assets. When his stocks rise, he experiences elation; when they drop, he experiences the opposite. Thus the same concern is the ground for different emotions.[13]

Since concerns or passions are values about which a person will have positive attitudes, emotional intensity reflects attitudinal intensity. If Martha believes strongly that abortion is murder (i.e., she values unborn life highly), the well-being of unborn children will be, for Martha, a passion. Her attitudes toward abortion clinics will have a negative valence and be strong. When abortion clinics run into difficulties (e.g., a clinic goes bankrupt), she experiences great joy. Conversely, lightly held attitudes evoke less powerful emotions.

Given this concept of intensity of attitude and emotion, one could plot attitudes on a scale of -3 to +3. If I am heavily involved in union activities, my attitude toward unions is +3. My attitude, in other words, is intense (3) and positive (+). How will I feel about the union member whose attitude is +1? He is in favor of unions, pays his dues, and walks out when a strike is called. But he is too busy with his bowling league to get involved in organizing activities. I may feel negatively toward this person, perhaps even regarding him with contempt. For me, any position from -3 to +1 is suspect; +2 is marginal.[14]

Suppose a farmer is pro-union but willing to live with any position from -1 to +3. This farmer has a wider *latitude of acceptance* than I. *Latitude of acceptance* refers not just to the spot I hold on the scale (say +3) but to all the spots I am willing to acknowledge as acceptable. If I accept anyone who is +1 to +3, that is my latitude of acceptance. Then 0 through -3 might constitute my *latitude of rejection*. Or I might have a *latitude of noncommitment* about which I am relatively neutral.[15] As the Minnesota Twins played the Atlanta Braves in the

13. Robert Roberts, *Spirituality and Human Emotion* (Grand Rapids: Eerdmans, 1982), 12–24.

14. Kenneth Anderson, *Persuasion*, 2d ed. (Boston: Allyn and Bacon, 1978), 91–102.

1991 World Series, one Minnesota public radio announcer, whose passion is classical music, said he did not care one way or the other who won—a latitude of noncommitment of -3 to +3!

When people differ in their attitudes, powerful emotions can arise. Religion and politics are the two forbidden topics in car pools because intense disagreements here create stress. These arguments can get personal: according to one study of British students, nonreligious people think religious people are brainwashed, unquestioning, and insecure.[16] Other sensitive spots include issues of culture, class, and race, for prejudices and misunderstandings along these fault lines cause many people great pain. Good apologists, therefore, must find ways to deal with attitudes and ventilate the emotions they evoke. They master strategies like these:

I can cultivate the habit of asking, "Is what I am doing building or undermining trust?" This is "the prior question of trust."

Acceptance breeds acceptance, and rejection breeds rejection. I should take the first step in self-disclosure and risk an offer of trust to the other. This can elicit a positive response.[17]

Openness to new ways of seeing things, new categories for organizing information and experiences, new perspectives from which to view problems will help me grasp the other's views. I need to be a flexible thinker, willing to ask, "What if . . ."[18]

I can deliberately stretch my latitude of acceptance by trying to see the other side of things when disagreements arise. Though not every view is true, I build rapport when I try to see the other's view from the inside.

Description is not the same as judgment. I should understand and show that I understand the strengths of any view that I must in the end criticize.

15. Muzafer Sherif and Carl Hovland, *Social Judgment* (New Haven: Yale University Press, 1961), 127–45; Carolyn Wood Sherif, "Social Values, Attitudes, and the Involvement of the Self," in *Beliefs, Attitudes, and Values*, ed. Monte Page, Nebraska Symposium on Motivation, 1979 (Lincoln: University of Nebraska, 1980), 27.

16. Kate Loewenthal, "Factors Affecting Religious Commitment," *Journal of Social Psychology221* 126 (1986): 123.

17. Marvin Mayers, *Christianity Confronts Culture*, rev. ed. (Grand Rapids: Zondervan, Academie, 1987), 7.

18. William Gudykunst, *Bridging Differences: Effective Intergroup Communication* (Newbury Park, Calif.: Sage, 1991), 108.

I must rid myself of stereotypes. I cannot, in the normal course of life, tell ethnic jokes, for example, and suddenly turn off those attitudes like a spigot as needed. I must deliberately cultivate genuinely accepting attitudes toward persons of every kind.

Empathy is powerful. (In sympathy I retain my point of view, but in empathy I do not.) I express empathy and gain insight if I use imagination to place myself in the other's shoes.[19]

A special problem related to apologetic dialogue is fear. Apologists are fearful of offending others. Others are fearful of being offended. In discussions of religion, people get wound too tightly. The ineffective and counterproductive methods used by some evangelists contribute to this problem. Everyone expects conversations about faith to be painful—which is why car pools outlaw them! Becky Pippert's solution for this problem is magic: admit it. Once when someone felt uncomfortable, she said, "Look, I feel really bad. I *am* very excited about who God is and what he's done in my life. But I hate it when people push 'religion' on me. So if I'm coming on too strong will you just tell me?"

Pippert's friend was shocked. She assumed Christians had no idea that those they talked with resented being blasted by running monologues. Pippert assured her that many Christians never enter the dialogue precisely because of their fear of offending others. Her friend's response showed great insight: "As long as you let people know that you're aware of where they're coming from, you can say anything you want! . . . And you just tell Christians that I said so."[20]

Just admitting my own fear of offending sends positive messages. I show empathy. I reveal sensitivity to how the other person feels. I can be honest and genuine about my own feelings. I express the joy and excitement of the Christian faith. And I give the other person an out. Because of reactance, people resist a hard sell just to retain their freedom. A person who feels trapped will do anything to feel free. But if the apologist gives him some elbowroom, he no longer needs to struggle for freedom. And the apologist need not feel badly about keeping him cornered. Dialogue is a two-way matter that requires permission from both parties. Forced conversations are monologues, and most people do what they can to avoid them.

19. Ibid., 121.
20. Rebecca Manley Pippert, *Out of the Saltshaker and into the World: Evangelism as a Way of Life* (Downers Grove: InterVarsity, 1979), 25.

Making the Case

Up to now I have covered affective matters primarily. The next subject is building the argument. But this is not a move from *pathos* (the emotional) to *logos* (the rational). In the past, people sharply divided *logos* and *pathos*, associating argument with logic and persuasion with emotion. This is the so-called *conviction/persuasion duality*. But the distinction is greatly overdrawn.[21] I assume a more integrated view. Informing, reasoning, and persuading are all closely intertwined. While setting the stage is largely relational, personal, and emotional, these factors are also clearly present in what follows. An apologist rightly attends to all these dimensions of dialogue in making the case.

Exerting Influence

Everyone has had the experience of talking with (or talking to?) someone who is thinking about something else. (Come to think of it, this might be a good description of hell.) Obviously, a good communicator needs the attention of a dialogue partner. Giving attention is the ongoing process of selecting from the environment the things that are relevant to personal needs. Thus except in complete dreaming (night or day), there is no such thing as inattention. If another is not attending to me, he is not usually attending to nothing, but to something else.[22]

Unlike monologue, dialogue requires the other's permission. I cannot coerce another's attention. But I can do several things to help earn his attention. Displaying empathy and maintaining positive tone invite the other's attention. Offering him my attention draws out a similar response. Talking about things that matter to him (e.g., his felt needs) and talking at a level that he understands also stimulate his interest. An attractive person, not physically necessarily, but in character and reputation, draws others to give attention.

21. Winston Brembeck and William Howell, *Persuasion: A Means of Social Influence*, 2d ed. (Englewood Cliffs, N.J.: Prentice-Hall, 1976), 14; Gerald Miller, "On Being Persuaded," in *Persuasion: New Directions in Theory and Research*, ed. Michael Roloff and Gerald Miller, Sage Annual Reviews of Communication Research, vol. 8 (Beverly Hills, Calif.: Sage, 1980), 14–15.
22. Brembeck and Howell, *Persuasion*, 269–70.

A related problem is getting started in an apologetic dialogue. Assuming that some rapport has already been established, my favorite way to begin is simply to ask, "Would you mind telling me about your spiritual journey?"[23] This does several things:

It asks permission. One who does not want to talk about this can say, "I'd rather not." Since I have given her an out, I need not feel nervous about forcing her to talk.

Everyone knows enough about himself to speak with authority. Since this is probably his favorite subject, he is usually happy to comply.

It assumes that the other is moving, not stationary. It is easier to steer a moving ship than to get it moving. The other person will often accept this assumption and attribute it to himself. "It is not out of character for me to talk about spiritual things; after all, I am on a spiritual journey," he thinks to himself.

It implies that process is acceptable. The question signals that I will not jump all over the other person if she is less than perfect or is still on the way.

It suggests that a destination is out there but has not yet been reached. More journeying lies ahead; more change or commitment may be required.

While I was writing my dissertation, people sometimes asked me the Dissertation Question: "So, what is your dissertation about?" (A Dissertation Question is a broad, open-ended question to which people do not want a full answer.)

"Do you want the thirty-second, the three-minute, or the ten-minute version?" I answered. People always chose the middle option. No one wanted to seem stupid (thirty-second version); no one wanted the whole thing (not really that interested). I gave them the thirty-second version anyway. But a Dissertation Question can be turned to good advantage. An answer that points out some benefits while remaining a bit vague can pique interest. This is a Mystifying Answer.[24]

23. Paul Little suggested a less open-ended variation: "Have you ever personally trusted Jesus Christ or are you still on the way?" This too has pluses. It recognizes three options (I am a Christian; I am on my way; I am uninterested), and asks the other to choose one of the first two. Paul Little, *How to Give Away Your Faith*, 2d ed. (Downers Grove: InterVarsity, 1988), 69.

24. See John Downes, *How to Be Irresistible Through the Power of Persuasion* (Wilmington: Enterprise, 1982), 129–31.

"What do you do?" someone asks me. (This is a Dissertation Question.)

"I'm professor of theology at Bethel Seminary. I teach philosophical theology and apologetics." This answer is really unhelpful. It gives true information, but it sends all the wrong signals. It is standoffish.

"Oh, that sounds interesting!" he says with a blank look. In his heart of hearts, he wants to talk to me about religion about as much he wants his house to burn to the ground.

But suppose I take a different tack:

"What do you do?" (Dissertation Question.)

"I help people understand the most important book ever written." This is a Mystifying Answer. It is a bit vague, but it may stir some interest. He is thinking to himself, "What is he talking about? I didn't know there was a book that important. This might be something I need to know about."

"What book?" (Another Dissertation Question.)

"It's the world's best seller. But best of all, it helps millions of people like you and me cope with everyday problems."

Here is another Mystifying Answer that gives some good reasons why this book is important and why he should become familiar with it. I do not present an argument that this book is the inspired Word of God (and back it up with a recitation of 2 Timothy 3:16 from the King James Version). Rather, I say that this is something he needs to help him with things that trouble him. So he asks me to tell him what I want to tell him:

"How does this book tell people how to cope with life?"

Consider this interchange between a Christian minister and a new acquaintance:

"What do you do?"

"I have the world's best job."

"How is that?"

"I help people find the support they need to solve some of the problems in their lives."

"How do you do this? Are you a psychiatrist?"

"I help people discover how Jesus Christ relates to the struggles we all have every day."

"Sounds interesting."

"It really is. In fact, just the other day . . ."[25]

Using Mystifying Answers for Dissertation Questions is not devi-

25. Adapted from Little, *How to Give Away Your Faith*, 61.

ous in any way. It is simply waiting until the other person really wants to hear the answer before giving it. It is connecting the message to his sense of need—even though the person has not yet revealed that area of need. Given that an argument carries the most weight the first time a person hears it, waiting until the audience is really interested and ready to listen simply maximizes the effectiveness of the message.

As a negative example, think of the doomsday preacher standing on the city street corner and screaming at rush hour passers-by. He produces total avoidance and zero communication. In contrast, consider the conversation between Jesus and the woman at the well (John 4:7–14):

"Will you give me a drink?"

"You are a Jew and I am a Samaritan woman. How can you ask me for a drink?"

"If you knew . . . who it is that asks you for a drink, you would have asked him and he would have given you living water."

"Sir, you have nothing to draw with and the well is deep. Where can you get this living water?"

"Everyone who drinks this water will be thirsty again, but whoever drinks the water I give him will never thirst."

Talk about Mystifying Answers! Mystifying Answers point out important advantages and then ask the other to work at gaining those pluses. This is just good communication. It acknowledges reactance. (People want what they cannot get, but they do not want what they are forced to take.) It recognizes the commodity theory. (Something scarce seems more valuable.) It encourages the other to pursue what the apologist wanted to tell him all along—except that now he is really ready to listen because his interest is piqued.

To get a person thinking about how the gospel would benefit him, I can ask this question: "If there were good evidence that what Jesus said and did was really true—and I said *if*—how might Jesus make a difference in your life?" The fit of the gospel to his felt needs is subjective. Only he can really say how he thinks the gospel will help him. Later on, I hope he will begin to consider objective evidence in which he now has no interest. But if he focuses attention on the ways in which Jesus could help him, *if only* the evidence were solid, then he may look at the reasons more seriously. Then as the evidence mounts, I can remind him of the benefits as he sees them: "Remember, you said if we could find some good evidence, then Jesus could really help you . . . ?"

In pointing out the advantages of faith, however, it is important *not* to oversell or overstate. Advertisers sometimes use lofty platitudes, making exaggerated claims about their products. Lofty platitudes cause negative attitudes: "Well, it can't really be *that* good." Given that a major objection against the faith is that Christians are hypocrites, lofty platitudes invite disaster. Thus if I come across as a stuffy, holy person, the effect will very likely be negative. Paradoxically, when I admit that I am not perfect, that I have struggles, or that I too am on a spiritual journey, I establish rapport and deflate critical negative attitudes about Jesus.

Admitting that some Christians act holier-than-thou sends lots of good messages. Such Christians are trying to help God look good (which is noble) by pretending to be perfect. But unfortunately their assistance is counterproductive. God does not need that sort of help. This is not what the gospel is about. It is about God helping people with their deepest need—forgiveness. Though I am not perfect, I can admit that God accepts me and helps me. This implies to the other that I will accept him as he is. And God will too.

This whole dynamic is complicated by differences of social class. Lower-class people *assume* that higher-class people think themselves better (mostly they do). According to studies, differences in status lead people to expect differences in belief.[26] Speaking with those in a different age range, social class, racial group, or cultural status requires being attuned to this problem. Any apologist who comes across as the great Bwana ("I've got my life together; now I'll help you get yours together!") does more harm than good.

Consider age differences. If a teenager observes *for herself* that God has straightened out my life, I am ahead in the game. This may help attract her to Christ. Perhaps if the relationship is positive, I can say God has helped me along the way. But if I tell her I have arrived, the game is over and I lose—especially if the evidence suggests I have not. Condescension is a first class ticket to failure.

Using Evidence

Traditionally, apologetics has been too heavily weighted toward building philosophical arguments. But I do not suggest going to the opposite pole; apologetic dialogue must use evidence. A student once

---

26. Paul Secord and Carl Backman, *Social Psychology* (New York: McGraw-Hill, 1964), 414.

asked how many points a good sermon should have. A wise pundit responded, "At least one." Relationship building is worthless if an apologist cannot articulate and defend the main point. Questions, diversions, and conversational interruptions will take dialogues all over the countryside. An effective apologist must discipline himself to remember where home base is. Discussing side issues is not always bad. But once they are hashed out, one must return to the main point.

Critical to presenting the case is speaking right to the point. That means repeating and reviewing basic distinctions. This is obvious, but it is difficult. I often talked with a woman who forced me to realize the importance of getting right to the point and giving my best argument. She asked questions like, "Why does God allow evil in the world?" Then she gave me about thirty seconds to answer before her mind flitted to another topic. Though frustrated, I took it as good discipline. What precisely am I trying to say? What exactly is my point? Having the main point solidly in mind makes it easier to get back on track after rabbit hunts.

This requires knowing the message well. Although in this book I have ignored apologetic arguments, understanding the meaning of and reasons for the Christian world view is critical. At some point, perhaps after a Mystifying Answer, a person will sometimes ask, "Well, then, what do you think?" That is the window of opportunity. A good apologist will be ready with several good reasons why faith makes sense and will benefit this person. The game is tied; the clock reads 0:00; I am on the freethrow line. What I say must have punch if I am to communicate effectively and give the other the maximum opportunity to grasp and accept the message.

Effective communication at this point uses language the person understands. Christians have a subculture all their own, and this subculture has its own language—"Protestant Latin," Eugene Nida called it. This is not the place for Latin, for words like *depravity*, *justification*, *election*, or *eschatology*. Concrete, need-related language is best. To a bitter, divorced woman, driven toward feminism by a violent husband, say: "Jesus is the most positive force for women in world history. He can heal wounds most men never heard of. Would you like to know how Jesus responds to women?" This, not the cosmological argument, is her agenda at this time.

The reason evidence should be need-based and person-relative is this: research shows that what the listener does with evidence is most important. *Self-created messages persuade.* Memorizing someone else's arguments has little effect over time. Arguments, developments, connections, and implications the audience produces will endure.[27] So I like to ask, "If this were true, what difference could it make to you?" A person begins thinking about the benefits as she sees them. Once she sees some benefits, she may ask, "How do you know it's true? What if it's false?" At this point, the rest of the cumulative case comes in. When a person sees value in believing, she is willing to expend energy to give the evidence a more honest hearing.

One way to help people develop their own reasons is to use concrete imagery. A major reason academic types fail to communicate is that scholarly communities become abstract. They deal every day with technical concepts and broad generalizations. These academic abbreviations are perfectly in order in the classroom—just like the linguistic shortcuts in the tuna boat, the attorney's office, or the welding shop. But moving from the classroom to real life is crossing a cultural fault line. In the real world, most do not have the interest, patience, practice, or skill to deal with academic abstractions. So they glaze over. Far better to follow the lead of C. S. Lewis, whose writings have endured due in part to the concrete imagery he employed.

According to the literature on persuasion, concrete images make persuasion more effective in inducing a person to be open to new evidence. Recall the experiment where a smoker enters a simulated medical office where she role plays with a "doctor" a conversation about smoking and "her" cancer.[28] Another study asked people whether they would take a vaccine with possibly risky side effects. Experimenters found that vivid visual aids significantly affected the attempted persuasion.[29] Evidence presented this way is not illogical. It is rational. But its mode of presentation is concrete. It uses practical examples and specific details, and thus it engages the mind.

Role play is not always feasible. But an alternative exists: stories. By telling stories, an apologist can present vivid, dramatic, concrete, engaging arguments. I first like to make a point sharply, abstractly, as

27. John Cacioppo and Richard Petty, "Effects of Message Repetition on Argument Processing, Recall, and Persuasion," *Basic and Applied Social Psychology* 10 (1989): 3–12.

28. Irving Janis and Leon Mann, "Effectiveness of Emotional Role-Playing in Modifying Smoking Habits and Attitudes," *Journal of Experimental Research in Personality* 1 (1965): 84–90. See chapter 7, pp.163–64.

29. Robert Kaplan, Bonnie Hammel, and Leslie Schimmel, "Patient Information Processing and the Decision to Accept Treatment," *Journal of Social Behavior and Personality* 1 (1986): 113–20.

briefly as possible. Then, I give my best reason to support the point. Next, I take the most time to tell an engaging story to drive the idea home. Finally, I recap abstractly, using different words to repeat and summarize what I am saying.[30] Over time, an apologist can collect vivid stories to drive home points that often come up in dialogue.

Studies show these results relative to evidence:

Evidence can help achieve short-term attitude change when the apologist has low credibility, as long as the evidence is well delivered and is novel for the audience.

Novel evidence has more punch. Evidence is most powerful the first time it is heard, which is why it should not be delivered before the other is really ready to hear it.

Even when well delivered and novel, evidence does not improve short-term attitude change when the source has high credibility.

Evidence is critical for long-term change, however. An intellectually persuaded person is more permanently convinced than someone persuaded *only* dramatically. An apologist must augment story telling with understandable reasons.[31]

Messages that contain cues about the importance of logic are more convincing—even when they are actually illogical. Trying to be logical pays off.

Recognizing both sides of an issue is more influential with fewer specific arguments, but one-sided presentation is more powerful when combined with many arguments. Higher source expertise compensates for fewer arguments, especially with a hostile audience.[32]

---

30. I use this strategy in teaching, preaching, and writing as well as in apologetic dialogue. But I apply it with audience sensitivity. The amount of concreteness and imagery increases with a more popular audience and decreases with a more academic audience.

31. James McCroskey, "A Summary of Experimental Research on the Effects of Evidence in Persuasive Communication," in *The Process of Social Influence: Readings in Persuasion,* ed. Thomas Beisecker and Donn Parson (Englewood Cliffs, N.J.: Prentice-Hall, 1972), 318–28; Charles U. Larson, *Persuasion: Reception and Responsibility* (Belmont, Calif.: Wadsworth, 1973), 109.

32. Jean-Charles Chebat et al., "Compensatory Effects of Cognitive Characteristics of the Source, the Message, and the Receiver Upon Attitude Change," *Journal of Psychology* 122 (1988): 609–21.

Overheard conversations persuade effectively. Apologists should not lose heart when talking to a skeptic, especially if others are listening.[33]

In presentations containing (1) no evidence, (2) evidence only, (3) evidence plus a citation, and (4) evidence plus a citation that is evaluated positively, (2) was most effective.[34]

Clear organization helps make a message more persuasive apparently because it signals that the presenter is more credible.[35]

The better people understand something, the more likely they are to accept it.[36] Comprehensibility, especially when understanding of abstract concepts is increased by using concrete illustrations full of vivid detail, enhances persuasion.

Requesting Response

A good argument offers an invitation. In one sense, of course, every conversation includes lots of responses. Listeners always give nonverbal feedback, and good apologists monitor it continuously. Verbal responses are obviously important as well. But an invitation offers a dialogue partner a chance to do something specific. It may not be asking him to trust Jesus on the spot. It may be asking him to agree to talk again, to meet for lunch for further discussion, to come to a Bible study, to take and read a book, or to come to a special church-related event. But whatever it is, say it. Offer an invitation sensitively but clearly.

If my dialogue partner is not a Christian, eventually I should pop the faith question. Here an apologist becomes an evangelist.[37] Not offending a person is important. But so is not being intimidated by the question, "I wonder if the time is right?" A good way to get things

33. J. Allyn and Leon Festinger, "The Effectiveness of Unanticipated Persuasive Communications," *Journal of Abnormal and Social Psychology* 62 (1961): 35–40.

34. Robert Bostrom, *Persuasion* (Englewood Cliffs, N.J.: Prentice-Hall, 1983), 146.

35. Ibid., 176.

36. Barbara O'Keefe and Gregory Shepherd, "The Communication of Identity During Face-to-Face Persuasive Interactions," *Communication Research* 16 (1989): 375–404.

37. A person can shift from apologist to evangelist—no harm there. This does not mean apologetics *is* evangelism. A plumber can pound nails, but this does not mean that plumbing is carpentry. Apologetics and evangelism are theoretically distinct, even though, like my heart and lungs, they are practically inseparable. See chapter 5, pp. 114–15.

started and to give the other the maximum opportunity to come to Jesus is to make a series of requests. Start small. Ask the other to come to a dinner or a party, then to an outing with people from church, and then to a Bible study group or lunchtime conversation.[38] Work up to the question of faith.

When offering an invitation, do not set up a negative response. Something like this is a disaster: "I don't suppose there's any way you'd consider becoming a Christian?" Remember the Brownie who asks, "You don't want to buy any Girl Scout cookies, do you?" This expects a negative answer and admits only the remotest possibility of a positive one. Here is an alternative: "Do you still have some things to think over or are you ready to trust Jesus and become a Christian?" This does not offer the negative option. It presents two choices: continue to think about it or make the commitment.

In general, skillful apologists ask others to take a step at the edge of their latitude of commitment. Asking something outrageous ensures a turndown. Asking something they have already essentially agreed to makes no headway. Stretching their latitude of commitment just a bit can precipitate attitude change in that direction.

Good apologists make the invitation count. They spend credibility capital wisely for "every successful persuasive interaction causes us to lose credibility."[39] (E.g., parents of teenagers should rarely debate clothing styles, but save their ammunition for the really important issues.) Good apologists consider what I call the *hierarchy of apologetic needs*: Where does this dialogue partner need to make his next move? Different people need different discussion. I may debate relatively minor theological points with advanced seminarians. I will concede a wider latitude of acceptance with lay people, debating only relatively important points. With non-Christians, I allow wide ranges of opinion on all but the really critical issues. Good apologists do not sweat the details when the major issues are unresolved.

On the other hand, devaluing the core message by making it easier to accept can have a reverse effect. Concessions make any product less valuable. A take-it-or-leave-it attitude is good; I must not water down essentials hoping to improve chances of acceptance. If I am so afraid of a negative response that I downgrade the product, I actually make it less appealing. In fact, making its essential core more difficult to achieve makes it all the more attractive—*if* the person wants

38. See chapter 7, pp. 165–66, on the foot-in-the-door strategy.
39. Bostrom, *Persuasion*, 128.

it. If I am not overly concerned that the other person might give me the turndown, I actually have a better chance of receiving a positive response. "The paradox remains that the more uncompromising [Jesus] is the more appeal he has."[40]

A Sample Dialogue

Adam the Apologist 1 (a pastor): Since we talked before, I just want to make sure I understand your position on the resurrection of Jesus—correct me if I'm wrong—but you said you believe there is a God?

Fred the Friend 1 (a young man): Well, right. I believe there is someone, or something, out there, a superior being or something, but we really can't know much about him.

Adam 2: Okay. So, you believe there is a God, or something out there, that is responsible for what we see around us. Right?

Fred 2: Yes.

Adam 3: Good. Now, you have also said you believe that Jesus lived as a man, right?

Fred 3: Yes.

Adam 4: And you believe he was crucified by the Romans, he died on the cross, was buried, and then was gone from the tomb on the third day, right?

Fred 4: Yes.

Adam 5: Now you have also said you don't believe he rose from the dead.

Fred 5: Well, we just can't know that.

Adam 6: What do you think happened?

Fred 6: I don't know.

Adam 7: The last time we talked, you seemed to think that the disciples stole the body. Do you think that is what happened?

Fred 7: I don't know, but I don't think so. The book you gave me to read talked a little about that. What do you think of that book?

[Adam had given Fred a book to read. It was a small request designed to lead to larger requests later.]

Adam 8: I thought it was very good. What did you think?

Fred 8: I didn't think so at all. First, there weren't two lines in a

40. Pippert, *Out of the Saltshaker*, 62.

row that I understood. Maybe it's my intelligence level or something, but I didn't know what he was talking about. And he said some very unfair things about Freud. I have studied a lot of Freud, and this guy doesn't know much about him at all.

Adam 9: I can see what you're saying. Boy, I'm sorry you didn't find the book helpful. And it's good for me to know how people respond to these books. I thought it was very helpful, but it must not have been the right kind of book for you to answer the questions you have right now. I'm really sorry.

Fred 9: That's okay.

[Note: Adam does not try to defend the book's discussion of Freud. Given Fred's *hierarchy of apologetic needs*, that is utterly unimportant at this time. Adam accepts responsibility for making a bad judgment. It might be a great book, but inappropriate for a particular individual. And he gained something from this interchange. In one comment, he has defused Fred's displeasure about the book. "A soft answer turns away anger."]

Adam 10: Well, maybe as we talk a little further, we can figure out what kind of books will help you more. But let's get back to the empty tomb. It seems the best explanation, when you consider all of the evidence, is that Jesus did rise from the dead. I need to know why you don't believe this to be the case.

[Fred's discussion of the book took them off course. Adam lets that rabbit hunt play itself out, but gets the discussion back on course. He does not forget the goal.]

Fred 10: Well, because I've never seen anybody rise from the dead, and it goes against everything we know about science.

Adam 11: So you're saying you don't believe miracles can happen?

Fred 11: I don't think so.

[Notice how Adam reflects Fred's position back, asking for clarification. This is dialogical listening.]

Adam 12: So you don't think miracles ever happen in our world? You seem to admit that there is a God who created all of this, then why couldn't that God step in and perform a miracle once in a while?

Fred 12: Well, I guess I have heard of one thing that I would consider a miracle. My sister's husband's mother had serious cancer and was not expected to live for over a couple of months. But when she went back to the doctor, she was completely free of cancer. There was no other explanation except that it was a miracle. And she had never stepped foot in a church more than six or so times in her whole life. So how do you explain that?

Adam 13: Well, I believe God can, and does, heal people however and whenever He wants to. So, are you saying that miracles are at least possible?

Fred 13: Yes, I suppose so.

[After reflection and with Adam's nudging, Fred suggests evidence that makes sense to him. Persuasion happens when people use their own ideas to build an argument. After Fred offers the evidence, Adam uses the evidence to help Fred reach his own conclusion.]

Adam 14: Okay, that's very good. We've got a good place to start. Fred, let me ask you this. Do you think it is possible, just *possible*, that the reason the tomb was empty on the third day was because Jesus actually did rise from the dead? Is it just possible?

Fred 14: I suppose so.

[Adam presses the edge of Fred's latitude of acceptance. He does not ask Fred to adopt the position, but to acknowledge it as a real possibility.]

Adam 15: So what would it take to convince you that this is exactly what happened? Would it help you to see that the historical evidence, if we examine it objectively, is very strong in supporting that Jesus did rise from the dead?

Fred 15: Yes, I suppose so. But it's like in your sermon yesterday, you're supposed to have faith, but I need to know for sure before I can believe something. I don't want to be a fool.

[Adam is exploring the sort of evidence *Fred thinks is relevant.* Fred has also revealed something important on the emotional side. He is concerned about giving up his intellectual integrity. And he may also be worried about what others will think.]

Adam 16: Fred, I think I've really misunderstood where you're coming from. I hear you saying exactly what I said several years ago. We have so much in common. I guess I thought you were having problems with the philosophical side of things, but what you really need, just like I did, is to see some hard evidence and good reasons for believing. The book does a very good job at looking at various aspects of life and then suggests, and I agree with the author, that Christianity does the best job of dealing with all of the data, and that's what a lot of people need to see. But people like you and me, we need to get ahold of some pretty hard evidence so we can trust in something.

Fred 16: That's right.

[Adam is still listening hard and reflecting Fred's thoughts. He also expresses empathy with Fred.]

Adam 17: Fred, remember when I said that before we can really *believe in* something, we first have to *believe that*. Does that make sense?

Fred 17: Yes, I think so.

Adam 18: You see, Fred, what I can help you do is to examine the data for yourself, to see if the best explanation for the resurrection is that Jesus rose from the dead. But all I can help you do is to *believe that*. The next step is to *believe in* Jesus as a person, and that's between you and God. You see, Jesus said we need to *believe in* him. Faith and trust in him will save us from our sins and give us eternal life. Let me ask you this, Fred. If we can look at the evidence and you come to the conclusion that Jesus probably did rise from the dead, do you think that then it might be possible for you to *believe in* him—to accept him as your Lord and savior?

Fred 18: Yes, I think I would be able to believe in him.

[Again, Adam is stretching Fred's latitude of acceptance. He gets Fred to accept the idea that trusting Christ is possible. This is a small step that helps prepare for another step later on.]

Adam 19: Well, then the place to start is to begin to examine the evidence. There's a lot of evidence, even outside of the Bible itself, that points to the life of Jesus and shows that the best explanation of the empty tomb is that Jesus actually did rise from the dead. Would you like to read about that?

Fred 19: Sure.

Adam 20: Good. Here's a book that talks about evidence outside the Bible. Let me show you some of the best parts in the back of the book. Remember yesterday when I described the P.A. system at the high school? Do you believe it exists?

Fred 20: Yes.

Adam 21: Why? Have you ever seen it yourself?

Fred 21: No. But I believe it because you told me it is there.

Adam 22: Do you understand how I described the way we know much of what we accept as true based on the testimony of others, usually people who are trustworthy and knowledgeable?

Fred 22: Yes.

[The P.A. system at the high school is not a glorious illustration, but it makes the point *concretely*. And Fred clearly understands the point.]

Adam 23: Well, here is a lot of evidence from many people, many of them eyewitnesses of Jesus, who knew him, and touched him, and felt him. They tell us he was really here and he really did rise from the dead. Now, if we have any doubt as to whether their testimony is true or accurate, we can compare the evidence regarding their accuracy with the manuscript evidence for other historical documents. (Adam and Fred run through some of the lists of evidence about manuscript evidence. Fred is impressed.) But again, Fred, I can show you all of the evidence in the world, but eventually *you* will have to *believe in* Jesus for yourself—to trust him as your God, your Savior—the one to give you eternal life.

Fred 23: Well, I know everyone—you and my sister—tells me that if I would just believe, I could be a lot happier. You know I've had a lot of psychological problems, and I would be a lot happier if I would just believe. I guess it's just so hard for me to believe in something I can't see or touch or feel.

[Fred responds positively to the novel evidence about the reliability of biblical manuscripts. Further, Fred's personal needs are important as well. He needs Jesus. This motivates him to consider the evidence.]

Adam 24: Fred, that sounds exactly like something that is in the Bible. Remember the story about the person we call "doubting Thomas"? Let me read this to you. (Adam reads from the Bible.)

Fred 24: Oh, yeah, now I remember that part.

[Adam's reading the story is effective just so it is not long and not in King James English. It is concrete—it is something Fred can identify with and participate in imaginatively. Note how Adam expresses empathy.]

Adam 25: Thomas is a lot like you and me—we all need to see and touch for ourselves. Jesus said that those who believe without seeing are more blessed. Now, maybe Jesus is going to appear to you, but he never has to me. But I believe in him because of the testimony given by those people who did see him. We have been given a lot of evidence, in the Bible and outside of it, enough to believe that Jesus lived, died, and rose from the dead. That evidence can lead us to *believe that* he did those things. But we have to take the next step and *believe in* him.

[Adam has repeated the distinction between *believing that* (understanding) and *believing in* (faith) three times.]

Fred 25: That's another thing that is hard for me to accept about

God. Do you mean I'm supposed to believe that God loves me and every starving kid in Bangladesh the same? Well, how is that even possible?

Adam 26: It is true, Fred. God is so much bigger. . . .

Fred 26: (sarcastically) He must be, I mean, how could he even know everybody, or keep track of them? I mean, he must be bigger and better than the best computer made by man.

[Suddenly, a big, new objection arises. But the problem is unclear. Is Fred concerned about the problem of evil ("starving kids in Bangladesh") or about God's omniscience ("keeping track of them"). Adam assumes the latter. In his response, note how he tries to use ideas Fred has already accepted.]

Adam 27: Fred, you've admitted that whoever God is, he is the one who has created everything. He created your brain, and that is more marvelous than any computer man will ever make. God is much greater than we will ever be able to comprehend. But that's where I really believe it's more important first to examine the evidence regarding the resurrection of Jesus, because if we can believe that he rose from the dead, we can then believe his words and his teachings. If we trust in what he tells us, it will be easier for us to accept some of the more difficult things to understand.

Fred 27: Well, like I said, I know I would be a lot happier and maybe be able to put my life together.

[Fred quickly drops the objection. Sorting out God's omniscience is important, but not to Fred at this moment. Adam is not morally obligated to discuss it completely at this time.]

Adam 28: Fred, I do believe Jesus is the only way for any of us to put our lives together, but I want you to believe first because it's true, and then because you can reap benefits. Jesus said to "seek first his kingdom and his righteousness, and all of these things will be added to you as well." Remember?

Fred 28: Yes. Boy, that's a nice Bible! Where'd you get it?

Adam 29: I got it for myself a few years ago, and I really like it. We'll have to get you one like this sometime soon. Fred, you seem so open-minded and receptive today.

[Adam pays Fred a compliment. He also attributes to him a characteristic that he hopes Fred will apply to himself.]

Fred 29: Well, I do think I am open-minded.

Adam 30: Fred, you've said you might be willing to believe in Jesus if you could see the evidence and it seemed convincing. Do you feel ready to accept him just now and to put your faith in him, or do you think you need to go home, read this book, and have some of your intellectual questions answered first?

[Notice that although Adam has asked for a definite response, Fred is not offended in the least.]

Fred 30: I need to go home and read this and think about it. My sister really appreciates what you're doing with me, but she's afraid you'll get discouraged.

[The persuasion process includes Fred's sister.]

Adam 31: Well, you don't have to worry about that. I think you do need to go home and read through this book, and don't be afraid to call me anytime if I can help. I personally believe you are going to trust in Jesus as soon as you answer some of these questions. I think the Holy Spirit is working on your heart and you are very close to believing in Jesus. And I won't get discouraged because I think this is why God has called me here.

Fred 31: I do, too.

[Adam attributes to Fred the response he hopes Fred will make. Fred agrees with this attribution.]

Adam 32: I'll keep praying for you, and we'll keep talking.

Fred 32: Thanks for your time—and have a safe trip this week.

[Fred does not feel put upon. He thanks Adam. Even though Adam has pressed some very direct arguments and asked for a definite response, Fred feels that Adam has done him a favor.]

Adam 33: Thank you, Fred. God bless you.

Fred 33: God bless you, too.

Summary

Preparing oneself for apologetic conversation means developing a proper set of attitudes about the process of persuasion and about the other. The other is a dialogue partner and friend, not a roaring lion stalking an apologetic gazelle.

Those who listen carefully hear at several levels—conceptual, attitudinal, cultural, and emotional. Listeners can serve the other by clarifying and by sending signals of openness.

Emotions are powerful—powerfully good or powerfully bad—and they influence apologetic conversations. Apologists who admit their feelings and cultivate empathy can defuse negative emotions and encourage positive ones.

An apologist can exert influence by waiting until the other is ready, willing, and wanting to hear the message, by connecting the message to the other's needs, and by engaging the other's imaginative thinking processes.

Apologists must use evidence, for evidence is what makes persuasive influence last. The reasons that make the best impact are understandable, novel, balanced, concrete, logical, and organized.

Almost all dialogues should end with an invitation. A good invitation engages the other, asking her to make a commitment that is neither too big nor too small. Properly done, it is not offensive in the least because it expects a positive answer but allows an out. No one is left turning on a spit over hot coals.

This discussion of dialogue, however, has left out one thing. From a biblical point of view, it might be the most important. It relates not to technique (what I do), but to character (who I am). To this issue we turn briefly in the conclusion. What difference does my own spiritual relationship to Jesus Christ make?

CONCLUSION

Who You Are Counts Most

We have come a long way. I have tried to develop an approach to Christian defense that is multifaceted and well-rounded. On the theoretical side, apologists can welcome a window of intellectual opportunity opened by recent developments in the world of scholarship. I emphasized these in part 1. On the more practical side, apologists can gain from several important fields a set of perspectives and understandings that will greatly enrich apologetic dialogue. I stressed these in part 2.

Does the necessity of faith entail that no reasons can be given for Christianity? No. Faith as personal trust is an act of the whole person, and this includes the mind. Does philosophy show that Christian thinking is substandard? No. Important developments in philosophy today show the viability of Christian thought. Does the success of science prove that religious thinking is defective? No. Philosophy of science suggests that science is not the only way to knowledge. Does the fact that absolute proof seems impossible mean one cannot build a case? No. All large-scale, interpretive grids use probabilist arguments. Does the presence of other religions preclude a Christian defense? No. Genuine dialogue with other persons is possible and rewarding.

Developments in philosophy of religion, philosophy of science, epistemology, and religious studies do not preclude Christian defense. If these problems need not cause apologists to pause, then how should they proceed? Does logic help the apologist? Yes. Although every argument needs content, attention to matters of form is important and will repay careful study. Do attitudes play any role in apologetics? Yes. An apologist's attitudes toward the dialogue partner as well as the other's attitudes toward Christianity and toward the apologist all powerfully affect dialogue. Do cultural issues enter apologetics? Yes. All conversations are saturated with racial, social, and cultural dimensions. Social class identity must not be ignored.

Christian apologists stand at a point in history when they have greater opportunity than at any time in the last several centuries. The demise of secularity—politically, intellectually, and culturally—has reached epidemic proportions. Secularism is in a shambles around the world to a degree no one could have anticipated just a few years ago. Christian defense has unparalleled relevance today. A method consonant with the times, one that is situationally and personally sensitive, can give Christian defenders the courage, determination, and skills to enter the great dialogue.

If this is so, what sort of persons does Jesus need? I have spent little time discussing this point. As has been true for centuries, however, the apologist's character is critical. Many of the points I made regarding attitudes and cultural sensitivity will require not just new understandings, but personal growth. A commitment to defending the faith is *not* a promise to argue whatever, however, whenever, and with whomever. It is *a commitment to be, to the highest degree possible, what God wants his servants to be—intellectually, relationally, and spiritually*.

Researchers studied what makes life insurance sales people effective. Knowledge of the product and smooth speaking ability, it turned out, did not predict success. The most important factor is the salesperson himself *as the client saw him*. Only the quality of personal interaction between the salesperson and the client correlated positively with purchases of life insurance.[1] Christian apologetics is about something far more important than selling insurance. Yet in both cases, a firmly established principle in communication applies: *"The probability of change in beliefs is directly proportional to the credibility of the source or sender."*[2]

A classic way to tap into the apologist's personal credibility is, of course, the personal testimony. This simply means sharing one's own spiritual journey, telling one's own story. This has always been an effective way to share the Christian world view with others. What I

1. Franklyn B. Evans, "Dyadic Interaction in Selling—A New Approach," an unpublished study; quoted in Winston Brembeck and William Howell, *Persuasion: A Means of Social Influence*, 2d ed. (Englewood Cliffs, N.J.: Prentice-Hall, 1976), 184–85.

2. James F. Engel, *Contemporary Christian Communications, Its Theory and Practice* (Nashville: Nelson, 1979), 192.

highlighted in this book shows why the personal testimony is so potent. It establishes rapport with the other through self-disclosure. It models the choice the apologist hopes the other will make. It is concrete and captivating, not abstract. It counts as legitimate evidence of the power of God to make a difference in a concrete situation. And it is irrefutable: no one can doubt what Jesus has done in the life of a real human being. If all this is so, a wise apologist will learn to tell his own story in a clear, vivid, concise, self-effacing, and winsome way as part of his defense.

More importantly, every apologist will seek not only a clearer conceptual grasp of Christian ideas and arguments, but also a richer personal experience of the Savior those ideas point to. He will seek to grow in grace, to develop godly character that consistently expresses itself in the details of life. He will continue to grow as a person who is consistent, sacrificial, mature, completely honest, and genuinely caring. For in the last analysis, *the apologist himself is the best evidence* for the truth of the Christian world view.

"Be wise in the way you act toward outsiders," wrote Paul. "Make the most of every opportunity. Let your conversation be always full of grace, seasoned with salt, so that you may know how to answer everyone" (Col. 4:5–6). Who you are counts, and it counts heavily!

Our conversation—yours and mine—about apologetic dialogue has come to an end, although I could write much more. Perhaps you will find in this approach to apologetics a perspective and a method that feel comfortable. Perhaps it will allow you to enter dialogue without feeling that you might wilt like a cut pansy. Or that you must crush your opponent as you might squash a Minnesota mosquito. If so, please use it. Perfect it. And then write another book that will sharpen more clearly than this one has the idea of dialogical apologetics.

INDEX

Abraham, William J., 45n, 97n
Absolute
    knowledge, 58, 59, 61, 75, 100
    proof, 90, 113
Acceptance, 213
Accuracy, 64, 148
Adler, Alfred, 60
Advertising, 219
Aesthetics, 12
Affirming the consequent
        (fallacy), 58–59
Agnosticism, 30, 33, 34, 46
Ajzen, Icek, 157n
Allegiance, 96, 97
Allport, Gordon, 156, 188n
Allyn, J., 223n
Alston, William, 34n, 44
Ambiguity, 67, 201
Anderson, Kenneth, 212n
Anomalies, 63, 68
Antirealism, 53–54, 56, 95
Anxiety, 207
Apologetics, 17, 38, 74, 75
    audience–centered, 100, 110,
        112–14, 125
    and dialogue, 99, 100, 117–18
    emotional dimensions, 206
    and evangelism, 114–15, 223
    goal, 122–24
    method, 110–12, 125
    traditional, 103
Aquinas, Thomas, 8, 9, 10, 11, 14, 16,
        17, 36, 111

Argument from design, 106–7
Ariarajah, S. Wesley, 118
Aristotle, 21, 55, 62, 132, 133–34,
        137, 154, 169
Arrogance, 114
Asch, Solomon, 162–63
Assumptions. See Presuppositions
Atheism, 23, 30, 33
Attitude, 155–57, 165–66, 177, 186
    and behaviors, 160–61
    and beliefs, 158
    assumptions, 149
    change, 158–64, 166, 167–69,
        170
    object, 156, 159
Attitudinal listening, 231
Attribution theory, 164–65
Audience sensitivity, 103, 115
Augustine, 9, 105
Authority, 96–98, 100
    of the church, 8, 10
Autonomous reason, 14, 22, 28, 84
Auxiliary hypotheses, 63, 68, 69, 73

Backman, Carl, 219n
Bacon, Francis, 56
Baillie, John, 89n
Bandura, Albert, 163
Barbour, Ian G., 57n, 70n, 86
Barnes, Barry, 68
Barth, Karl, 6–7, 16, 79n, 103
Basic beliefs, 23, 34–36, 39, 40, 41, 42,
        44, 50

Bayly, Joseph, 209n
Beatific vision, 17
Beck, Aaron, 196n
Behavior change, 163–64
Belief, 15–16, 26, 157–58, 229
    and action, 29, 121n
    in God, 42, 45–46
    and intellect, 31–32
Bem, Daryl, 164n
Best explanation, 88–89
Bible, 10, 13
Bliks, 79
Bloor, David, 68
Bormann, Ernest, 211n
Bostrom, Robert, 157n, 222n, 223n, 224n
Braithwaite, Brian, 79n
Brehm, Jack, 166n
Brembeck, Winston, 215n
Brock, Timothy, 168n
Brown, Harold I., 69
Brunner, Emil, 6
Butler, Joseph, 87–88

Cacioppo, John, 221n
Caird, G. B., 196n
Calvin, John, 9–11, 14, 16, 23, 28, 43, 50, 105
Cappella, Joseph, 170n
Carnap, Rudolf, 57–58, 134n
Carnell, E. J., 105
Categories, 141–43
Certainty, 10, 29, 37
Chaiken, Shelly, 167n, 210n
Channel, 169
Character, 234, 235
Chebat, Jean-Charles, 222n
Chesterton, G. K., 87
Childlikeness, 20–21
Chilton, David, 140n
Circular reasoning, 48, 65, 104, 145, 146, 149, 154
Claim, 136, 138, 139, 140, 154
Clark, David K., 85n, 92n, 141n
Clark, Gordon, 48
Clark, Kelly James, 28, 36n, 44n, 45n 98n

Classical apologetics, 108–9, 111, 125
Classical foundationalism, 34–41, 42, 44, 45, 46, 49–50, 51, 82, 100, 110n, 136
    and dialogical apologetics, 113n
Classification, 198–99, 204
Clifford, W. K., 28–30, 36, 50, 55, 86, 92, 96, 106, 121
Cobb, John, 118–19
"Cogito ergo sum," 35
Cognitive consistency, 160, 161, 177
Cohen, Arthur, 166n
Coherence, 46–49, 85–86, 94, 148
Coherentism, 46–51
Coleman, Lerita, 191n
Commitment, 15n, 23, 25, 26
Commodity theory, 167–68, 218
Common
    coordinate system, 81
    ground, 105, 125
    sense, 43
Communication, 218, 220
Comprehensibility, 223
Comprehensiveness, 85–86
Conceptual
    listening, 231
    relativism, 66–68, 72, 77–78, 80–82, 84, 93, 100, 101, 148, 185
    schemes, 76–78, 80–81, 93, 100
Concerns, 212
Concrete illustration, 221, 223, 228
Confirmationism, 57, 59, 61–62, 75
Conformity, 162–63, 166
Congruence, 85, 86
Consistency, 64, 85–86
Contextual factors in science, 62
Contextualism, 46
Control beliefs, 77–78
Conventionalism, 68, 78, 101
Convergence, 87
Conversion, 64
    as paradigm shift, 73–74, 75
Conviction/persuasion duality, 215
Cooper, Joel, 190n
Coping v. copying, 53
Correspondence, 47–48, 94
Corroboration, 60, 61

Cosmological argument, 88n, 111
Cosmology, 89
Counter-attitudinal advocacy, 160–62
Counterexample, 142
Craig, William Lane, 22n, 46n, 108,
    123n
Creativity, 56–57
Credibility, 169, 224, 234
Credulity, 86, 87
Crisis state, 63
Critical realism, 54
Critical thinking, 134
Cross-cultural communication, 195–96,
    198–204
Cultural
    adjustment, 199–200
    identity, 179–80, 186
    relativism, 192–94, 204
    sensitivity, 198–99, 204, 231
Culture, 66–67, 93, 114, 115, 179, 181
    definition, 180, 203
    and stereotypes, 188–89
    and world view, 204
Cumulative case argument, 87–90, 96,
    100, 147

Data beliefs, 77–78
Datum, 136, 138, 139, 154
Davidson, Donald, 81
Dead option, 31
Decategorization, 199
Deduction, 55, 57
Deductive certainty, 110n, 121
Defensiveness, 209–10
Descartes, René, 35–36, 55
Dialogical
    apologetics, 102, 109, 113–16,
    125–26, 132, 154
    and cross-cultural communication,
    198, 200, 204
Dialogue, 114n, 116–17, 123–24, 126,
    130–31, 153
    and apologetics, 117–18
    and change, 119
    and pluralism, 118, 120
Dierks, Friedrich, 184
Dispositional influences, 191

Dissertation question, 216–17
Downes, John, 216n
Drees, Willem B., 71n
Dualism, 89
Duck-rabbit figure, 64, 67, 80
Dyrness, William, 194n

Elegance, 86
Emotional listening, 231
Emotions, 157, 169, 177, 211–13,
    231–32
Empathy, 201, 214, 228, 229, 232
Empirical criteria, 85–86, 100
Empiricism, 56, 62, 69, 75, 91–92, 100
Engel, James F., 156n, 157n, 167n,
    234n
Enlightenment, 4, 13, 14, 28, 33–34,
    37, 58, 61, 71, 75, 82, 90,
    109
Enthymemes, 133–35, 141
Epistemological
    subjectivity, 111n
    warrant, 44
Epistemology, 12, 28, 54, 110
Equivocation, 140–42, 146
Ethical relativism, 192, 193, 194n, 204
Ethics, 12, 89
Ethnocentrism, 192–93, 204
Ethos, 132, 154, 169
Evangelism, 209, 223
    and apologetics, 114–15
Evans, C. Stephen, 33n, 88n, 98n
Evans, Franklyn B., 234n
Evidence, 17–19, 23, 29–30, 31, 42–44,
    86–87, 90, 93, 97, 100, 219,
    220, 222, 232
    anecdotal, 144–45, 154
    circumstantial, 145–47, 154
    demonstrative, 145–46
    historical, 108
    novel, 169, 222
Evidential apologetics, 106–7, 111, 125

Evidentialism, 28–32, 34, 36, 41–42, 46, 50, 51, 56, 71, 75, 79, 82, 86–88, 91, 100, 111
Exclusivism, 120, 123
Existential apologetics, 103–4, 125
Existentialism, 37n
Experience, 43, 44, 49, 50, 69, 91–93, 100, 103–4, 122, 125, 163, 164, 173, 177
Experimentation, 27
Explanatory power, 86, 135

Facts, 33–34, 68, 69, 82
    and theory, 78, 80, 94, 147n
    and values, 37n
Faculty psychology, 157
Faith, 4–5, 8–11, 14–15, 18–19, 26, 74, 96–97, 229
    biblical, 16, 19–20, 22
    formed, 9, 14
    and knowledge, 120
    New Testament on, 18–20, 96
    object of, 20, 22
    and reason, 4–11, 16, 22–25
    unformed, 9, 10–11, 14
Faithfulness, 19
Fallacies, 143–45, 149
Falsification, 59–62, 75
Fazio, Russell, 159n
Fear, 214
Felt needs, 166–67, 177, 210, 218
Ferré, Frederick, 84n, 86n
Fertility, 86
Festinger, Leon, 161, 223n
Feyerabend, Paul, 81
Fideism, 37–38, 45, 49–50, 74, 79, 80, 82, 84, 101, 104, 109, 110, 113
    and presuppositionalism, 105–6, 125
Finiteness, 21–22, 107, 113
Fishbein, Martin, 157n, 169
Flew, Antony, 30, 79, 88
Foot-in-the–door persuasion, 165–66
Forgiveness, 219
Form and meaning, 193–94
Foundationalism, 34–38, 48, 49

Fraser, Scott, 165n
Freedman, Jonathan, 165n
Freedom, 4, 5
Friendship evangelism, 114
Fruitfulness, 64
Functional theory of persuasion, 166–67
Geisler, Norman L., 85n, 92n, 94n, 108, 118n
Gill, Jerry H., 37n, 91n, 98n
God
    as Creator, 10
    experience of, 91–92
    as Redeemer, 10
    ultimacy of, 21
Great Pumpkin Objection, 44, 50
Griffin, Em, 157n, 209n
Griffiths, Paul J., 120n, 123n
Grounds, 42–44, 50, 91, 92
Group influence theories, 162, 177
Groups, 183, 186, 188, 189, 191
Grunlan, Stephen A., 182n, 193n
Gudykunst, William, 192n, 196n, 213n

Hall, Edward T., 180, 192n
Hammel, Bonnie, 221n
Hard core theories, 68–69, 73, 93–94
Hard rationalism, 50, 82, 100
Hare, R. M., 79–80
Harnack, Adolf von, 7
Harrison, Randall, 197n
Hartshorne, Charles, 87n
Hasty generalization, 143–44, 154
Hayakawa, S. I., 190n
Hedonistic paradox, 124n
Hesselgrave, David J., 117n, 157n, 184n, 186n, 187n, 196n, 200n, 207n
Hick, John, 12n, 79n, 118
Hidden pathways, 180–81
Hierarchy of apologetic needs, 224, 226
History, 89
Holism, 46
Holmes, Arthur F., 15n, 37n, 48, 72n, 89n, 98n, 111n, 122n
Holy Spirit, 10, 11, 24, 25, 38, 104
Hoover, A. J., 143n

Hovland, Carl, 157n, 168–69, 213n
Howell, William, 210n, 215n
Hume, David, 79, 90
Humor, 199
Humpty Dumpty, 76–77, 82, 83
Hypothesis, 57–58, 60
Hypothetico-deduction, 57, 82

Idealized logic, 135–37
Ideology, 93
Illumination, 11
Impression management theory,
    161–62
Incoherence, 81
Incommensurability, 64–66, 80–82,
    100
Incommensurate paradigms, 64–65
Incorrigible propositions, 35, 39, 40
Individualism, 4
Inductivism, 44, 55, 56, 75, 78
Infinite regress, 23
Informal logic, 132n
Information, 167–68, 169
Information integration theory, 169–70
Integrity, 123
Intellectual imperialism, 41
Intensity, 158
"Interprefacts," 78
Invitation, 223–24, 232
Irrationality, 6

Jackson, George, 167n
James, William, 30–33, 34, 50, 97,
    121n
Janis, Irving, 163, 221n
Jesus Christ, 24, 89
    as object of faith, 20
    use of language, 209n
Jussim, Lee, 191n
Justice, 123

Kant, Immanuel, 4–6, 25
Kaplan, Robert, 221n
Katz, Daniel, 156n, 166n, 167n, 210n
Kekulé, August, 57
Kelman, Herbert, 159n

Kierkegaard, Søren, 103
Kinesics, 197
Kluckhohn, Clyde, 179n, 180
Knitter, Paul, 118
Knowledge, 17, 18, 36, 229
    and commitment, 15n, 23–25,
        120, 122
    person-centered, 98, 99, 100, 110
    and truth, 99, 100, 110, 111n
Kraft, Charles H., 184, 194n
Kuhn, Thomas, 55, 62–69, 72, 75, 80,
    81, 82, 121, 136
Kuyper, Abraham, 105

Lakatos, Imre, 58n, 61n, 68–70, 75
Language, 132, 136, 185–86
Lapide, Pinchas, 107n
Larson, Charles U., 222n
Latitude
    of acceptance, 212–13, 228
    of commitment, 212–13, 224
    of rejection, 212
Learning approaches, 168–69, 177
Lerch, Lauren, 191n
Leslie, John, 89n
Lewis, C. S., 18n, 42, 87n, 97n, 108,
    109, 121n, 122, 145
Liberalism, 7
Lippmann, Walter, 188
Listening, 209–11, 231
Little, Paul, 216n, 217n
Livability, 106, 148
Live option, 31
Lochhead, David, 120n
Loewenthal, Kate, 213n
Logic, 12–14, 21, 47, 85, 87, 122, 132,
    133–35, 137, 139, 222
Logos, 132, 154, 215
Losher, D. Jay, 187n
Louw, J. P., 141n
Love, 123
Loyalty, 17, 19, 20, 22, 74, 97, 119
Lucas, J. R., 90n
Luther, Martin, 22n

Mandelbaum, Maurice, 66–68, 80
Mann, Leon, 163, 221n

Maslow, Abraham, 166
Mavrodes, George I., 23n, 34n, 46n, 98n
Mayers, Marvin, 182n, 193n, 213n
McCroskey, James, 222n
McDowell, Josh, 107
McGuire, William, 168–69
McMullin, Ernan, 55
Meaning, 195–96
Meaningfulness, 85
Messages, 169–70
Metaphysical subjectivity, 111n
Metaphysics, 12, 77
Mild incommensurability, 80
Miller, Arthur G., 189n, 190n
Miller, Gerald, 215n
Mind, 157
Miracles, 4, 5
Missiology, 184
Mitchell, Basil, 66n, 72n, 79, 86, 87n, 88n, 120n
Modeling, 163
Monologue, 116–17, 118, 120, 125, 210, 214, 215
Montgomery, John Warwick, 107, 135n
Moody, D. L., 209
Moral obligation, 5
Moreland, J. P., 108
Mormons, 77–78, 92, 94
Mueller, George, 14–15
Murphy, Nancey, 70n
Murray, Henry, 179n
Myers, David G., 191n
Mysticism, 91, 103
Mystifying answer, 216–18, 220

Naive inductivism, 82
Naive realism, 54
Nash, Ronald, 48n
Natural revelation, 6–7, 11, 24
Natural theology, 4, 7–9, 37, 38, 103, 108, 111
Naturalism, 89
Needs, 166–67, 171, 177, 218, 224, 229, 232

Negative messages, 169
Neutrality, 65, 69, 80, 82, 122
Newcomb, Theodore, 159n
Newton, Isaac, 5, 21
Nida, Eugene, 220
Niebuhr, Reinhold, 79n
Noetic effects of sin, 22, 103, 105, 106, 111, 113, 125
Nongenuine option, 31
Nonverbal communication, 196–97, 208, 211, 223
Normative judgments, 193
O'Hair, Madalyn Murray, 23
O'Keefe, Barbara, 223n
Objective knowledge, 68, 80, 121, 122, 125
Objectivity, 65, 66, 69, 75, 90, 107
Observation, 27, 57, 61
Olthuis, James, 211n
Ontological argument, 45
Options, 31–32
Ordinary language, 136
Organization, 223

Paley, William, 106–7
Pantheism, 89
Paradigm, 62–68, 70, 72, 76, 77, 80, 82, 100, 121
    shift, 64, 65–66, 69, 73–74, 75
Paradox, 103
Paralanguage, 197
Pascal, Blaise, 33, 103
Passions, 212
Pathos, 132, 154, 215
Paul, 20, 24
Permission, 216
Personal testimony, 234–35
Persuasion, 126, 132, 134, 159–60, 163, 165, 168, 170, 171, 206–7, 222, 223, 224, 227, 231, 232
Peterson, Michael L., 44n, 45n
Petty, Richard, 221n
Phillips, D. Z., 79n
Philosophy, 8, 9, 12–14
Pietists, 103

Pippert, Rebecca Manley, 214, 225n
Placher, William C., 119n
Plantinga, Alvin, 28, 34, 35, 36, 40n, 41, 42–45, 50, 73n, 84n, 136
Plato, 131–32
Pluralism, 116, 118, 123, 125
Point of view, 72–73
Polanyi, Michael, 55, 71
Polarization, 166
Polkinghorne, John, 71n
Polysemy, 140, 141
Popper, Karl, 59–61, 71
Positive messages, 169
Positivism, 37n, 71
Possible truth, 60, 61, 75
Practical apologetics, 115–16
Practical logic, 133–34
Pragmatism, 95, 100
Prayer, 5, 43
Prejudice, 189, 191, 192
Presuppositional apologetics, 104–6, 111, 125, 148
Presuppositions, 65, 104–6, 111, 125, 147–50, 154
Primacy effect, 169
Primary inductive principles, 86, 96
Probabilist argument, 147
Probability, 58, 60, 61, 75, 121
Proclamational apologetics, 116, 120
Proof, 110
Proportionality, 121–22
Proxemics, 197
Pseudo-science, 60, 71
Psychological factors, 62, 93, 115
Puns, 140

Qualifier, 138, 139, 154
Question-begging, 104, 145
Quine, W. V. O., 71–72, 75, 87–88

Racism, 188, 192, 201
Rank, 182–83
Rational criteria, 84–86, 87, 100
Rationalism, 37, 38, 45, 49–50, 79, 82, 107, 113, 125
Rationality, 22, 28, 45–46, 105, 107, 108–9
    and world view, 104

Rationalization, 22
Reactance, 168, 209, 218
Realism, 56, 95
Reardon, Kathleen, 196n
Reason, 4–5, 6–9, 11–14, 22–23, 26, 100
    ambiguity, 26, 84
    neutrality, 20, 85
Rebutter, 138, 139, 154
Receptor, 169, 170
Reformed
    epistemology, 26, 28, 33–46, 49, 50–51, 75, 82, 91–92, 104, 110n, 136
    and internal philosophy of science, 55
    and presuppositionalism, 105
Regan, Dennis, 159n
Reid, Thomas, 43, 50
Rejection, 213
Relativism, 67, 68, 77, 78–79, 99, 100
    in Kuhn, 65–66, 75
Religion
    and culture, 187
    as myth, 54, 70
    and science, 75
Religious experience, 6, 89, 91–92
Research program, 68–69
Response, 223–25, 231
Results, 95, 100
Revelation, 4, 6, 36, 38, 43
Rhetoric, 131–32, 135
Risk, 32, 33, 36, 97
Ritschl, Albrecht, 7
Roberts, Robert, 212n
Rokeach, Milton, 157n
Role play, 163, 164, 221
Rolston, Holmes, III, 78n, 93n, 122n
Rommen, Edward, 184n, 186n
Rosenberg, Milton, 157n
Ruggiero, Vincent Ryan, 143n, 155n, 162n

Salvation, 11
Sapir, Edward, 197n
Saving faith, 19, 24
Schaeffer, Francis, 14, 54n, 105

Schimmel, Leslie, 221n
Schoepfle, G. Mark, 186n
Science, 53–54
    history of, 55, 63
    normal, 63, 64
    metaphysics of science, 53, 55, 56
    philosophy of, 51, 53–57, 62,
        70–72, 74–75, 82, 87, 90, 95,
        100
    and religion, 70–71, 79
Scientific evolution, 69–70
Scientific methods, 5
Scientific revolutions, 64, 69–70
Scope, 64
Scriven, Michael, 30, 33n, 88n
Secord, Paul, 219n
Secularism, 234
Self
    centeredness, 123–24
    created messages, 220–21
    defeating propositions, 39, 40, 41,
        149–50, 154
    evident propositions, 35, 39, 40
    excepting fallacy, 67, 80
    image, 180
Sennett, Richard, 167n
Sensitivity, 214
Sharpe, Eric, 117n
Shepherd, Gregory, 223n
Sherif, Carolyn Wood, 157n, 213n
Sherif, Muzafer, 213n
Sherry, Patrick, 71n
Simplicity, 64, 86, 170, 190
Sin, 10, 22, 25, 103, 105–6, 107, 111,
    113, 125
Situational influences, 191
Skepticism, 32, 55, 90, 113
Skinner, B. F., 163
Smith, Mary John, 157n, 161n, 162n,
    170n
Smith, Wilfred Cantwell, 118
Snyder, Mark, 190n
Social
    class, 219
    consensus, 188
    learning, 163
    reality, 165

Sociological factors, 62, 64, 66, 68, 69,
    74, 75, 93
Soft rationalism, 48–50, 51, 82–83, 87,
    88, 90–92, 94–95, 100–101,
    113, 148
Sound argument, 133
Source, 169
Special
    pleading, 61, 144, 146
    revelation, 5, 11, 13, 24, 104–5
Spencer, Herbert, 195
Spiritual journey, 216, 234
Sproul, R. C., 108, 109, 110
Stangor, Charles, 167n, 210n
Stereotypes, 188–91, 198–99, 204, 208,
    214
Stories, 118, 221–22
Stott, John, 114n, 123
Street, Richard, Jr., 170n
Style, 132
Subcultures, 181, 182, 183
Subjectivism, 33n
Subjectivity, 56, 75, 80, 120
    in Kuhn, 65–66, 68
    in religion, 78
Sumner, William Graham, 192
Swann, William, Jr., 190n
Swinburne, Richard, 6, 10n, 16, 86,
    87n, 89n, 90n, 92n, 96, 147
Sykes, Rod, 33n
Syllogism, 133–35, 137
Sympathy, 214
Systemic criteria, 85, 87

Tabula rasa, 56
Tedeschi, James, 161–62
Teleological argument, 88n
Tennant, F. R., 87n
Tertullian, 6
Theism, 89, 122
Theistic proofs, 8, 42, 45, 103, 108
Theory and practice, 115–16
Thiselton, Anthony, 187n
Tillich, Paul, 21, 79n
Toulmin, Stephen, 55, 121n, 135–39,
    144, 147, 154
Transcendental argument, 148n

Translatability, 81
Triandis, Harry, 159n, 191n
Trueblood, Elton, 25, 48, 87
Trust, 17, 19, 20, 22, 25, 74, 97, 213
Truth, 10, 46, 94, 99, 118
　　and knowledge, 99, 100, 110,
　　　111n
Twain, Mark, 17

Unwarranted assumption, 147

Valence, 158, 177, 186
Valid argument, 133
Values, 62, 63, 64, 65, 186
Van Til, Cornelius, 105
Veatch, Henry, 54, 71n
Vincent of Lérins, 29n

Wakefield, Norman, 210n
Warrant, 56, 60, 136, 138, 139, 154
Ways of knowing, 16–17
Web of belief, 72–73, 75, 88, 90, 92
Wellhausen, Julius, 145
Weltanschauung. See World view
Werner, Oswald, 186n
Weyl, Herman, 60n

Whorf, Benjamin Lee, 81
Wiles, Maurice, 82n, 83n
Will, 157
Wittgenstein, Ludwig, 23n, 79n, 136
Wolfe, David L., 24n, 83n, 84n, 85
Wolterstorff, Nicholas, 34n, 38, 54
Word, Carl, 190n
Words, 130, 140–41, 143, 195
Working logic, 135, 139
World view, 12, 14, 21, 76, 77, 78,
　　80–81, 161
　　anthropological sense, 184–85
　　change, 74, 210
　　criteria, 83–84, 86, 87, 100
　　as glasses, 94, 109
　　as paradigm, 72–73
　　as point of view, 72
　　and truth, 106
Wykstra, Stephen, 92n, 97n

Yale theory, 168–69
Yandell, Keith E., 62n, 80
Yankelovich, Daniel, 167
Yielding, 169

Zanna, Mark, 190n